First Taste of Freedom

Sports and Entertainment
Steven A. Riess, *Series Editor*

SELECT TITLES IN SPORTS AND ENTERTAINMENT

Black Baseball Entrepreneurs, 1902–1931: The Negro National and Eastern Colored Leagues
Michael E. Lomax

Invisible Seasons: Title IX and the Fight for Equity in College Sports
Kelly Belanger

Joining the Clubs: The Business of the National Hockey League to 1945
J. Andrew Ross

Legends Never Die: Athletes and Their Afterlives in Modern America
Richard Ian Kimball

The 1929 Bunion Derby: Johnny Salo and the Great Footrace across America
Charles B. Kastner

The Rise of American High School Sports and the Search for Control: 1880–1930
Robert Pruter

(Re)Presenting Wilma Rudolph
Rita Liberti and Maureen M. Smith

The War of the Wheels: H. G. Wells and the Bicycle
Jeremy Withers

First Taste of Freedom

A Cultural History of Bicycle Marketing in the United States

Robert J. Turpin

SYRACUSE UNIVERSITY PRESS

First Edition 2018
18 19 20 21 22 23 6 5 4 3 2 1

∞ The paper used in this publication meets the minimum requirements of the American National Standard for Information Sciences—Permanence of Paper for Printed Library Materials, ANSI Z39.48-1992.

For a listing of books published and distributed by Syracuse University Press, visit www.SyracuseUniversityPress.syr.edu.

ISBN: 978-0-8156-3573-4 (hardcover) 978-0-8156-3591-8 (paperback)
978-0-8156-5439-1 (e-book)

Library of Congress Cataloging-in-Publication Data

Names: Turpin, Robert J., author.

Title: First taste of freedom : a cultural history of bicycle marketing in the United States / Robert J. Turpin.

Description: First edition. | Syracuse, New York : Syracuse University Press, 2018. | Series: Sports and entertainment | Includes bibliographical references and index.

Identifiers: LCCN 2018012455 (print) | LCCN 2018024402 (ebook) | ISBN 9780815654391 (E-book) | ISBN 9780815635734 (hardback : alk. paper) | ISBN 9780815635918 (pbk. : alk. paper)

Subjects: LCSH: Cycling—United States—History. | Cycling—Economic aspects—United States—History. | Bicycle industry—United States—History.

Classification: LCC GV1041 (ebook) | LCC GV1041 .T87 2018 (print) | DDC 629.227/20688—dc23

LC record available at https://lccn.loc.gov/2018012455

Manufactured in the United States of America

To the loves of my life: Julia, Mabel, and Lydia

Contents

List of Illustrations *ix*

List of Tables *xi*

Acknowledgments *xiii*

Introduction: *Conceptions of Bicycles* *1*

1. Cycling's Rise and American Manhood *11*

2. Automobiles and a World at War *35*

3. Cooperation and Confusion *53*

4. The Child Consumer *74*

5. The Postwar Slump *95*

6. The Safety of Cycling *117*

7. Surviving the Great Depression *136*

8. Bicycles in the Age of Affluence *158*

9. High-Risers and Multi-Geared Redeemers *193*

Conclusion: *Consumers as Derailleurs* *213*

Notes *221*

Bibliography *263*

Index *277*

Illustrations

1. A woman on her tricycle followed by men on high-wheelers *16*
2. *Her Choice. The Young Man's Slave (Five Years Later)* *33*
3. A. W. Nourse in his bicycle shop *67*
4. *Gee! It's a Hum-Dinger* *85*
5. *Spring Is on the Wing* *86*
6. *The Boys behind the Army* *89*
7. *One Boy in 1918 Is Worth 3 Boys of 1914* *91*
8. *Does Your Boy Have This Opportunity?* *107*
9. *How the Boy Market Stacks Up for Size* *109*
10. Annual bicycle purchases in the United States, 1921–33 *137*
11. *Ride 'Em Rough Fellows, They Thrive on It!* *149*
12. 1953 Mead "Juvenile Ranger" *171*
13. *108.92 Miles per Hour on a Bicycle* *180*
14. 1968 Schwinn "Orange Krate" high-rise model *198*

Tables

1. US Bicycle Production, 1888–1902 *14*
2. US Bicycle Consumption, 1898–1909 *37*
3. Price of Model T and Number Sold, 1908–21 *38*
4. Bicycle Consumption versus Car Registration, 1909–19 *39*
5. Foreign Trade in the United States, 1914–21 *102*
6. Unemployment, Bicycles Sold, Cars Registered, 1929–37 *139*
7. Bicycle and Automobile Consumption, 1947–55 *160*
8. US Bicycle Sales, 1961–69 *196*
9. US Bicycle Sales, 1970–77 *199*
10. US Bicycle Sales, 1979–92 *205*

Acknowledgments

I AM REALIZING NOW that I should have maintained my acknowledgments just as I (theoretically) maintain my vitae. I should have opened the file from time to time and added a few new lines of names that have helped this book see the light of day. A research project that takes years to complete is surely going to accrue countless debts to librarians, friends, family, colleagues, mentors, other scholars, and so on. My failure to provide a full list of those debts here does not mean I have forgotten all the help and support I have received along the way. I do, however, want to acknowledge some of the crucial resources, as far as this book is concerned.

My wife has supported me since day one and while our writing relationship is not quite the same as F. Scott's and Zelda's, I have certainly bounced ideas off her and been enriched by her input. She has also allowed me to shirk my household duties, like cleaning toilets and folding laundry. That will change. I have been fortunate to have a mother that encouraged me academically; a father who told me, "you can't eat a football so you better focus on your grades"; and a brother who led me to work harder in school than I would have otherwise. My in-laws, Tom and Diane, were also a key in helping me finish this project.

Karen Petrone has gone out of her way to mentor, and counsel me long after graduate school ended. I am lucky to have her in my corner. I have also been encouraged by my colleagues at Lees-McRae College—Scott Huffard, Ken Craig, and Todd Lidh in particular. Marvyn Rieger spent his summer vacation reading my manuscript and translating German works on bicycle marketing. Sadly, those did not make their way into this book but his help was valuable. David High used his graphic design wizardry to help me edit images. This saved me a considerable amount of precious time. Frank MacKenzie and Jon Psimer consistently answer my calls and drive long distances to help me move, repair cars, hang drywall, et cetera. It is an incredible gift to have friends like these.

The librarians and staff at the Shelton Learning Commons have gone out of their way to help me locate and obtain sources. There are numerous libraries and archives without which this book would lack sufficient sources. Some of the critical materials came from the Benson Ford Research Center, the Cincinnati Public Library, the New York Public Library, the Chicago Public Library, the Library of Congress, the Leavenworth Public Library, the Appalachian Regional Library, the William T. Young Library at the University of Kentucky, the Belk Library at Appalachian State University, and the Bicycle Museum of America in New Bremen, Ohio. Trips to many of those locations were funded by the Whalen Research Grant from Lees-McRae College and the George C. Herring Research Grant from the University of Kentucky.

This book was significantly improved by suggestions from Steven Riess and anonymous readers. I am also grateful for those that helped me with quick questions or encouraged me along the way, like Margaret Guroff, David Herlihy, Glen Norcliffe, Thomas Burr, Deborah Beckel, and Bob Flynn. Finally, I am extremely thankful for all the work the excellent team at Syracuse University Press has put into this book. Suzanne Guiod has been the absolute best editor. Her support, encouragement, work ethic, and excitement for this project have kept me motivated more than she will ever know.

First Taste of Freedom

INTRODUCTION

Conceptions of Bicycles

IN 1958 CAPTAIN KANGAROO (Bob Keeshan) began regularly taking time out from his show to tell kids all about the virtues and value of Schwinn bicycles. Schwinn was, after all, an important sponsor of the show. That was no coincidence. Schwinn had been exploring the potential benefits of advertising bicycles on the radio, in children's magazines, and in comic books since the 1930s. It soon found steady returns on its investment in Captain Kangaroo, who adamantly proclaimed, "Schwinn bikes are best!" In fact, according to a survey conducted in 1963, two out of three Schwinn dealers gave Captain Kangaroo direct credit for bicycle sales.[1] When the Federal Trade Commission took steps to stop children's television hosts from directly promoting consumer items on-air, Captain Kangaroo responded by adding a new character to the show—Mr. Schwinn Dealer. The show afforded Schwinn the ability to reach over ten million children.[2] It was a smart move on Schwinn's part. By the 1950s, the bicycle had become an indelible part of childhood in the United States. So pervasive was the idea that bicycles and children belonged to each other that there was little room for anyone else.

The bicycle has long been a part of American culture but its image and significance have been ever changing. Cycling was so popular in the United States by 1896 that Representative Thomas Reed of Maine proclaimed that learning "how to dodge a bicycle" was the most important problem confronting Americans.[3] Two decades later, among the dwindling number of cyclists in the United States, the biggest concern was how to dodge an automobile. Beyond simply serving as an alternative to the car, many Americans, particularly those who were white and middle class, began to see bicycles as backward, emasculating, and unbecoming. It is this image of the bicycle that seems to be the most pervasive in popular forms of entertainment, which have used bicycles for childhood adventures and to show characters as emotionally stunted and/or eccentric. As early as 1939, we see bicycles used in movies to signify otherness. This is certainly true in *The Wizard of Oz* when Miss Almira Gulch rides her bicycle to Dorothy's farm to forcibly remove Toto and have him "destroyed."[4] Among more recent examples, one need only think of *The 40 Year Old Virgin*, in which the main character, Andy, (played by Steve Carrell) is shown falling off his bicycle or using it to chase down his girlfriend's Volvo.[5] The bicycle seems more natural in settings where precocious juveniles use it to solve mysteries or find treasures. Movies like *The Goonies*, *E.T.*, *BMX Bandits*, and the Netflix series *Stranger Things* all use bicycles as a child's only option when they need to get somewhere far away or fast. Today, adults who regularly ride bicycles are still often considered odd, or at least unconventional. Many Americans associate the bicycle with transportation for those unable to afford a car. Some see it as the preferred choice of mobility for middle-class environmentalists, or a means for health and adventure among the upper class. Of course, there are also those who see it primarily as a child's toy. The bicycle's ability to represent such different ideas is the result of its relatively short, yet dynamic, history.

In 1893, there were close to one million bicycle owners in the United States, a number that would more than double by 1896.[6] By that time, the US cycling industry was experiencing a major boom, which peaked in 1899 with a total output of around one million bicycles produced domestically.[7] The United States has experienced several cycling revivals since the boom of the 1890s and each one has been somewhat unique. The changes bicycles and cycling have experienced in the United States were, and continue to be, symptomatic of larger changes in ideals of gender, mobility, and consumerism. First introduced to Americans around 1869 but not popularized until the 1880s, the bicycle represented ideas that evolved during industrialization, two world wars, the birth of child consumerism, suburbanization, and the growth of environmentalism. These developments contributed to alterations in the symbolic nature of the bicycle and the ways in which Americans consumed it. Even though, generally speaking, Americans prefer cars over bicycles, the bicycle remains popular. Its longevity as a fixture in American culture is due to its malleability as a consumer item. The bicycle has satisfied the needs of a diverse assortment of people. This book examines how and why it has been representative of such a wide array of ideals from the 1880s to the present. It offers fresh insights into the bicycle's history by focusing on actions taken by the bicycle industry, the demands of bicycle consumers, and the connections between childhood and bicycles that developed over time.

In both 1898 and 1899 the American bicycle industry produced around one million bicycles. Try as they might, bicycle and parts manufacturers would not experience a similar volume of sales until 1936, at which point the US population was significantly larger. At the turn of the twentieth century, the market for bicycles contracted as drastically as it had expanded. Of the works that examine the history of the bicycle in the United States, most give a great deal of attention to the "boom" years in the 1890s, yet little to the "bust." This book devotes the bulk of its attention to the years in which the bicycle was least popular, particularly among adults. It shows that understanding a consumer item that moves to the fringe of cultural interest is just as important as understanding those that are dominant. Therefore, understanding the bicycle's history in the United States is just as important as understanding the automobile's history. Since the bicycle was a precursor to the automobile, it is often attributed with laying the groundwork for the automobile's success. In many ways, the history and relevance of the bicycle and car converge, but there are also ways in which they diverge. Understanding the multiple facets of bicycle marketing and consumption in the United States as well as the contested ideals the bicycle was representative of, offers insight into our understanding of the interplay between consumerism and identity.

This study focuses on urban areas in the Northeast and Midwest, where cycling was prevalent over a considerable period. It maps important changes in American culture since the 1880s to understand why American adults' interest in the bicycle declined for several decades while children's use of bicycles grew, and why that trend has seemingly reversed more recently. It will do this by focusing on trends in bicycle production, design, and marketing campaigns, which, in turn, affected how society used the bicycle. While this book examines the bicycle's history from 1880 to the present, it is particularly attentive to the 1910s through 1950s because these years are crucial for understanding conceptions of the bicycle that still linger today. It is during this time that the bicycle became intrinsic to childhood—a product that adults were supposed to give, not receive.

Histories of the bicycle often discuss the boom and bust of the United States' bicycle market in the 1890s, but this book shows that the bicycle has had an impressive ability to recover and remarkable staying power. It is true that there was a long period in which the bicycle industry struggled to stay afloat, but the history of bicycle sales in the United States reveals a general upward trend, albeit with several dips and spikes. The bicycle avoided a fate like that of the roller skate, the coonskin cap, or the pet rock through its ability to represent multiple and often contested and/or contradictory meanings throughout history. In his anthropological study of the bicycle, Luis Vivanco says that answering the question of what a bicycle is, depends on the "when of the bicycle."[8] He argues that "specific technological conditions, practices of life, social relations, cultural meanings, and political-economic dynamics . . . help produce important variations across cities, countries, and social groups in how people think about and interact with bicycles in their everyday lives."[9] Similarly, Jeremy Withers and Daniel P. Shea describe the bicycle as a rolling, or floating, signifier as it is "perpetually taking on new and varied significations."[10] The symbolic complexities of the bicycle are key to its cultural significance.

Buying, riding, and racing a bicycle all demonstrated different norms and ideals depending on the specific moment in history and how the consumer understood their own position in the social hierarchy. For instance, the bicycle represented upper-class masculinity in the 1880s but by the 1890s it could also represent women's liberation. Alternatively, by the 1950s it was primarily demonstrative of juvenile masculinity. Industrialization, suburbanization, economic downturns, and the unique climate of both postwar periods all resulted in cultural changes that are illuminated by tracing the history of the bicycle. The shifts in American ideals that occurred over time had direct influence not only on bicycle consumption, but also on industry marketing practices and design. These shifts instigated changes in the symbolic nature of the bicycle and the public's use of it to attain and affirm socially constructed ideals.

A critical examination of cycling's loss of status—from one of the most popular forms of sport and recreation among middle-class white adults in the United States during the 1890s to one of unfashionable insignificance for that same user group by the 1950s—illustrates changes in American ideals and has broader implications for American national identity. Prior to, and during the 1920s, many velodromes closed and competitive cycling moved beyond the purview of the American public. Similarly, there was a resulting downturn in the profits of the American cycling industry and a decrease in the frequency of cycling events. Previous works that have touched on this period in the bicycle's history attribute the downturn solely to the emergence of the automobile and growing car culture in the United States.[11] This book shows that those explanations are overly simplistic. They fail to fully explain why car sales grew and bicycle sales declined, or to consider factors other than the car in the bicycle's loss of consumer appeal. One need only look to France, Belgium, Great Britain, Germany, the Netherlands, and other countries to see that the car did not have the same impact on the bicycle's image around the globe. Evan Friss's recent study of the bicycle and urban America in the 1890s argues that Americans did not stop cycling because they started driving cars. "Rather, in the end, distinct social groups held competing, and ultimately unsustainable, notions about the bicycle."[12] This study adds further complexities to the story of the bicycle's fall by arguing that many other factors contributed to a dismantling and reconstruction of the bicycle's image. In the process, it demonstrates how the bicycle-industry elites who tried to manage the bicycle's image embraced a changing, yet specific, set of national virtues.

As bicycle production increased and prices fell, the bicycle industry's target market—white middle-class males—lost interest. In response, manufacturers began a series of attempts at redefining the bicycle and broadening its market. Each attempt at manipulating the image of the bicycle had significant repercussions that altered its appeal among American consumers. Attempts at first to broaden the market from elites to the middle class resulted in elites' loss of interest in the activity. The industry's subsequent turn to female consumers in the first decade of the twentieth century threatened the masculinity of cycling. Finally, the industry's decision to begin targeting America's youth—beginning in the in the 1910s—had an adverse impact on adult participation in cycling. This book argues that the bicycle industry itself was culpable in the bicycle's loss of status among adults. Thus, the car's destiny to supplant the bike was neither natural, immediate, or inevitable. Instead of completely displacing the bicycle, automobiles influenced the way it was marketed and designed. By the late 1930s, bicycle designs were noticeably changing to appear more like cars, motorcycles, and airplanes. This development not only signaled the capitulation of the bicycle industry to the internal combustion engine, but also worked to instill in children a desire for consumer items that would be in opposition to the bicycle as they competed for space on public roads. Cycling became an activity for white middle-class children, which damaged the status it once enjoyed—as a legitimate means of transportation and popular recreation for adults.[13]

The automobile is indeed an important factor to consider when examining cycling's decline in the United States but the argument that cars replaced bikes, however, must be interrogated more fully.[14] This study proposes we include, but look beyond, bicycle production to also consider industry marketing schemes and the changing symbolism of the bicycle based upon popular usage. It adds depth to our understanding of the bicycle's history by considering the broader social, cultural, and economic developments affecting the bicycle in the first half of the twentieth century. Most notable is the attention this book gives to mobility, consumerism, nationalism, and gender.

Trade journals often show how the bicycle industry perceived itself, defined its goals, and in some cases, how it planned to achieve those goals. They discuss pricing, marketing, and the general state of the industry. They are also important because their audience is the shop owner and manufacturer, who actively worked to alter the bicycle's image. Consumers, on the other hand, were thought to merely accept or reject the appeals of the advertisements but it is important to keep in mind that perceptions of social norms and the connected ideas about what consumers wanted drove the creative strategies of those who commissioned and executed the advertisements and marketing strategies.

Advertisements are particularly useful sources of evidence because they demonstrate how the bicycle was marketed and, to a degree, how it was perceived. They effectively illustrate the differing tactics bicycle producers used to make the bicycle appealing. In turn, they also demonstrate how members of the bicycle industry understood ideals of class, race, and gender. Advertisements also give insights into how a specific industry attempted to influence society. At the same time, however, advertisements and marketing tactics are merely prescriptive. Women did not necessarily run out to buy a bicycle just because the advertisements told them that it would make them healthy and beautiful. Indeed, attempts to alter the bicycle's image were not always successful. Tactics considered ineffective were quickly abandoned while those deemed effective had a longer life-span. The public's reception of those advertising and marketing tactics is also demonstrated by the way individuals used bicycles and how industries wholly unrelated to bicycles used cycling to promote their products.

The bicycle was inspired by an earlier invention called the draisine, or hobbyhorse—a crude walking machine consisting of two wheels connected by a board that the rider would straddle and propel by pushing off the ground with their feet. The bicycle would be lauded as superior to horses, whereas the hobbyhorse was a substitute for the horse. The next major development for cycling was the introduction of the velocipede, which popularized the idea of using pedals for propulsion. The pedals were affixed to the front wheel and the rider sat between the two wheels, which were only slightly different in circumference. Due to its lack of comfort, the velocipede was dubbed the "boneshaker" and it was therefore soon exceeded in popularity by the high-wheel (subsequently called the *ordinary*). With its massive front wheel powered by pedals attached directly to its front axle, the high-wheeler was relatively common by the 1870s. It was appealing because it was more efficient, more comfortable, and could achieve higher speeds than the boneshaker. In 1878, Colonel Albert A. Pope, owner of the Pope Manufacturing Company, was first to begin producing high-wheelers in the United States.[15] There were other versions of bicycles but the ordinary was the most common style until the rise of the Rover–style safety bicycle. The Rover quickly outmatched all other models of "safety" bicycle and eventually became synonymous with the term *safety*.[16]

First produced in the mid-1880s, the safety bicycle is the basis for the most common model of bicycle seen today. It incorporated a triangular frame with two wheels of equal circumference that were propelled by the rear wheel, which was driven by chain. This allowed for some choice in gear ratios, which could lead to greater efficiency and, ultimately, faster speeds. It was called the *safety* because it was safe compared to the ordinary, which was prone to "headers"—throwing the rider over the handlebars when its large front wheel was forced to a sudden stop by potholes or debris. Because the safety bicycle was relatively easy to ride and less dangerous, cycling soon became a much more popular form of recreation—especially after the introduction of pneumatic tires. With the standardization of frame design that accompanied the invention of the safety bicycle and the recognition by entrepreneurs that bicycles were en vogue, bicycle manufacturing and consumption both escalated.

The independence bicycles granted was important, particularly because it differed from that of horses in cost and upkeep. The expense of the bicycle resulted in its ability to denote class. Early cyclists could demonstrate their wealth through the purchases they made and simply by participating in a leisure activity. As bicycle manufacturing increased it became more affordable and more popular, particularly among the middle class. By 1896, there were close to 250 bicycle factories and nearly 2.5 million cyclists in the United States.[17] The price of a new Vanguard bicycle in 1896 was eighty-five dollars. By 1898, Acme Bicycles was selling bicycles via mail order for $39.50. At the same time, most workers were earning less than $800 per year.[18] Bicycles were a considerable investment for working-class men, but there was also the potential for cheaper, used bicycles since wealthier cyclists preferred to buy a new bicycle every year and sell their old models. This allowed them to stay up-to-date with the latest trends, thereby flaunting their economic position.

The act of cycling during the late nineteenth century was also a social statement. Initially, it was a statement of wealth, as the working class did not have the financial means to spend $150 on a luxury item like a bicycle. As the number of manufacturers increased and prices decreased by more than half, greater numbers of people were able to participate in the activity. It was at this point that cycling became an expression of manhood for classes other than the wealthy elite. Thus, cycling has demonstrated multiple, often competing, masculinities over time and the way the bicycle was used as an expression of manhood has experienced several shifts over time, just as ideals of manhood were undergoing significant alterations. In the 1870s and early 1880s, the bicycle represented men's adventurism and pioneering spirit because it allowed them to maintain a sphere that was separate from feminine domesticity. Men could ride their bicycles outside of the city into nature and get back in touch with their primitive self-reliant ancestry. After the invention of the safety bicycle, however, women began cycling in greater numbers and definitions of manliness as reflected by cycling were thereby modified. Men could no longer simply ride a bicycle to prove their masculinity. To set themselves apart, they had to ride safeties regularly and go farther and/or faster than what was common on ordinaries. Cyclists had been interested in demonstrating speed, pluck, and endurance from the very beginning but with the safety, what constituted fast, far, or daring had changed. As the bicycle entered the twentieth century, however, its connection with manhood was significantly diminished.

The 1910s through the 1950s represent an extremely important span for the bicycle because this is when the child consumer becomes an important force in advertising and marketing. The bicycle industry was at the forefront as one of the first to market their products to children. The story of how and why the bicycle industry focused on young consumers, boys in particular, is crucial to understanding the bicycle's trajectory in the United States. With that purpose in mind, the first chapter of this book lays the foundation for subsequent chapters by looking at the American bicycle industry's boom and bust. Chapter one maps the direction of cycling industry innovations and marketing at the turn of the century and how it related to simultaneous changes in American culture. It covers the 1880s and 1900s and centers on industrialization, urbanization, the rising need to be strenuous, and intensification of conspicuous consumption. While other works of cycling history have covered this era, it is important to this study because it is critical for understanding the zenith of cycling's popularity in the United States. From there, this book flows chronologically ending with a discussion of the bicycle in the current era.

The bicycle has many different associations today based on location, socioeconomic status, and many other variables. However, the image of the bicycle as a child's toy, which was cultivated by the bicycle industry during the first half of the twentieth century, has held considerable sway over public opinion in the United States. More recently, it has showed signs of escaping the confines of that image but only through directly confronting that stereotype. This is the story of the attempt to manage the image of the bicycle in reaction to societal changes in the early twentieth century and the long-term implications of those efforts.

1

Cycling's Rise and American Manhood

THE GENESIS OF WHAT could truly be described as a market for bicycles in the United States began late in 1868. For a little over a year, the velocipede, or boneshaker, a primitive version of the bicycle, captivated American's attention. Riding schools sprang up from Portland, Maine, to San Francisco, California. Carriage makers and independent blacksmiths shifted focus in their trade toward bicycle production as well. Soon their efforts brought production up to around one thousand bicycles per week and even then, the demands for this new machine were not satisfied.[1] The velocipede was indeed popular but so was the spectacle of velocipede riding. People crowded to riding tracks, often indoor, to see these riders attain great speeds. The Grand Velocipede Academy of New York boasted that their *gymnacyclidium* included over eight thousand square feet for riding and a gallery with seating for about fifteen hundred people.[2] The swirling motion of unsteady riders around the track and the frequent collisions proved entertaining, but the speeds did not always turn out to be that impressive. In one race with twelve competitors, only one rider was able to travel a mile in less than six minutes.[3] Even though riders were notorious for crashing, men, women, and children all took part in the craze.[4] Dubbed the boneshaker because of its harsh ride, even after affixing a solid rubber tire to the rim, the velocipede was better suited for smooth tracks, many of which were indoors. Riders' attempts to impress spectators with their speed were less successful when they ventured out onto open public streets and roads. There were some notable exceptions but the average rider was not capable of pushing the velocipede very fast nor very far.

While it did have widespread appeal among the upper classes, in the United States the velocipede would prove to be a passing amusement. Its inability to redefine the way people thought about mobility certainly limited its long-term appeal. In the United States, it was written off as a toy more than a serious pursuit. In fact, its roots may have begun in a toy factory when Pierre Lallement began experimenting with children's tricycle designs moving toward a larger two-wheeled version.[5] The velocipede craze also struck around the same time in France, Great Britain, Germany, and Italy but interest soon dwindled in those countries as well. Paul Smethurst argues that the bicycle was able to establish itself in the public's imagination but it did so more positively in France and Great Britain than in the United States.[6] In France and Great Britain the velocipede seemed to prove itself a little more; such was the case in well-publicized exhibition rides from Edinburgh to London—a distance of around four hundred miles.[7] In the United States, on the other hand, the bicycle experienced a significant amount of bad press with headlines that read, "The velocipede idiocy has again broken out" and "The velocipede mania rages in South Norwalk, greatly to the disgust of the sedate citizens."[8] One journalist, who was convinced the velocipede was unhealthy, went so far as to propose a "reward be offered for velocipede scalps." He implored residents of Leavenworth, Kansas, to take action, writing, "Let us ride them down. Don't vote for anybody who rides a velocipede. . . . Down with the velocipedes."[9] There were also numerous stories about velocipedists injuring pedestrians or themselves. Consequently, their attempts to use the smoother surfaces afforded by sidewalks were met by an increasing number of bans on such activities.[10] Bicycle historian David Herlihy argues that a combination of factors caused the velocipede to suffer in the United States. There was the bad press, and there were patent issues that effectively limited innovations in velocipede design in the United States. Those same issues did not impact Europe in the same way. He sees the poor roads in the United States as well as the safety concerns, and "inflated popular expectations" as playing a role, as did the lack of leadership. The one man who seemed particularly suited to take the helm of the fledgling velocipede industry in the United States, Calvin Witty, was too busy enforcing legal fees regarding patent issues to actually promote the velocipede.[11]

There would be several outbreaks of velocipede mania in the early 1870s but none to rival what happened in 1868 and 1869. Mostly the bicycle seemed to remain dormant in the American imagination until an undisputed leader did emerge. That man was Colonel Albert A. Pope, owner of the Pope Manufacturing Company. He was an early advocate for a new model of bicycle that would soon replace the velocipede—the high-wheeler. After seeing a high-wheeler at the Centennial exhibit in 1876, Pope was enthralled. He began formal production of the Columbia high-wheeler in 1878.[12] By this point, the United States seemed much less interested in the bicycle compared to other countries. In 1877, England produced 30,000 bicycles, yet there were comparatively few cyclists in the United States.[13] One year later, nearly 2,500 Americans purchased bicycles.[14] It would not be until 1890, however, that American bicycle production would near the 30,000 units England produced in 1877, but sales and production would skyrocket soon thereafter (see table 1).[15]

The high-wheeler that Pope mass-produced was powered by the directly driven axle of an inordinately large front wheel. In part, this solved the problem of attaining significant speeds that the velocipede had faced. The larger diameter of the front wheel would mean more ground could be covered with each revolution of the pedals. It also smoothed out the ride by rolling over small holes, rocks, or other such impediments more easily. The high-wheeler was commonly referred to as the *wheel* and later as the *ordinary* because of the assumption that it would be the default model amongst all the other new designs emerging. Those were often seen simply as experiments. During the 1880s, the high-wheeler became a mainstay in the United States in large part because of Albert Pope. By 1882, he boasted the ability to produce one thousand bicycles a month and estimated that there were around twelve thousand high-wheelers in the United States.[16] Even still, the design was flawed and served to keep cycling somewhat exclusive.

TABLE 1: US Bicycle Production, 1888–1902 (x 1,000)

Year	**1888**	**1890**	**1892**	**1894**	**1896**	**1898**	**1900**	**1902**
Estimated US production	16.75	29.89	60.7	109.3	437.2	928	997	620

Source: Bruce Epperson, "How Many Bikes: An Investigation into the Quantification of Bicycling, 1878–1914," in *Cycle History 11: Proceedings of the 11th International Cycling History Conference*, ed. Andrew Ritchie and Rob Van der Plas (San Francisco: Van der Plas Publications, 2001), 49.

The high-wheeler positioned the rider so that most of his weight was over the large front wheel, thereby making it prone to "headers." This occurred when the front wheel came to an abrupt stop and the rider's momentum carried the body forward, causing him to fly off the saddle and over the handlebars. The saddle was also relatively high, making riders unable to touch the ground with their feet (see fig. 1). In fact, simply mounting an ordinary bicycle was considered a courageous act requiring great skill. The rider's distance from the ground combined with the prevalence of headers gave ordinaries the reputation of being dangerous, which resulted in perceptions of cyclists as daring and extraordinarily athletic. This had the effect of dissuading all from cycling except those who were coordinated and physically fit. The potential for injury combined with the relatively expensive price of an ordinary, at $150, seemed to exclude all but upper- and middle-class males. These men formed elite riding clubs that had distinct uniforms, which often appeared militaristic, and they organized parades to publicly demonstrate their prowess. Their parades and rides regularly included a bugler leading the adventure.

The ordinary's cost, its reputation as dangerous, the independence it inspired, and social norms all worked in unison to make female cyclists a rare sight. The greater range of movement ordinaries offered, in and away from civilization or domesticity, was particularly important. Even though the velocipede's cost was also prohibitive to all but those who were white-collar or beyond, and despite the perception that velocipede riders were destined to break their necks, both women and children rode them. The same was not true for the ordinary. The ordinary made it easier to go faster and farther than what was possible on a velocipede, all while placing the rider farther from the ground. It quickly took on an image of a serious machine, not a toy or a mere amusement. The ordinary made cycling seem much more masculine than it did during the velocipede craze. Pope and others promoted it as a revolutionary form of movement. These factors led to a vast reduction in the numbers of women riding bicycles. Even so, while they were less common than men, there were certainly a number of women who rode ordinaries with great aplomb. This was true even though the ordinary all but necessitated the donning of bloomers. Their position over the front wheel meant there was a distinct possibility that a dress would become entangled in the spokes. The women who were bold enough to ride ordinaries aroused a great deal of controversy. At that time, athleticism was considered unbecoming in a lady and the independent nature of cycling, which afforded women the freedom to move beyond their family's surveillance, evoked protest from men.[17] Most expected women, if they were to cycle at all, to ride tricycles (see fig. 1).[18] The tricycle's steering was operated by levers and the front wheel was slightly off center so that women did not have to straddle a bar or worry about ensnaring their dresses in the wheel. It was at a noticeable disadvantage to the ordinary, however. By design, tricycles were heavier and less efficient. Some were even designed so that a man could accompany his wife—riding alongside her. Consequently, like the velocipede, the independence tricycles offered was relatively limited. It would not be until the advent of the safety bicycle that women would constitute a significant portion of the cycling market.

Shortly after manufacturers began mass-producing and promoting the safety—which closely resembled modern bicycles—American cycling experienced unprecedented growth. Soon fenders, dress guards, and chain guards could be installed on safety models with a sloping top tube. All of these advancements made cycling more accessible to women. They could safely ride while wearing dresses even though some adopted the more controversial fashion of wearing bloomers.[19] As the name suggests, the safety took an element of danger out of cycling. Its

1. A woman on her tricycle followed by men on high-wheelers. Bicycling/Hy Sandham; aquarelle print by L. Prang & Co., 1887. Courtesy of the Library of Congress.

wheels were closer in size to one another (they were eventually equal) and the positioning of the rider, nearer the rear wheel, greatly reduced the chance of headers. The safety was also lower to the ground, which not only meant a less severe fall; it also added an aerodynamic element. It did not need such a large front wheel because it was powered by the rear wheel, which was turned by a chain and sprocket connected to cranks in the center of the frame. This made it possible to utilize different gears while not changing the geometry of the bicycle, unlike the velocipede or ordinary. By 1890, this new design and the incorporation of pneumatic tires began a period of rapid growth—culminating in a bicycle boom from 1896 to 1898. Demand peaked in 1898 and production did the same one year later with a total output of just over 1.1 million bicycles.

Cycling had quickly become one of the most popular urban sports in the United States. At a time when baseball was drawing fewer than three thousand spectators, bicycle races drew crowds of over twenty thousand.[20] That popularity proved to be somewhat short-lived, for the 1890s saw both a boom and bust for American bicycle consumption. Historians have attributed much of the growth experienced during this period to female cyclists. Albert Pope was in fact very excited about the prospect for greater numbers of female cyclists. Their full potential as a consumer demographic was relatively untapped.[21] David Herlihy argues, "The vast majority of new purchasers, many of whom were female, favored the new-style safety bicycle."[22] This, however, made the safety a source of controversy, especially for those who believed it improper for women to cycle. The implication of women's entry into cycling is a topic that has received some examination.[23] Historian Robert Smith points out that the thought of women on safety bicycles created "vigorous debates." He contends, "As long as the tricycle was the only thing available to her, a woman could sit between the two rear wheels and travel sedately down the street with a minimum of effort and a maximum of ankle coverage. However, with the advent of the safety bicycle the debate erupted, with some people stoutly maintaining that cycling was not for women."[24] While works focusing on the history of the bicycle in the United States have traced the bicycle's exponential growth in popularity during the 1890s and how women came to participate in the activity, the connection between the cycling boom and the broader "cult of fitness" that occurred simultaneously has been ignored.

Public participation in sports and leisure was on a significant upswing at the turn of the century. John Higham argues that this rise in sport, which occurred primarily among young males, was part of a "growing cult of masculinity." The "urge to be young, masculine, and adventurous" was evident in the growing popularity of boxing, football, and cycling.[25] It was part and parcel of a "profound spiritual reaction" to the mechanization of industrialized living.[26] As a matter of public opinion, sports were considered beneficial because they offered physical training and diversion from the stresses of city life. American author Price Collier contended in 1898 that "Not only are muscles and sinews strengthened and hardened, but the temper and the will are trained as well. The man who learns to spar, for example, not only schools his eye, his hands and his feet to respond quickly when called upon, but he learns also, and what is far more important, to keep his temper under control and to take a pounding cheerfully."[27] Collier considered sports beneficial for boys and young men, more so than fully matured adults. For mature men, the most valuable benefit of sport was the diversion of mind and body it provided.[28]

By the end of the nineteenth century, many men increasingly believed that industrialization and the new lifestyle it offered—one that was overmechanized, overcivilized, and entirely too urban—was robbing them of manly experiences. Gail Bederman highlights how white middle-class men at the turn of the century learned that "the excessive brain work and nervous strain which professionals and businessmen endured as they struggled for success in an increasingly challenging economy" made them subject to contracting the recently discovered "disease," neurasthenia.[29] Neurasthenia, commonly referred to as nervousness, "led many to fear that middle-class men as a sex had grown decadent. Working-class and immigrant men, with their strikes and their 'primitive' customs, seemed to possess a virility and vitality which decadent white middle-class men had lost."[30] To combat these fears, men turned to sport, particularly cycling. Kevin Hayes argues that George B. Thayer, who was too young to participate in the Civil War, used bicycle touring in the 1880s as his "substitute for going to war" because "both cycling and soldiering provided ways for men to test themselves."[31]

The growth of cycling in the United States was an intrinsic part of the aforementioned alterations in an American culture that had become increasingly concerned with the health and manhood of the nation.[32] American men sought sport as a means of rejuvenating a vigorous lifestyle, which had become extremely important among urban middle-class men. These men found themselves compelled to discipline and improve their own bodies. Bicycle manufacturers and cycling advocates took advantage of the rise of sport to promote bicycles to those men who had become convinced of a need to improve their physique. To that end, bicycle promoters employed the use of doctors to convince the public that cycling was a "health stimulating exercise . . . a powerful means of strengthening the human body . . . an exercise acting as a preventive and curative . . . of certain bodily ailments."[33] One doctor argued that the greater sense of balance that the bicycle instilled in cyclists was a distinct advantage. He wrote, "Those who possess it will be able to jump ditches with greater precision and safety, pass along narrow paths, mount more difficult staircases, climb up and descend precipitous mountains, and will also carry themselves more erect, than those who do not possess this power of preserving an equilibrium." In addition, the bicycle could help develop strong chest, abdominal, and arm muscles, as well as encourage cyclists to expel the "stagnant air" in their lungs.[34] These traits were beneficial because they made men healthier and good health was a requisite of manliness. Doctors and health advocates promoted a steady regimen of exercise as both good for the individual and, in a subtler manner, good for the nation.

An attorney, Charles E. Pratt, was one of the leading advocates of cycling in the 1880s and 1890s. With a large mustache and receding hairline, Pratt was described as intense, morose, well-educated, and in desperate need of exercise.[35] He was cofounder and president of the League of American Wheelmen (LAW) and the editor of *Outing*. He also authored an instructional bicycling manual, *The American Bicycler*, which attempted to arouse interest in cycling and to put common misconceptions about the activity to rest. He romanticized cycling writing, "As a means of exercise, it calls every muscle and nerve and faculty into alert and healthful activity, without fatigue, in the open air, the sunshine, and the natural beauties of a rapidly-changing landscape."[36] His description illustrated how bicycles combined the health benefits of vigorous exercise with those of nature. Pratt continued, "As a sport, bicycling is manly, innocent, humane and rational. The companionable 'run,' the club 'meet,' the amateur 'race,' are all full of refreshing enjoyment and healthful excitement. The friendly emulation and the voluntary struggle compel regular and temperate habits."[37] Here, Pratt extolled the benefits of club membership and fraternization as well as the benefits of self-control that exercise granted individuals.[38]

The focus on self-control over one's own body was particularly important to those of the burgeoning temperance movement. In turn, the temperance movement was based, in part, on gendered ideals of the middle class. For them, a man was expected to have complete control in his life, not just control over his family, home, and social inferiors, but also over his own body. This contrasted with the stereotype of the hard-drinking factory worker of the lower classes.

Self-control was also a requisite of good health. Connections between good health, temperance, and cycling even led some to believe rising bicycle sales were cause for dwindling sales of alcohol and tobacco. In June 1896 an article in *Scientific American* titled "The Ravages of the Bicycle Boom," claimed that the increasing popularity of bicycles had a negative impact on various pastimes and consumer goods, such as a drop in the sale of cigars by over seven hundred million dollars.[39] Robert Smith argues, "Instead of idling the Sunday afternoon, smoking a cigar and drinking a schooner or two of beer, the young bloods were out on their bicycles, scorching through the streets and breathing nothing but clean air. And this hurt the tobacco business."[40] Many cyclists cut out drinking all together and those who continued to drink did so with moderation. Kennedy Childs, the secretary of the National Board of Trade of Cycle Manufacturers, felt that the issue of drinking and smoking was important enough to directly address in his suggestions for those who were training for cycling competitions. He wrote, "The question of drink is one that should receive, in an article of this nature, a statement of opinion. . . . We incline to the belief that in many cases the moderate use of malt liquors at table can do no harm, and may be of positive benefit." Smoking, on the other hand, was strongly discouraged.[41] There were a variety of opinions regarding drinking. Childs specifically mentions some of the more popular racers of the era to point out that there were some who drank and some who did not, all with mixed results. The most important thing for those who did drink was that they did so in moderation. Whether the rider was a moderate drinker or a teetotaler, there was a necessary component of self-restraint and self-discipline.

W. Gordon Stables, MD, was another influential figure who touted the benefits of the bicycle. In his book, *Health on Wheels*, he argued that the best method for attaining healthy manhood was "by being temperate not only in eating and drinking but in everything; and by taking a proper amount of exercise of the kind most suited for individual health—the best by far at the present day being what we term Cycling." In his opinion, cycling was a "means of preserving and restoring the vital powers."[42] The concept of moderation was something that was to be practiced by *healthy men* in all aspects of life. This even applied to the amount of exercise and muscle building in which one partook. Many held the opinion that a healthy man was not overdeveloped or disproportionately muscular. For these individuals, the ideal body was a strong, but natural one. There was also a clear rejection of the overcivilized shut-in whose muscles had atrophied. Dr. Stables desired the idealized body type of his self-reliant ancestors—men, who lived in an increasingly glorified time when things were more primitive, work involved sweat, and the landscape of the natural countryside was home. Even those who were born weak could "strengthen and vivify their systems, by adopting a plan of judicious and rational living; by steering clear of that rock on which so many lives are lost . . . the abuse of medicine; by proper attention to cleanliness; by drinking only pure water; by breathing, as far as possible, only pure air; by avoiding worry as much as they can."[43]

Charles Pratt also attempted to define contemporary ideals of manhood, arguing that the bicycle was a means of achieving "The training of eye and ear, the alertness and suppleness of limb and joint and muscle, the quick observation, the prompt decision in emergency, the strength and courage and self-reliance."[44] As president of LAW and a magazine editor, Pratt was able to disseminate his opinions to a large but somewhat narrow audience composed mainly of those who already owned and enjoyed bicycles. His book was unlikely to have been read by many outside of the white middle to upper classes and seemed designed primarily to legitimate bicycles. It may have been, however, a bit confusing for readers.

In some respects, Pratt's argument about the bicycle was similar to what many consider the seemingly contradictory goals of Progressivism—the political milieu in which the bicycle was blossoming.[45] In the 1890s, bicycles were still something of a technological marvel. They represented many of the same things cars and airplanes would come to represent ten to twenty years later. With that in mind, Pratt appeared to define the bicycle in contradictory terms that embraced modernity and yet, at the same time, had the capability of restoring the primitive qualities of manhood, which were perceived as endangered by modern industrialized, urban lifestyles. Curiously, cycling was an activity associated with modernity and technological advancement in the 1880s and 1890s, yet it was often celebrated as a vehicle that could restore nature and the waning sensibilities of the self-reliant man.[46] Historian Richard Harmond made note of this fact in his study of the bicycle, writing, "it was this paradoxical attraction of the bicycle—as an instance of inventive progress and as a means of flight from the consequences of such progress—which substantially explains the great cycle craze of the years between 1893–96."[47]

Pratt seemed to recognize this paradox and so he advocated a specific form of manhood wherein men could embrace modernity and civilization without compromising their natural, primitive manliness. His instructional manual argued that cycling was manly because it did not need a spur, whip, or those "ungentlemanly associations, and even excesses and cruelties, which are so often objectionably attendant upon boxing, billiards, trotting, pedestrian races, and other public exhibitions of physical training or endurance." Cycling, he argued, was a "gentlemanly recreation, a refined sport."[48] The sporting magazine *Outing* also supported the idea of cycling as a refined sport. An editorial, possibly written by Samuel Sidney McClure, proclaimed, "Bicycling in both England and America is largely on the increase, and is probably at the head of all the graceful recreations."[49] The opinion that cycling was manly because it was civilized contradicted the idea that men were becoming effeminate because they were overcivilized. One reason why Pratt stressed the genteel nature of cycling was due to the ongoing struggle for acceptance that cyclists waged among the general public during the 1870s and 1880s. This reflects a particular conceptualization of manliness based on the ideals of the white middle and upper class. As cycling entered the 1890s and became more affordable, the stress of "gentlemanly behavior" and "graceful movement," as manly characteristics would be drowned out by magazine and newspaper coverage that emphasized the long distances and great speeds cyclists were riding. Speed and distance were somewhat important during the 1880s—the heyday of the ordinary bicycle—but the safety model changed what was considered far or fast. Frank Lenz, for instance, set a regional record, when he covered 162 miles in twenty-four hours on an ordinary in 1891. In 1893, his best friend, Charles Petticord, easily smashed that record on a safety when he covered 216 miles in twenty-four hours.[50]

While the ways in which advocates promoted cycling in books and articles was changing in the 1890s, so were advertisements. Health concerns, which were directly related to perceptions that Americans were growing more nervous and effete, were important themes in bicycle advertisements of the 1890s. Their appeals employed modern advertising techniques to promise good health and economic prosperity for consumers. In his study of advertising's history in America, Roland Marchand argues that advertising matured and took on a new scope during the 1920s and 1930s. He explains that advertisements "increasingly gave predominant attention to the consumer rather than the product."[51] Bicycle advertisements show, however, that this was happening well before 1920. They had clearly "matured" and focused on consumers rather than the product as early as 1892. An advertisement for the Pope Manufacturing Company promoted bicycles as a means of increasing enjoyment and rewards in life not only through the health benefits it bestowed on cyclists but also through the monetary rewards of that good health. In an attempt to lure business away from public transportation, one of Pope's ads proclaimed, "Save $60 a year—have [an] elegant time doing it—never felt so well—can do ten hours' work in seven—salary raised yesterday—employers like healthful men."[52] This ad also shows that by 1892 advertising campaigns were attempting to broaden appeal beyond elites, to white-collar workers.

This particular advertisement focused not only on the bicycle's ability to define and alter one's social position, but also highlighted how men could use bicycles to demonstrate vigor. The bicycle could help men succeed in life by impressing their bosses with their healthful manhood and by helping them save money that would otherwise be spent on public transportation. Here, the Pope Manufacturing Company was targeting a specific class ideal of masculinity.[53] While the bicycle was considered a toy of the elites during the 1860s through the 1880s, by the 1890s, members of the bicycle industry urged the bicycle's transformation into a utilitarian device of the middle classes.[54]

Manufacturers took advantage of urban middle-class men's feelings that they needed to strengthen and discipline their own bodies by promoting bicycles as a means to gain health *and* experience nature. T. J. Jackson Lears shows how those commenting on Americans' problems at the turn of the century "traced the rise of nervous illness to 'modern civilization.' The unprecedented speed with which railway and telegraph allowed people to transact business, the barrage of information from magazines and newspapers, the monotony of routinized, subdivided labor—all were cited as causes of nervousness or insanity."[55] To combat those ailments, as Lears argues, many turned not only to "martial bellicosity" or boxing and football—they also sought "bicycling and outdoor life in general."[56] The Harbison and Gathright Bicycle Company capitalized on the masculine ideals outdoor life provided by marketing their bicycles as analogous to nature. One of their advertisements told consumers:

> Nature intended every human being to be perfectly developed. Since the hurry and hustle of our American civilization first swallowed up the healthy life of the Indian, the people have had no time to completely develop themselves. Nature saw that this couldn't go on, and her solution of the problems was the Tribune Bicycle, a wheel built for health, joy and economy, and to annihilate time.[57]

Harbison and Gathright directed this ad at those who saw the city and industry as a deteriorative force that stifled men's muscular development, joy of life, and health. Evan Friss argues that the "back-to-nature movement intensified in the late nineteenth century. . . . It became an obsession for many in the urban middle class. The countryside was glorified. And it was atop bicycles that crowds of urban worshippers flocked to the temple of nature."[58]

Other articles suggested that "real" men stood apart because they actually *craved* exercise. An article from the *Toledo Medical and Surgical Reporter* claimed, "The locomotor apparatus of man craves exercise as the stomach craves food, and the gratification produces similar good feeling in the respective organs."[59] Since any "proper" man would crave exercise, bicycle promoters believed all they needed to do was prove to them that the bicycle was the best means of exercise and then make it available. Michael McGerr argues that indeed a "rage for cycling" did result from the middle class, who were "caught up in a cult of fitness."[60] Because of the exercise boom that was occurring at the time, bicycle ads had to do relatively little work; they did not need to convince, or change men's minds, they just needed to give them a nudge toward the bicycle.

There was ample propaganda from bicycle manufactures and cycling enthusiasts to promote cycling as a natural exercise and a means of getting men out of doors. A cartoon in *Puck* demonstrated how the bicycle was an "agent of reform." In it, there are two drawings of the same man. In one, he sits in an armchair staring at a newspaper while other papers are piled around. In the other drawing he rests on the side of a country road with his bicycle leaning against a fence. There he sits staring at a flower, pondering "nature's book."[61] Cycling was advocated as a "sanitary pastime," which brought "health to those who by its means found themselves able to escape from the close and vitiated air of town life into the pure and life-giving air of the meadows and open fields."[62] Not all men were drawn by promotions that connected the bicycle to nature and health, particularly those that did not ascribe to a strict middle-class understanding of manhood.

As the number of advertisements targeting men's insecurities proliferated, it is clear that bicycle promoters believed American men were turning to the bicycle in attempts to affirm their manhood. Even companies outside of the bicycle industry were aware that insecure men were turning to sport and the bicycle to affirm manhood. Their advertisements often appeared alongside advertisements for bicycles. Similar to bicycle manufacturers, medical companies exploited fears that manhood was waning. One ad for the Erie Medical Company read, "Four out of five who suffer nervousness, mental worry, attacks of 'the blues,' are but paying the penalty of early excesses. Victims, reclaim your manhood, regain your vigor. Don't despair."[63] The ad featured a half-nude female, kneeling down drawing water from a well. Those in the medical profession often spoke of "nervousness" as one of the most rampant side effects of industrialization and urbanization.[64] Another advertisement from the same company used the headline "Weak Men," and pictured a scantily clad woman sitting on top of a prostrate lion.[65] The fact that these ads often ran in the same sections that reported on bicycling news, and near advertisements for bicycles, highlights that—at least in the opinion of the Erie Medical Company—men who were insecure about their manliness were prone to turn to sport, particularly cycling, in attempts to reclaim their manhood.

By the mid-1890s—as cycling became more common due to the growing popularity of the safety—the physical act of riding a bicycle was not enough, in and of itself, to demonstrate manhood. This was particularly true after a massive influx of female cyclists. Still, cycling was an activity associated with certain notions of manhood because it remained a somewhat exclusive activity. In fact, that exclusivity was an intentional and important aspect of cycling. It allowed white male cyclists a chance to secure their own idealized version of manhood through attempting to control access to the activity. This could be done through club membership and/or race participation. A commonly used template for club rules and bylaws stated that membership should be open to "any gentleman who is not a professional bicycler."[66] The use of the word *gentleman* was not only an expression of the exclusion of women from the club, but it was also a subtle and yet very loosely defined term that could be used to exclude those perceived to belong to other races, ethnicities, and classes. The exclusion of professional cyclists from clubs, for instance, was an attempt to maintain class-based ideals of manhood. It denoted that members must participate in the activity solely because they enjoy it, not because they are talented enough to make money from participation. This language of amateurism, popular among all "respectable" sports at the time, particularly Olympic sport, was simply a means of excluding all except those that had the free time and discretionary money to invest in leisure. Additionally, these clubs often included a membership fee of around five dollars, which could work to achieve the same exclusionary ends. That does not mean that all those outside the white middle class were necessarily prevented from participation. In fact, groups who were excluded occasionally created their own clubs but even then, they were still denied access to events organized by whites.

Similar to recreational riding, competitive cycling was another area in which organized and unorganized white male cyclists sought to maintain certain ideals of masculinity. The characteristics of manhood demonstrated in competitive cycling, however, were different from those of cycling as leisure. In the case of competitive cycling, white men attempted to exercise control over access to races and participated in acts of intimidation against individuals who defied the norms of the sport. Cyclists were generally not permitted to simply show up at a venue and enter the contest. They had to be a member of the organization or sanctioning body that was governing the race. Initially, this was the responsibility of the LAW, which openly denied individuals the right to participate, especially if they were black—the most well-known case being that of Marshall "Major" Taylor.[67]

Exclusionary practices were not only directed toward racial and ethnic minority groups. It is clear that women were also strongly discouraged from participating in races or even riding their bicycles with significant speed. Rigorous cycling was only seen as suitable for men. All women, however, did not embrace those standards. In many ways, the women's movement for greater independence and suffrage was apparent in cycling. Women, who were once discouraged from cycling, continued to confront social convention by pedaling their way toward greater liberation. In fact, the suffragist Frances Willard referred to her bicycle as an "implement of power."[68] She and other women did not merely seek access to the bicycle; they struggled for complete and total freedom to use it in whatever manner they saw fit. In this struggle, they often had to overcome men's attempts to limit their access to cycling. In her endeavor to cycle around the world, the infamous female cyclist Annie Londonderry faced incredulity and scorn. There were those who denied her accomplishments because she used steamships and trains liberally, and those who saw her merely an immoral woman running out on her husband and family.[69]

As did many of the debates concerning the propriety of women's activities during this era, opposition to female cyclists was often couched in terms of health. In her essay on bicycles and gender, Ellen Gruber Garvey shows "Both defense and attack took medicalized form: antibicyclers claimed that riding would ruin women's sexual health by promoting masturbation and would compromise gender definition as well, while probicyclers asserted that bicycling would strengthen women's bodies—and thereby make them more fit for motherhood."[70] One such "antibicycler attack" came from opposition to women's adoption of the "scorcher" position, which was necessary in attaining faster speeds. This position was the most common posture of men who raced with their chest bent over the handlebars, backs arched, and their bodies in a forward position on the nose of the saddle. Such posture decreased wind resistance and added power by positioning the rider's weight more directly over the pedals. In this instance, objections to women's participation were framed in terms of both hygiene and health. Medical experts claimed that the position, coupled with strenuous exercise, could lead to physical deformations of women's bodies as well as potential damage to their reproductive organs. An article in the *Brooklyn Medical Journal* was direct in its claim that "the bicycle teaches masturbation in women and girls" because of the angle of the saddle.[71] Dr. Robert Dickinson was more elaborate in explaining how the saddle could be angled and manipulated to result in a "hammock—like connectivity which would fit itself snugly over the entire vulva and reach up in front [and] bring about constant friction over the clitoris and labia."[72]

Ellen Garvey argues, "Riding was a threat to gender roles; while it would be safe for healthy men to do so, it would be dangerous for women to expend so much of their strength on physical activity."[73]

Expectations were that a "proper" woman's first priority would be to her duties as a wife and/or mother. While some doctors opposed cycling for women all together, others argued a moderate amount of cycling was beneficial because it maintained health and could make them more attractive. Peter Zheutlin posits that some of these doctors may have been on bicycle merchants' payrolls.[74] While it is easy to make that assumption, it is a little more difficult to find conclusive evidence. Regardless, there was certainly a fine line between a healthy amount of activity and too much. Too much cycling would have detrimental results.

Attempts to limit women's access to cycling were not unique to the United States. An anonymous English writer argued that there was to be "one unwritten axiom . . . it is that the gentler sex must on all occasions consult appearances in a special manner not demanded of men."[75] This particular writer's concern was whether women could ride tricycles without sacrificing their appearance. He did not even consider the possibility of women on bicycles, for "obvious reasons," which was undoubtedly an allusion to the fact that women could not efficiently ride the common bicycle in a sidesaddle mount or otherwise without inciting controversy. He described himself as repulsed by the sight of women on bikes with their "bodies bent well forward, knees up and down anyhow—struggling along with purple faces and hair awry."[76] To him and many others, the thought of female athleticism was improper and unattractive.

The article voiced a common objection to women's participation in what was seen as a male domain. The author, like many men of the era in both the United States and Europe was, however, willing to accept women's participation in cycling so long as it was limited strictly to leisure. It must not compromise a woman's appearance, whether that be through signs of physical exertion or the impropriety of straddling of a bicycle. Kennedy Childs offered a similar opinion in his article "Training for Cycle Competitions." He wrote, "for the purpose of this article the writer will, forgetful of his past flattery of the fair sex, assume its practice by the lords of creation only."[77] Initially, men admonished women for riding bicycles all together, but by the 1890s, with the invention of the safety bicycle and women's refusal to let men enjoy bicycles by themselves, men were forced to concede to women's participation. Still, women did not immediately gain free reign to ride the bicycle in the same manner as men. Articles from the era show that men only approved of women cyclists as long as they did not do so strenuously or excessively. In March 1898, the New York Central Wheelmen voted to ban women and children from participating in centuries—one-hundred-mile bike rides completed in a single day.[78] The fact that the club imposed such a ban illustrates that women were indeed capable and eager to demonstrate their own vigor. It also shows how cycling elites tried to negotiate the changing image of the bicycle. Women's entrance into the sport certainly opened up that share of the market Albert Pope was so eager to tap, but the tapping of that market had to be done in a manner that did not sacrifice male consumers. Such restrictions and regulations were the direct results of efforts to maintain the manliness of cycling.

In spite of the debate and attempts to implement limitations, women took to bicycles in growing numbers, actively refuting fears that cycling would damage their bodies. Sarah Hallenbeck focuses on women's agency during this period arguing that during "the later years of the bicycle craze, women riders began to undertake longer rides, outside of indoor arenas, through which they made displays that often overtly challenged doctors' prescriptions for women's bicycling."[79] By 1896, views were beginning to change as "moderate cycling was even being recommended for expectant mothers."[80] In their study of bicycles and women's rights, Lisa S. Strange and Robert S. Brown have argued that the safety bicycle was an important vehicle for women's liberation. "Heralding the bicycle as a tool of emancipation, [Elizabeth Cady] Stanton linked cycling to dress reform, the collapse of the distinction between the public and private spheres, and religious liberation."[81] Frances Willard celebrated the bicycle in her book, *A Wheel within a Wheel.* At first, she praised it for its ability to lure young men away from saloons and into the outdoors but after she received a bicycle as a present from Albert Pope she soon advocated cycling as a worthwhile endeavor for women as well.[82]

Men may have been reluctant to accept women cyclists at first, but some found a way to counteract the threat to their masculinity through a patriarchal belief that they could "allow" women access to bicycles. During this moment, cycling norms mutated in order to accept women, as cycling became a gift that men could give to women. One advertisement exemplified this attitude proclaiming, "These are days of doubles—two's company—two Columbias are better than one. Let that lady of yours feel as sprightly as you do. Buy her a Columbia Bicycle."[83] The art shows a man and woman riding side by side on their bicycles, sitting upright and socializing. This was more an act of courtship than participation in a strenuous lifestyle. In this particular advertisement, the manufacturer was appealing to men as patriarchs by showing that their acceptance of women on bicycles would win women's favor.

Advertisements told men to "let" their women ride bicycles but many women did not wait for approval—using the bicycle to gain opportunities for freedom and independence.[84] While women such as Frances Willard, Annie Londonderry, and Elizabeth Cady Stanton employed bicycles to liberate themselves from the domestic sphere, bicycle marketing attempted to appeal to this new woman without upsetting traditionalists. Ellen Garvey argues, "The discourse of consumption constituted by the advertising articles, and fiction within the developing mass-market magazine of the 1890s subsumed both feminist and conservative views in the interest of sales. In effect, these advertising dependent magazines asserted a version of women's bicycling that reframed its apparent social risks and benefits."[85] Even as magazine advertisements and literature attempted to "diffuse the threat" by focusing on "scenarios in which [the bicycle] upheld and renewed the traditional social order," there was concern that it afforded women too much independence.[86] There were still those who believed it was a direct threat to manhood. A poem published in *Outing: An Illustrated Monthly Magazine of Recreation* titled "In These Bicycle Days" offered a satirical reflection of the societal changes that were occurring during the bicycle boom, as well as men's attempts to maintain authority. One verse of the poem reads, "Peter, Peter pumpkin eater, Had a wife, and couldn't keep her; Took an axe and smashed her bike, So she had to stay home at night."[87] Similarly, a cartoon in *Puck* showed a reversal of gender roles brought on by the bicycle where the husband took care of the children while the wife went for a ride (see fig. 2).[88] The bicycle's ability to free women from their homes to enjoy the same spirit of adventurism that men enjoyed was a privilege that men were often reluctant to share. The idea that the woman's sphere was at home with the children, preparing food while men were free to venture out into the unknown with their bicycles, was a concept that was clearly being challenged.

In making appeals to gendered ideals, the bicycle industry effectively shaped the image of the bicycle so that it symbolized health and manhood. Pamela Laird's study of American business and consumer marketing verifies that bicycle advertisements were indeed successful. The bicycle industry offered "an attractive illustration of advertising's powerful impact in helping to build a new and quite respectable industry."[89] The Pope Manufacturing Company alone invested over $500,000 a year in advertising by 1897.[90] Bicycle advertisements appeared in a myriad of sources. Their art and copy linking notions of health with the bicycle set the tone for "modern advertising" techniques. In the process, bicycle advertising not only helped to shape the bicycle's image, the artwork it employed diffused the act of cycling to a broader audience.

The high volume of sales and sheer popularity of cycling in the 1890s established this era as the "golden age" of the bicycle. This was the high-water mark that the industry would continue to compare itself to throughout the following decades. Consequently, this period also set the tone for the future of bicycle advertising and marketing, which would focus on the male sex. The heightened concern with masculinity in the face of industrialization and urbanization was beneficial for the bicycle industry because of cycling's ability to affirm white middle-class ideals of manhood. Not only could cyclists show off their purchasing power and their access to leisure—they could also use bicycles to develop their bodies and get out into the fresh air. This association of cycling with muscular development and nature is one that the cycling industry would continue to try to maintain, long after

2. *Her Choice. The Young Man's Slave (Five Years Later).* Print-lithograph, illustration in *Puck*, July 7, 1897, 16. Courtesy of the Library of Congress.

the boom and bust of the cycling industry, and after American adults nearly abandoned the activity altogether.

By the end of the nineteenth century, the bicycle appeared to have lost a great deal of cultural relevance. To be sure, the rising importance of strength and vigor in the 1890s played well for bicycle promotion. Simultaneously, however, the bicycle seemed merely a faddish means of exercise. American bicycle manufacturers' output peaked at just over one million units in 1899, after demand had already begun to dwindle. The next few decades would find the industry desperately trying to get back to the golden days of cycling in the 1890s. Production would fail to reach five hundred thousand from 1904 to 1914. Sociologist Thomas Burr argues that the bust was caused by an overabundance of new companies entering the US market leading to overproduction and a severe drop in prices.[91] There were nearly 50 manufacturers in 1892 but that number rose to over 2,800 by 1898. A majority of these were small manufacturers producing fewer than 500 bikes a year, but there were over 300 manufacturers with an annual production well above that number.[92] The average price was around $150 at the beginning of the boom but new bicycles could be purchased for as little as $10 after the bust.[93] The rise of bicycle manufacturing and the resulting lowering of prices changed the way Americans thought about cycling leading to the bicycle's loss of appeal. Those who remained in the industry, after the bust in 1898, began to question how they could revive sales to peak levels.

The bicycle came of age during a specific moment in which calls for participation in sport and physicality came from a multitude of directions. Bicycle proponents and industry elites effectively used cultural ideals and concerns to create an image of the bicycle that offered an opportunity for conspicuous consumption as well as a physical and psychic means of reclaiming manhood. Sales were further aided by the bicycle's malleability as a consumer item, which allowed it to simultaneously represent manhood and demonstrate the independence of the new woman. As fears of contracting neurasthenia subsided, and women effectively made their claim, the bicycle seemed to have served its purpose. In short, the cultural changes underway at the turn of the century were a boon to the bicycle industry. At the same time, those changes inspired overconfidence in the ability to move a product, which was ultimately detrimental to long-term success. By 1904 production fell to 252,923 and stayed below 500,000 for the next ten years. The dramatic boom and bust of the 1890s left an indelible impact on the bicycle industry. Within the institutional memory, there would remain not only a desire to get back to the production levels of 1896–99, but to do so by building a consumer base that was more stable than that of the golden era. It would take until the 1910s before any sense of cohesion appeared within the industry. By that time, it was not only saddled with the problem of trying to increase the bicycle's appeal, but to do so in the face of rising competition from the automotive industry. The attempts it would make to increase business throughout the first half of the twentieth century were reminiscent of those directed toward white middle-class males in the 1880s and 1890s. The targeted demographic, however, would change.

2

Automobiles and a World at War

IN THE 1910S, bicycle boosters continued promoting the bicycle as a curative for the ill effects of overmechanization and urbanization. Magazine articles that celebrated cycling as a healthy activity and a means of returning to nature also gave a voice to Progressive's adulation of the yeoman farmer. One such article described a multi-day bicycle trip in which a group of riders stopped at a farmer's house. Upon arriving, they were happy to find food cooked and prepared "the good old-fashioned way." There was, "None of the small, overseasoned portions of the city restaurants often unfit to eat, and surely not the thing for the healthy appetite of a bicycle rider, but huge slices of home-made bread, with freshly churned butter, chicken, tender and cooked to a turn, with heaps and heaps of beans, corn, tomatoes and potatoes, all products of the farmer's own bounteous fields."[1] The article explained that all riders had "the same intent and purpose—to get out, out into God's own glorious country where the air is clear, the sky blue, and where they could, without fear of censor, throw aside the mask of artificial civility one is forced to assume in his daily intercourse with those that go to make up the many thousands that inhabit the great city."[2] There were already 153,622 miles of surfaced road in the United States by 1904.[3] The bicycle provided an opportunity to travel those roads and get away from city life, where one could move about in a more natural setting at whatever pace they desired. Using the bicycle to escape the confines of the city gave one the ability to breathe "fresh air" and interact with and/or conquer nature.

What the bicycle needed in the 1910s, however, was new business, not a return to the pastoral emphasis and worn-out concentration on ideals of white middle-class masculinity that defined bicycle marketing of the 1890s. Slowly, it became apparent that targeting white middle- and upper-class males alone was no longer sufficient. The bicycle industry wanted to increase business and many of the leaders believed the best way to do so was by expanding their market. Making appeals to those who were thought to appreciate nature and healthy exercise was a poor tactic for broadening the consumer base because it continued the status quo. Bicycle marketing needed to diversify, and using the same marketing tactics on the same consumer group was not the way to do so. Sales increased significantly when cycling became popular among women in the 1890s but by the 1900s it appeared that the phenomenon of the female cyclist was a temporary trend. Appeals to women therefore, when they were made, came primarily through efforts to make cycling fashionable again (discussed in further detail in the following chapter). For the most part, that meant the industry waited for any news of women on bikes and then hyperbolized and publicized those stories. The tactic did not work, as sales remained low. Overall consumption of the bicycle had clearly fallen in the course of ten years and everyone in the bicycle industry desperately hoped for salvation (see table 2).[4]

A resurrection of any sort would require different methods of marketing. The consumers of the 1910s would not respond the same way as those of the 1890s. The industry could no longer count on the cycling fad or public fascination with bicycles now that bigger, faster machines at increasingly affordable prices were on the horizon (see table 3). Even those who praised the virtues of cycling referred to it as the "old bicycle." Automobiles were quickly changing the way people thought about movement. Initially considered a rich man's toy, they proved more than a passing curiosity and members of the bicycle industry soon took notice. In an attempt to quell fears that the bicycle's day was done, bicycle supporters supplied evidence that bicycles were still more popular than cars. A trade magazine informed readers that of the 2,681 tags issued in Richmond, Indiana, 1,254 were to bicycle

TABLE 2: **US Bicycle Consumption, 1898–1909**

Year	**1898**	**1899**	**1900**	**1904**	**1909**
US bicycle consumption	928,250	1,182,250	997,000	252,923	233,707

Source: Bruce Epperson, "How Many Bikes: An Investigation into the Quantification of Bicycling, 1878–1914," in *Cycle History 11: Proceedings of the 11th International Cycling History Conference*, ed. Andrew Ritchie and Rob Van der Plas (San Francisco: Van der Plas Publications, 2001), 49.

riders. "One-horse rigs" accounted for 840 of the tags while only 245 belonged to automobile owners and another 52 for motorcycles.[5] The number of cars registered each year compared with the number of bicycles purchased, however, suggests that the days of bicycles outnumbering automobiles on city streets were quickly coming to a close (see table 4). The 1910s show that some of the forces affecting bicycle sales were outside of the industry's dominion. Realizing their limited power made members of the industry recognize the need to work together in attempts to recover sales.

There were merely 8,000 automobiles registered in the United States in 1900, but by 1909 that number would reach 306,000. In 1919 the number had grown to 6,679,000.[6] From 1904 to 1907, the average price of automobiles rose steadily but it began to fall by 1908.[7] In 1912 the average price of a car was $1,083—the lowest it had been since 1903. In response, sales soared.[8] A combination of decreasing prices with increasing reliability spawned a long span of sustained growth for the automotive industry. The number of cars registered in 1919 was twenty-one times the number in 1909. Car sales quickly outpaced bicycle sales, a development that aroused a sense of panic among members of the bicycle industry.

Increased bicycle sales during the second half of the 1910s, however, show that the automobile had yet to supplant the bicycle entirely but it is important to consider why sales picked up at that time. Even though sales were decidedly less than those experienced in the 1890s, cycling seemed to maintain some of its popular appeal. In the sporting

TABLE 3: **Price of Model T and Number Sold, 1908–21**

Year	1908	1910	1912	1914	1916	1921
Price of Model T	$850	$780	$600	$490	$360	$260
Number of Model Ts Sold	5,896	19,293	78,611	260,720	377,036	...

Source: Clay McShane, *Down the Asphalt Path: The Automobile and the American City* (New York: Columbia Univ. Press, 1994), 135.

world, for instance, cycling had diminished but not gone away. Six-day and other track races continued to enjoy sizeable crowds. A *New York Times* feature, "Topic of the Times," questioned whether this fact alone meant people were still excited about bicycles. With the headline "Hypnotized by the Thousands," the article proclaimed that a "duller and less pleasing spectacle" than six-day races was unimaginable.[9] It suggested that spectators were simply in the habit of going to the races. They did not find the races exciting. Rather, it was the thought that thousands of other people would be present that attracted spectators. Therefore, attendees were merely demonstrating a desire to attend social functions, not an interest in exercise, health, or even bicycles.[10] According to this view, even though six-day bicycle races continued to enjoy a degree of popularity, there would not necessarily be a correlation in bicycle sales. Even if those attending the races were interested in cycling, the bicycle industry itself seemed less confident that the bicycle could continue to appeal to consumers without intervention.

Some of the fluctuations in bicycle sales that would occur were beyond the industry's control. Advertising and marketing were certainly important, but it was also apparent that changing ideals of mobility influenced the bicycle's successes and failures over the years. New dances such as the cancan and the mechanization of corporeal labor resulting from Taylorism represent developments that were "symptomatic of [these] wider changes in the sense of movement."[11] The automobile was a critical component. As it achieved faster speeds and the capability to travel greater distances, the car became the standard

TABLE 4: **Bicycle Consumption versus Car Registration, 1909–19**

Year	Bicycles consumed	Cars registered	Increase in registration	Cars produced
1909	233,707	306,000	112,000	127,731
1910	388,148	458,000	152,000	181,000
1911	393,894	619,000	161,000	199,319
1912	426,561	902,000	283,000	356,000
1913	464,080	1,190,000	907,000	461,500
1914	398,899	1,664,000	474,000	543,679
1915	...	2,332,000	668,000	895,930
1916	526,076	3,368,000	1,036,000	1,525,578
1917	606,918	4,727,000	1,359,000	...
1918	567,207	5,555,000	828,000	...
1919	479,163	6,679,000	1,124,000	...

Sources: Bruce Epperson, "How Many Bikes: An Investigation into the Quantification of Bicycling, 1878–1914," in *Cycle History 11: Proceedings of the 11th International Cycling History Conference*, ed. Andrew Ritchie and Rob Van der Plas (San Francisco: Van der Plas Publications, 2001), 49; US Census Bureau, *Statistical Abstracts of the United States: 2003*, "Transportation Indicators for Motor Vehicles and Airlines: 1900 to 2001," no. HS-41, 77.s.

by which all other forms of mobility would be measured. Encapsulated in this changing sense of mobility were ideals of race, gender, class, and citizenship.[12]

The decreasing price of the automobile changed the way Americans viewed cars. The car was associated with effeteness during its formative years, when it was merely a form of conspicuous consumption and fashionableness. In 1906 Woodrow Wilson described the car as a symbol of "arrogance and wealth."[13] As cars made their way onto the driveways of the lower classes, however, they became more representative of rougher masculine characteristics.[14] At the same time, the automobile also began to represent American national identity. In his cultural history of the car, Cotton Seiler argues, "In the first generation of motor touring narratives, we see automobility sanctioned as a vehicle of individual and national renascence—a means to resuscitate republican selfhood and reopen the frontier."[15] The public and federal sanctioning of the automobile, which widened the conception of mobility, required a reworking of all other forms of movement. For the bicycle, this process would take more than decade.

While cars had been growing in number on American roads steadily since 1900, the official endorsement they were given by President Taft in 1909 coincided with a 101 percent increase in automobile production—the largest increase in production in the fifteen years from 1901 to 1916.[16] Whereas Theodore Roosevelt refused to own a car, the White House garage included several cars and chauffeurs under Taft. He publicly celebrated the car declaring, "I am sure the automobile coming in as a toy of the wealthier class is going to prove the most useful of them all to all classes, rich and poor."[17] Christopher Wells argues that after 1910 there was a growing belief that the federal government should be directly involved in road construction. The culmination of these changing beliefs came with the passage of the Federal Aid Road Act of 1916, "which approved $75 million in matching funds for distribution among the states."[18] This piece of legislation was undoubtedly influenced by the two-million-plus cars registered in 1915.

The emergence of the automobile was important from a legal perspective because the definitions of bicycles and motorcycles, as codified by law, would hinge on definitions of the automobile. In turn, these definitions shaped the way citizens thought about movement and impacted sales. The decision of whether police departments and legislatures should consider the bicycle a vehicle played out in numerous states during the first years of the twentieth century. Peter Norton argues that "struggles to define the use and misuse of streets were at their hottest in the 1910s and the 1920s."[19] Some states categorized the bicycle as a vehicle while others did not. A cartoon commenting on one such debate in Connecticut pictured a character resembling an orangutan dressed in a police uniform holding a small bicycle in his hand. He asked, "What is that thing anyway?"[20] The caption below the image explained, "New Haven, Conn., police want to know if a bicycle is a vehicle."[21] Similar debates were occurring in Providence, Rhode

Island, and Springfield, Massachusetts.[22] Another cartoon pictured a Puritan looking over a motorcycle with sidecar. He commented, "That looks like an automobile to me." The accompanying caption read, "The Massachusetts legislature needs an oculist badly."[23] In these instances, the important question was how to classify bicycles and motorcycles in light of the growing production and consumption of automobiles. Classifying bicycles as vehicles would make them subject to many of the same regulations as automobiles, such as licenses, tolls, taxes, and safety precautions. New Jersey decided the bicycle was a vehicle and therefore all cyclists were required to have a lamp kept lit from a half hour after sunset to a half hour before sunrise and an audible signal.[24]

Increased regulation came with consequences but the alternative was potentially worse. If bicycles were considered something other than a vehicle, their legitimacy as a form of transportation would be called into question with the implication that they were simply for exercise or recreation. Cotton Seiler argues, "The flattering image of the automobile entailed, in turn, a general disparagement of the automobile's ancestor and erstwhile rival, the locomotive."[25] The same was certainly true of the bicycle. Judging all other forms of movement in relation to the automobile conferred a hierarchy of movement in which the car was king.

The way a bicycle was defined and the safety regulations it was subject to were not the only important developments beyond the bicycle industry's control. Another issue of great importance to bicycle sales, domestically and abroad, was the tariff placed on them. Of course, the tariff issue went beyond bicycle sales. Calls for lower rates came from farmers and others who wanted to see the duties on goods they exported lowered but they were thwarted by Grover Cleveland and ignored by Theodore Roosevelt. Taft campaigned on tariff reform but the Payne-Aldrich Act he signed came out of the legislature heavily revised by "protectionists," who favored the high tariff to cut down on competition. The act that emerged "saw prevailing duties firmly re-established, if not actually raised."[26] Real tariff reform would come under President Wilson with the Underwood Tariff Act in September 1913. Wilson declared, "The object of the tariff duties henceforth laid must be effective competition, the whetting of American wits by contest with the wits of the rest of the world."[27] The motorcycle and bicycle industry were understandably concerned about the potential effects of these reforms.

A quarterly report issued by the Department of Commerce regarding imported materials and US consumption compared the effects of lowered import duties on motorcycles and bicycles. There were fears that lowered import duties would lead to increased competition from foreign manufacturers by flooding the US market with imported goods and a likely lowering of prices, undercutting those produced domestically. The resulting increase in imports of motorcycles, however, was not quite as drastic as it was with bicycles. When the duty on motorcycles was decreased from 45 percent to 25 percent, "imports did not take the jump that might generally have been looked for. . . . On the other hand, immediately upon the reduction from 45% to 25% in import duty on bicycles and finished parts thereof, imports showed a striking increase." The value of bicycles and parts thereof imported in the July 1–October 3 quarter of 1913 when the duty was 45 percent was $12,095. When that duty was lowered to 25 percent for the last quarter of 1913 the value of bicycles imported rose to $65,640.[28] The higher import duty of 45 percent was indeed protecting American bicycle and parts manufactures from foreign competition. That foreign competition, however, came mostly from Germany and a few other European countries that would soon be embroiled in World War I. Subsequently, their metals and other materials used for bicycle production would be consumed strictly for militaristic purposes. This reduced the competition American bicycle manufacturers faced.

The automobile and World War I were two major forces that played havoc with the bicycle industry in the 1910s. The automobile's impact was adverse while World War I's was advantageous. World War I was beneficial to the US bicycle industry in a few ways. While there was a reduction on the duties for imports, US manufactures also enjoyed relaxed regulations on exports. This was especially important during the war. By 1915 much of the manufacturing and production of goods not specifically needed for war in European countries were dwindling in supply. Not only would those countries involved in the war effort have few materials and workers to produce bicycles to export to the United States, but they would also have fewer for their own citizenry. The increased need in Europe and eventual entrance of the United States into the war led to a period of "enormous industrial and agricultural expansion" that lasted from 1915 to 1920.[29]

Neutrality and mobilization did not lead to the kind of sales experienced in the 1890s but they did offer a ray of hope for the US bicycle industry. The cover of the trade magazine *Motorcycling* included a picture of Uncle Sam holding a bicycle and a motorcycle with a caption that read, "Is Uncle Sam to land a good slice of motorcycle and bicycle business from other countries? It looks so now, since the Washington authorities have ruled that cycles can be shipped without hindrance by our own authorities."[30] Another article triumphantly announced, "Record Foreign Trade: Motorcycles and Bicycles Shipped Abroad Show Great Increase."[31] While bicycles shipped abroad reached "unprecedented" figures, the article was also happy to announce, "Turning to the import side we are taking fewer motorcycles and bicycles than at any time in years. Just a few machines are coming in, directly due to the fact that all foreign made machines are being commandeered for war purposes."[32]

The prosperity of the wartime economy also meant that bicycle retailers could make more sales to skilled laborers.[33] Skilled workers' wages were on the rise and the number of hours they were required to work began to decline. The average wage per hour, excluding agriculture, was slightly up from 1914 but it would continue to rise to a nearly 80 percent increase by 1919.[34] Leaders of the bicycle industry were quick to tell merchants of this exciting opportunity to sell more bikes. By August 1915, *MotorCycling and Bicycling* was informing merchants that skilled laborers had more wages and more free time on their hands than they had ever had. One article asked bicycle dealers, "Doesn't it signify that these men, who are your best customers for motorcycles and bicycles, are now in position to buy these vehicles? Doesn't it tell you that this is the rising tide for your business?"[35] Merchants were told to be patient, that if increased sales had not made it to their store yet, they would, and that "The pressure for labor is steadily moving westward. If it hasn't struck your town now, it will within a month."[36] *MotorCycling and Bicycling* recommended that these dealers should seek to establish good relationships with local factories so they might have an "in" when factory production picked up. The suggestion that dealers concentrate on skilled workers and the middle class presented an opportunity for dealers to create new customers who were more likely to continue riding and buying bicycles after the war was over—provided the prosperity continued.

Somewhat conversely, another aspect of World War I that was beneficial to cycling manufacturers was the culture of sacrifice inspired by the war effort. Educators even incorporated the themes of "patriotism, heroism, and sacrifice" into elementary school classrooms.[37] Herbert Hoover, who was appointed head of the US Food Administration food by President Wilson in May 1917, proposed to dictate food policy by "Mobliliz[ing] the spirit of self-denial and self-sacrifice."[38] Hoover gained popularity by encouraging households to voluntarily participate in "meatless" and "wheatless" days rather than enacting a policy of food rationing.[39] The public response was proclaimed, "wholehearted and enthusiastic."[40] The idea that the citizenry should tighten up their belts and make do with what was available as an expression of their patriotism provided an excellent marketing opportunity for the bicycle industry. A particularly clever advertising and public relations campaign did precisely that and heralded cycling as patriotic. L. Stanton Pugh's article, "Ride a Bicycle and Do Your Bit," explained that in light of the "possibility of the government issuing 'gasoline tickets' to the joy-riding autoists, limiting the individual car owner to one gallon a week, it seems a most opportune time for the bicycle's appeal to patriotism."[41]

Pugh suggested that pleasure-riding in automobiles was unpatriotic. He also took the moment to argue, "A false pride has tended to convey the impression that the bicycle implies a loss of social prestige; this however, is refuted by the ever-increasing numbers of the elite who are taking up the bicycle at such aristocratic resorts as Palm Beach, Florida."[42] His comments reveal a shift in consumer society where elite status was now conferred by automobile consumption. As a result, the bicycle had moved down-market. While Pugh acknowledged that people commonly perceived the bicycle as having been downgraded in status, he believed that elites were coming back to cycling as an expression of their patriotism. The goal of the article, however, was not to admonish US consumers for their misperception but instead to suggest to bicycle retailers that a great opportunity was coming their way. It concluded, "This then is the opportune time for dealers throughout the country to make a decisive appeal to the patriotism of the public. A new field opens before the dealer, made possible and directly attributable to the war."[43]

A few months later, *MotorCycling and Bicycling* encouraged retailers to market bicycles as synonymous with patriotism. A two-page article titled "A Cycle Sign of the Times, Society Women 'Hooverize' by Going Back to the Bicycle" was included, complete with four large photos of well-dressed ladies and details about how four women of St. Paul, Minnesota, were back to riding bikes like "their sisters twenty years ago."[44] This revival of cycling among society women was also occurring in Palm Beach, Florida; Newport, Rhode Island; Lenox, Massachusetts; and Bar Harbor, Maine. The trend started in Palm Beach a few seasons prior "but war conditions . . . added their impetus all over the country. Like their sisters in England and including the nobility and members of the Royal family, American society women have made a war sacrifice by laying up their autos and substituting the efficient and economical bicycle."[45] Dealers only needed to encourage the trend. This was, no doubt, a great idea for marketing bicycles during the war and it made excellent use of the heightened sense of patriotism at the time, as it made a subtle point about making small sacrifices for the sake of the war effort. After all, the idea that women should make sacrifices for the improvement of their country was a fundamental precept of idealized notions about republican motherhood. Still, using the culture of sacrifice to promote bicycles was rather myopic.

The bicycle industry, perplexed by elite women's abandonment of bicycles, saw this as a great opportunity to pull them back. If society women were, however, simply substituting the bicycle because it was efficient and economical, what would be the point of riding bicycles once the war was over? Obviously, women of this class, and their husbands, would not be as concerned with what was economical. In fact, it would be their decisions to partake in activities and practices that were not economical that would set them apart from the lower classes. The wartime appeals to patriotism relied too heavily on notions of sacrifice and therefore only helped contribute to the diminished status of the bicycle among the well-to-do.[46] After the war ended, there was no apparent reason for them to continue riding bicycles. The end of the war meant a "return to normalcy" and citizens' return to spending freely, unconcerned with sacrifice or conservation.

In spite of this potential blunder, while the war raged on, the bicycle industry prospered. A leading member of the industry, the New Departure Company, reported that business was going so well by 1915 that their factories were running twenty-three hours a day and they were forced to expand their facilities.[47] C. F. Olin, the manager of advertising for the firm reported, "Our increased business is to some extent due to the war in stopping of the supply of European made bearings. . . . But the principal reason is that we are working on orders received before the war, indicating that we are making bearings equal to the best in the world and satisfactory to our customers."[48] Olin also posited that New Departure's success was potentially due to their new and vigorous advertising campaign. The explanation of the war's role in stopping the supply of European bearings, however, called the effectiveness of advertising into question. It also highlighted how the ebb and flow of American manufactured bicycle consumption was affected by outside forces. The war was not only good for US bicycles and parts traveling abroad, but also those sold domestically, as governmental entities incorporated bicycles into their services.

The bicycle industry profited from bicycle purchases for police officers, mail carriers, and even soldiers—all who were reportedly able to do their jobs more efficiently. The New York Police Department bought several hundred bicycles in the spring of 1915. The bicycle police proved so successful that the *New York Times* ran an article about their effectiveness, which *Bicycle News* then quoted so that members of the bicycle industry could have something to be proud of, but also to suggest that merchants sell bicycles to police officers in their own communities. Capitalizing on the efficiency of wheeled transport, there was also a comment about the New Yorkers' favorable impression of bicycle-mounted police because of their increased efficiency and productivity. One resident commented, "The bicycle corps, both pedal and motorcycle, is the finest idea ever put into practice. . . . Each man can cover more ground than ten of the ordinary patrolmen."[49] Because police officers could travel faster and farther on bicycles than they could on foot, many areas of the city soon took notice of the difference the bicycle made—some who never saw a policeman in a year were beginning to see them on a regular basis.[50] The police were using the bicycle to venture farther out into their districts, and to some it made a difference in crime rates. M. K. Nash, the field secretary of the Staten Island Civic League said, "Unlike all other summers, there was no 'crime wave' this year. It never got started. The police and detectives were on the job, and the crooks and light-fingered gentry have found it almost impossible to operate profitably."[51]

Police departments in Salt Lake City and Kalamazoo, Michigan, were also using the bicycle to great effect.[52] A police sergeant pointed out the advantages of the bicycle over other forms of transportation to local reporters asking, "Do you think a housebreaker or safe blower would hear me coming on that machine of mine . . . not on your life. But let me come panting and chugging on a motorcycle or in an automobile and see how near I get to them."[53] He also pointed out how no man on foot could outrun him on his bicycle. It is unclear whether he purchased his own bicycle or the police department supplied it. Regardless, he provided an argument that the police could use bicycles to stop crime more effectively.

Trade magazines made sure to play up the advantages of the bicycle over the car or motorcycle for this particular task. The prospect of police officers using bicycles was not only beneficial to the bicycle industry due to increased sales, but it was also an important promotional opportunity. As a symbol of respect and heroism, these officers were moving advertisements for the bicycle. Because of expectations that police officers should be able to get from one place to the next quickly, their use of the bicycle demonstrated that it was not an outmoded form of transportation—it was a source of civic improvement.

Another area in which the bicycle could help employees within the governmental sector was mail delivery. Unlike police departments, however, there was a degree of anti-bicycle sentiment at the top tier of the postal service. In 1915 Postmaster General Albert S. Burleson made a decision to prohibit mail carriers from using the bicycle in the Rural Free Delivery system (RFD) on the basis that they were impractical.[54] This, of course, was upsetting for members of the cycling industry. Both the bicycle and motorcycle industry had hopes of making sales to the 41,500 RFD carriers covering 1.07 million miles a day serving 21.5 million people.[55] A 1911 article in *Bicycling World and Motorcycle Review* described the RFD as a "field that affords great possibilities" not only because of the nature of their job—the average route spanned 25 miles—but also because of their pay. The minimum salary for an RFD carrier was $440 a year but the average salary was $965.[56] Members of the bicycle industry were truly upset about the lost opportunity resulting from Burleson's decision. Frank Eagan, a bicycle booster, responded, "Why should the poor, underpaid postman at Hick's Corners be permitted to deliver his mail in one-fifth the time he could if he walked? . . . Any rural postman who is so radical as to forsake shank's mare for a bicycle should be disciplined and your Uncle Burleson is the man to do it, by gosh!"[57] He suggested that the postmaster general go ahead and remove the bicycle from the special delivery stamp as well. Any governmentally endorsed use of the bicycle was, of course, great for the industry, but any rejection or specific action against using the bicycle in official capacities was a slap in the face.

The motorcycle and bicycle industry immediately reacted to the postmaster general's decision. T. W. Henderson, president of the Motorcycle Manufacturers' Association, organized a meeting in the same city and on the same date as the planned meeting of the National RFD Association. The hope was that by working together, they could persuade Postmaster General Burleson to reconsider his decision. In publicizing the meeting, Henderson tried to convey the urgency of the situation to other members of the motorcycling and bicycling industry. He argued, "It is urgent not only from the standpoint of the possible loss of the R.F.D. business but from the very bad psychological effect that would result from the unfavorable publicity which this action would be sure to inspire."[58] The publicity was critical because Burleson barred the use of motorcycles and bicycles in mail delivery on the basis that they were impractical, particularly when it was raining.[59] This directly contradicted a large part of the cycling industry's campaign to promote the bicycle as practical in nearly every situation. This was worsened by the fact that Postmaster General Burleson's new regulation gave approval to the use of automobiles, if "permission [was] obtained from a regular schedule approved by the department and where road conditions [would] allow uninterrupted service during a large part of the year."[60] The last stipulation, as well as Burleson's belief that motorcycles and bicycles would get stuck or prove useless on muddy roads, suggests that his primary concern was that the mail be delivered. However, his argument that in the case of bicycle and motorcycle deliveries, the materials would be unprotected from the elements demonstrated a lack of understanding. Cars would not be fully enclosed until the 1920s and the use of horses left carriers just as exposed to the elements as they would be on a bicycle or motorcycle. The motorcycle industry quickly pointed out that with the use of a sidecar, materials could be just as protected as they were in an automobile. Even those carrying mail via bicycle could devise a water- and wind-resistant vessel for the mail. The belief was that the carrying capacity of a motorcycle or bicycle was insufficient. Another important issue was the potential for accidents. This was especially the case since an act passed on March 9, 1914, entitled carriers to compensation in case of injury or death.[61] Postmaster General Burleson's decision certainly stung—all the more so since a major component of the industry's marketing strategy revolved around the bicycle's efficiency and convenience.

Undaunted, members of the bicycle industry continued their concerted effort to promote bicycles as efficient by marketing them as a way to increase business productivity. "Bicycle Usefulness in Business," told of the Pusch Grocery Store, which had gone from using two trucks for grocery deliveries to one truck and one bicycle. It used the truck for larger orders and the bicycle for the deliveries that were "within a radius of one mile of the store."[62] Stories also spoke of how doctors were using bicycles to make house calls, while others included pictures of messenger boys with bicycles to show business owners how they might use the bicycle to conduct business more effectively. A series of advertisements for the New Departure Company identified potential customers based on their occupations and explained how the bicycle aided them in their employment. The series included "the shopman, lawyer's clerk, bellhop, policeman, jobber salesman, and mail boy," among others, as customers to target.[63]

While the postmaster general may have been unconvinced of the bicycle's practicality, the US government was more open to the idea. The Pope Manufacturing Company, which had been trying to persuade the government of the bicycle's utility in war since 1891, had good reason to be excited in 1917.[64] In October of that year, the company was awarded a contract to provide ten thousand bicycles for the war effort, "mostly for messenger and dispatch work."[65] While this was certainly good news for the Pope Company—ten thousand bikes would have represented a significant portion of their yearly output—even better news came in the next issue of *MotorCycling and Bicycling*, which informed readers that the US government was now going to buy one hundred thousand bicycles. This order represented nearly one-sixth of the total sales in 1917.[66] Because this was such a substantial order and the time specified for its fulfillment was relatively fast, the order required that nearly every willing American bicycle manufacturer take part in the project. Colonel George Pope of the Bicycle Manufacturers Association (BMA) and Walter Rinck of the United Cycle Trade Directorate assisted the government in distributing the workload among the industry and overseeing the project.[67]

Aside from the obvious benefit derived from an immediate increase in revenue, the governmental contract for one hundred thousand bicycles would also provide a promotional benefit. A soldier's use of the bicycle to aid in the war effort was a welcome endorsement of the utilitarian benefits of bicycles. The same was true of using bicycles for delivering the mail, groceries, or medical assistance to the community. Each instance was a testament to the usefulness of a bicycle and a subtle reminder that there were times when bicycles were indeed more practical than any other means of transportation. This was another form of validation for an industry that had become increasingly insecure in light of the growing popularity of automobiles. Cars and trucks had distinct advantages over bicycles and so the bicycle industry struggled to find a proper niche. It focused on those who needed to make short trips with a lot of stops and in the case of the army, a vehicle that could mobilize hundreds at the lowest price using the least amount of materials. At the time, a Model T cost around $360, while Sears & Roebuck advertised Kenwood bicycles for $16.95.[68] An added benefit was that when roads were impassable by wheel, the bicycle could be pushed or carried, whereas the automobile would be forced to turn around or simply be abandoned. With the announcement that the US Army was going to purchase one hundred thousand bicycles, the industry had good reason to be excited. It was not necessarily excited because its own marketing worked but rather because of the marketing opportunities troops on bicycles would provide. In essence, this was more of a windfall than a product of the industry's efforts. Whether governmental entities such as the RFD or the army would embrace the bicycle was beyond the industry's control.

The United States and the world economies during World War I had a significant impact on the bicycle industry but it was more of a bandage than a curative for slumping sales. The onset of the war resulted in relaxed regulations on American exports. This, coupled with the rising scarcity of consumer goods in Europe, allowed American-made bicycles to flourish overseas. More importantly, the growing economy at home, beginning in 1915, provided opportunities for men and even women to work for steadily increasing wages. The increased sales of bicycles in 1914 breathed fresh life into the industry as it began working harder than ever on making systematic attempts to increase and diversify its consumer base, something which the automobile's growth in popularity also necessitated. The 1910s, therefore, brought about a cause for fear and excitement within the bicycle industry. The growing popularity of automobiles threatened to displace bicycles but World War I offered some unique opportunities. With less competition from overseas and the opportunity to sell more bicycles in Europe, the US bicycle industry saw some success but it had yet to figure out how to keep consumers interested as automobiles became more affordable.

Trade magazine articles and haphazard, often contradictory, marketing strategies that emerged throughout the 1910s reveal a genuine sense of alarm among members of the bicycle industry. Bicycle boosters' search for a solution to declining sales would send sales tactics in a myriad of directions. No longer new and exciting, the industry struggled to define the bicycle in a way that maintained relevance. This period of trial and error set the industry on a course that forever shaped the way Americans think about bicycles. The automobile's impact on ideals of mobility necessitated a response from the bicycle industry. The response given would appear confused and ineffective in restoring sales to levels achieved during the cycling boom of the 1890s.

It is clear that a significant number of juvenile cyclists existed. There were children's "sidewalk" models in the 1890s. Some were even using the bicycle for more serious pursuits. By 1910 there were nearly nine thousand telegraph messengers in the United States—a group that was predominately young and male.[69] Gregory Downey describes the popularity of bicycles among many telegraph messenger boys, yet the bicycle industry was not exactly targeting them as a group, aside from including them among the various groups that used bicycles.[70] It was these younger consumers that the industry would come to depend on but by the first part of the decade, the bicycle industry was a loosely defined entity that was doing very little collectively, other than reeling from the precipitous loss of sales experienced after the boom. Once the industry did coalesce, the marketing of bicycles to children would become much more pronounced.

3

Cooperation and Confusion

THE BICYCLE INDUSTRY was certainly confused about the proper direction for future advertising during the first decade of the twentieth century. In an effort to recover sales, the industry managed to initiate a cooperative bicycle-boosting campaign in 1915. It was at this point that the industry began devoting more attention to bicycle marketing than ever before. To that end, industry leaders suggested the use of universal tactics to sell bikes even though they were acutely aware that different locales and populations required different marketing strategies. Trade journals from the era reveal marketing trends but they also show that, to an extent, industry leaders were suggesting nearly any and every conceivable tactic. The bottom line was that they wanted to sell bikes to as many people as possible. Still, there was a palpable fear of directly marketing to nonwhites. Assuming that this was purely a by-product of class—because many nonwhites did not make enough money to afford bicycles—is wrongheaded not only because there was, in fact, a significant number of nonwhites who earned enough to afford bicycles, but also because merchants were indeed making appeals to "working men." Even though the industry did not specifically target minority cyclists such as African Americans, trade magazines show that black riders, black bicycle races, and black cycling clubs did exist. So why did news about those riders seldom appear in the major magazines?

Bicycle and motorcycle dealers feared that African Americans' participation in cycling or motorcycling would actually be detrimental to overall sales. An article entitled "Twixt the Nigger and the Devil" calls attention to the fact that dealers were reportedly "opposed to negroes riding motorcycles, as it is feared that recklessness in riding and the speed mania will get the best of them and they will do the trade more harm than good by disgusting white prospects."[1] This fear that diversifying their appeals would cause a forfeiture of other demographics was a powerful force. Operating under the assumption that consumer patterns would spread from the top down, the bicycle industry demonstrated their own ideals about the racial and gendered ordering of American consumers. First, it targeted elite white males, then middle-class men and women before broadening appeals to lower classes. It never made the move to nonwhites—regardless of class.

Due to a slight increase in sales experienced in 1913 and 1914, the bicycle industry was convinced that things would soon turn around. It was just a matter of time, the industry hoped, before bicycles were just as popular as they had been in the 1890s, but with more stability and even better sales—since the population in the United States was quickly growing. Still, sales were not nearly as good as they were fifteen years earlier. With a goal of complete recovery, the industry not only targeted business owners, it also used trade magazines to encourage bicycle merchants to consider female customers. Articles about women's enjoyment of bicycles and advertisements directed specifically at women became more prevalent. Women had long been riding bicycles but advertisements still treated them as an afterthought, since ads spoke more to white masculine ideals. This alteration of tactics was somewhat logical since it was becoming more apparent to the industry that it needed to diversify advertisements in order to draw customers from a broader portion of society. More importantly, the industry proved more willing to rework marketing strategies to embrace shifting gender ideals than it was willing to market their product to the lower classes in national advertising campaigns. After all, this tactic of marketing to women was now more feasible because of the increase in women's independence and the growing number of women with jobs. By World War I, two million women were working in business offices and when mobilization created a labor shortage, women stepped into positions they had never before occupied.[2] If Americans had clung tightly to Victorian ideals and the notion of separate spheres, marketing bicycles to women would have been entirely illogical.

Trade magazine articles scolded merchants for all their talk about the bicycle's comeback and hopes that a resurgence in velodrome races, road races, tours, and club runs would save the industry, while others were actively working to create new business. In spite of those who were trying to create new business, one bicycle booster suggested that *everyone* was failing to pay attention to women. He called readers' attention to the neglect of the female market by including a letter from Mrs. H. S. Darrall, who wrote, "There are so many ladies whom I know who wish so much to ride bicycles again, but have not the nerve to start the style. If some impetus was given they would certainly start like a pack of sheep."[3] The notion that bicycles were appealing because of the independence they afforded women was called into question by such appeals that treated women as mindless followers.

Dealers were told that all they needed to do to sell women's bicycles was "dig out that woman's machine you have in the back room, wipe the dust off it and put it in the place of honor in the show window. It has been so long since most of the women in your town have seen a bicycle built for skirts that they have almost forgotten there is such a thing. Get your wife or daughter or sister to start the style of riding."[4] As far as dealers' unwillingness or laziness in marketing their product to women was concerned, the article continued, "Thousands upon thousands of dollars have been expended in advertising campaigns but the proportion devoted to attracting women riders has been so small that few have noticed it, certainly not the women."[5] It is apparent that the industry was becoming fully cognizant of the need to target women as consumers, but this article shows that not all manufacturers and merchants had taken industry leaders' advice.

Another article gave notice that "society women" were indeed taking up the bicycle. It boasted, "There has been a growing demand for bicycles by women riders ever since the spring of 1915." It went on to explain, "The women of Evanston, one of the stylish suburbs of Chicago, are returning to the bicycle for pleasure, health and exercise. Automobiles, carriages and horseback riding are in the discard and the ladies may be seen daily on the streets both on errands and seeking exercise and recreation."[6] The emphasis on the fact that they were women of a "stylish" neighborhood is of particular note because again it shows that boosters were operating under the logic that if elites bought bicycles, then other classes would follow. The article concluded, "Now that society has once more taken to the wheel all that remains is for the live dealers to get busy and land the business while it is to be had."[7]

Bicycle sales also seemed to experience some benefits from the growing enrollment of women in college. In "Why College Girls Ride Bicycles," Elizabeth Skelding Moore explained that the women of Smith College had taken to the bicycle because it allowed them to go anywhere they wanted, "unlike an automobile."[8] This was not simply about women's ability to get around college campuses easily. After all, most campuses were not that big at the time. Rather, as Moore goes on to explain, the women of Smith College were using the bicycle to ride out into the countryside with their friends. Forming clubs, the women would organize "parties" in the woods and encourage incoming freshmen to bring a bicycle with them to school. While it is true that this portrayal of the bicycle as a means to get out into nature was somewhat played out with regard to men, it was still new and exciting for women. Moore argued that because numerous college women were taking bicycles with them to school, "bicycling among women is becoming more and more popular."[9] The potential of the college-aged market was somewhat important to the industry at the time, but as college enrollment increased over the next few decades—especially after World War II—the bicycle industry would give college students much more respect and attention as a consumer group. Another important point about this article is the fact that these women, or more likely their families, had the finances to allow them to attend college, which was undoubtedly favorable to those in the bicycle industry. Not only would they have the money to afford one of the more expensive models, but these women were, or would become, trendsetters. The bicycle industry believed women, as consumers, would do everything in their power to follow the most current fashion trends.

While the bicycle industry was actively trying to create new customers by going after women, they were also hopeful that the bicycle would return to the fashionable status it enjoyed in the 1890s. More importantly, in this instance, the industry was more willing to accept shifting gender notions associated with the bicycle than it was with the prospect of making direct appeals to lower classes. That is not to say that the cycling industry did not want the working class buying bicycles. At this point, however, it was still hesitant to devote too much time or money on national advertising campaigns for anyone below the middle class. Here, the maintenance of class associations with the bicycle was more important than the gendered and racial notions. Furthermore, the mention of automobiles and carriages in both the article about the Smith College women and in the article about society women is important because it shows the emergence of overt attempts to couch appeals for the bicycle in anti-automobile language. This makes the increasing threat of automobiles to the bicycle industry more apparent. The bicycle had an upper hand because automobiles were still relatively expensive, but that advantage was weakening.[10]

The culmination of the bicycle industry's effort to broaden appeals came with the formation of a cooperative organization named the Million Bicycles Committee (MBC). Bicycle boosters formed the MBC after an industry-wide convention in 1915 showed there was a desire for the "trade [to] establish a promotion committee to stimulate in every way possible the use and sale of bicycles."[11] An article proclaiming "Bicycle Dealers Organize" announced that on December 22, 1915, twenty-nine members of the bicycle industry met at the YMCA in Cleveland, Ohio, to organize this "association for the purpose of reviving and stimulating the bicycle trade throughout the United States."[12] The MBC's primary objective was to sell one million bicycles in 1916. The New Departure Manufacturing Company, who specialized in coaster brakes—an accessory that greatly improved the safety of cycling—was a leader in this promotional organization and reportedly an "exemplification of the genuine booster spirit to the nth degree."[13] The assistant to DeWitt Page (the president of New Departure) was the brainchild behind the MBC. That man was Charles F. Olin, a former newspaper contributor and editor with a legendary work ethic. In fact, he was reported to have worked his way to a nervous breakdown, which left him blind for three months. This happened while working for a paper in New York City and simultaneously trying to finish classes at Columbia University. When asked about his hobbies, he smiled and said he only had time for family and the "occasional quiet chat with friends." Olin had shifted his focus in life from the "art of writing to the science of selling," and he soon became recognized as "the power behind New Departure sales."[14] He brought those same skills and talents to the MBC.

To help boost bicycles a "comprehensive system" was "devised," in which "attractive folders [were] furnished [to] dealers for distribution, setting forth arguments and inducements that will sell bicycles to boys and their parents."[15] Within the system there was provided a plan "whereby the boy himself may earn his bicycle. Similar folders are prepared to win the girls to bicycle riding. Every class and condition is appealed to in the most effective way, through these folders, from the laboring man to the pampered children of the rich."[16] While actual advertisements may suggest that the industry was primarily concerned with white men of a certain class, desperation was leading them to treat nearly anyone as a potential customer—as demonstrated by the move toward advertising to women and then to children.

The New Departure Manufacturing Company went so far in the publicity campaign to publish their own advertisements giving notice to the rest of the industry about the push to sell more bikes than ever in 1916.[17] Because it was a parts manufacturer, New Departure was more concerned that bicycles be sold in general, with relatively little concern about which brand they were, since they could supply any bicycle manufacturer with brakes. There were a few other coaster-brake manufacturers in the United States at the time, but the New Departure Company was a powerhouse in the industry and in large part due to Olin, it had a strong voice in directing the MBC.

Similarly, Harry S. Quine, the manager of advertising for the Goodyear Company, supplier of bicycle tires, was another key member of the MBC. Quine had also begun his career in newspapers—after recovering from yellow fever, which he contracted while fighting in the Spanish-American War.[18] Under Quine's leadership, Goodyear advertisements encouraged others in the industry that the goal of one million could be met. It told other members, "You have simply let the automobile and motorcycle business scare you out. As a matter of fact, the automobile and motorcycle have taken only a small part of the former big demand for bicycles."[19] In attempts to foster the cooperative spirit that industry leaders thought was the cure for low sales, the advertisement contended, "Bicycles are better made today. Prices are better. Roads are better. Tires are better. The business will thrive if we all get together and pull."[20] The ad concluded by encouraging dealers to write to Goodyear for a plan that would increase sales.

Several ads encouraging merchants to link their business with Goodyear circulated. One such ad implored dealers to get on board with the Goodyear marketing plan highlighting the fact that 136,082,830 Goodyear ads would be published "in the great magazines and weeklies of the nation."[21] Their promise to any merchant's agreement to sell Goodyear tires was their "great trade-winning book for tire dealers."[22] The book included "ready-made advertisements, handle bar tags, package and envelope enclosures, advertising novelties, stationary, trade-winning letter service, mailing folders, booklets, moving picture slides, window displays, store signs, new schemes for winning trade, tire racks, and more."[23] These materials were, in fact, provided through the MBC, which Goodyear was helping support financially. Undoubtedly, the stationary and envelopes were for the dealer to mail to the prospects in his area directly, while the intention was that the dealer would display the slides in his store as proof that even stars of moving pictures enjoyed cycling. With the case of the moving-picture slides, the bicycle industry expected to cash in on the notoriety of the actors and scenes in the slides.

Parts manufacturers such as Goodyear and New Departure were noticeably more supportive of general campaigns to promote bicycles than bicycle manufacturers. The parts manufacturers contributed over $23,000 to the campaign, while the bicycle manufactures gave approximately $15,000.[24] This could have been because the parts manufacturers had more money, therefore more power, and control over the bicycle industry as a whole.[25] Parts manufacturers had an advantage in that they manufactured parts for several items. Tire manufacturers produced tires for motorcycles, bicycles, and automobiles. New Departure, which started out as a doorbell company, grew into a successful ball bearing manufacturer and ultimately became part of General Motors.

In addition to bicycle manufacturers and parts manufacturers, there were also wholesalers, or "jobbers." These multiple facets of the industry created some complications for cooperative attempts. Jobbers, for example, made large purchases from parts manufactures in order to undercut prices. This was a source of frustration for the rest of the industry. Cleveland bicycles called attention to this system and attempted to use it to their advantage by questioning the authenticity and craftsmanship of wholesalers' bicycles. Their catalog made sure to let the customer know, "All the component parts of Cleveland bicycles are designed and *made* in our own factory, each for its particular place, not bought outside and adapted to the desired purpose. In this manner is secured the well-rounded, perfectly proportioned, evenly balanced bicycle, which cannot be secured in bicycles which, as is the case with many machines, are *assembled* from parts bought here and there and fitted as best they can be."[26] Making such claims would obviously raise jobbers', and even parts manufacturers', ire. This was precisely the sort of divisive attitude that trade associations like the MBC wanted to get beyond. This is why one of their first campaigns would be to endorse more of a cooperative spirit in which there were no negative ads directed against one another and all dealers worked to create new business rather than stealing it from others. Prior to the MBC there was the Cycle Jobbers' Association of America. Cycle jobbers were concerned with increasing bike sales in whatever way possible. They worked to standardize parts, which would benefit the industry by making parts increasingly interchangeable. At the same time, however, it would result in generic bikes with one-size-fits-all–type components that were not necessarily best-suited for application on all frames—precisely what the Cleveland catalog attacked. Another issue with the jobbers association was that it did not include bicycle manufacturers. As long as associations for jobbers and bicycle manufactures remained separate, it is no surprise that there was tension between the two groups. This is why the MBC would work so tirelessly to convince bicycle and parts manufacturers to invest time and resources into cooperative boosting.

Ultimately, the goal of selling one million bicycles in 1916—which New Departure, Goodyear, and other members of the bicycle industry truly thought possible—was not achieved. The MBC focused on a one-year goal and was consequently short-lived as an organization. It was quickly succeeded by the United Cycle Trade Directorate (Directorate), which included many of the same leaders. In their opinion, the failure to meet the targeted goal was a result of not getting 100 percent cooperation from all the members of the industry, particularly when it came to funding the campaign.[27] Goodyear ran articles publicizing the progress of the campaign saying, "There can be no doubt that bicycle and part manufactures are interested in the slogan and fulfillment."[28] The campaign report, however, reveals that many were more interested in the committee's supply of free advertising materials than they were in making financial contributions. In a somewhat bitter and contemptuous tone, the Directorate rebuked merchants for failing to make monetary contributions to the campaign. Its report stated, "It must not be overlooked that this shortage of funds lies with you [the merchant] and not with us [the Directorate], and that, had we received it, much more effective results would have been accomplished through the use of this material. We realize now that, while it is our proper function to train the dealer to trim his window and brighten up his store with all the material available, it is not our province to furnish that material."[29] While it saw the window displays as having "some value" they were, for the most part, considered a mistake and a primary reason for the failure because nearly 55 percent of 1916's total budget went toward the creation and distribution of window displays to dealers.[30] The report included many letters sent to the director of the committee thanking him for the materials and giving the campaign credit for increased sales. Still, the campaign did not meet its objective. In the committee's opinion, their efforts were actually effective but it was the donors who failed to do their part to achieve the goal. The total number of bicycles sold in the United States in 1916 was 526,076, just barely over halfway to the goal of one million.

Apparently there was too much resistance and questioning of the campaign, even from those who contributed funds for the plan, and not enough "helpful spirit of co-operation."[31] This focus on cooperation was pivotal and so was the idea that individual businesses volunteer to contribute to the campaign, rather than being "conscripted." In a comment that reflected World War I's impact on the psyche of American businessmen, the treasurer wrote, "In these days of volunteering and conscription it seems appropriate that I begin my report with whatever recognition we attach to those who volunteer. True, with man, it signifies no lack of patriotism or willingness to serve, but we do recognize a difference, so here's to our volunteers, though they be but few."[32] Many of those who "fought" the modus operandi of the campaign favored spending the bulk of funds on a national advertising campaign. The Directorate, on the other hand, thought it a better idea to focus their attention on the retailers with the hopes that they would then give more and better quality attention to the potential customers in their specific locales.

After failing in 1916, industry leaders reinstated the goal of selling one million bicycles in 1917 with a projected campaign budget of $600,000, but it failed once again.[33] It was at this point that the change of name from the Million Bicycles Committee to the United Cycle Trade Directorate took place. The new name more accurately reflected their mission since their goals were scaled back after 1917 to simply increase sales, rather than trying to achieve a certain number. What the MBC and, subsequently, the Directorate, hoped for was a return to the kind of sales experienced during the bicycle boom of the 1890s, but with more stability.

In search of stable sales, the Directorate also published a series of booklets titled *The One Hundred Per Cent Bicycle Merchant*, which were issued with the goal of training bicycle merchants to be better salesmen by reaching out to a diverse array of consumer groups. Since the Directorate was a cooperative organization representing various bodies associated with the bicycle industry, its main objective was to help the entire industry by sponsoring works of general publicity for the bicycle. In its advertisements, the slogan printed in all ads was "Ride a

Bicycle." This campaign was "based on the fundamental points of the utility, convenience, economy and health obtained in the riding of a bicycle. The workman [was] advised to get rid of strap-hanging. The appeal to the business and family man [was] based on the exercise and health angles. The women [were] reminded of the convenience of a bicycle for running errands, etc."[34]

As part of their work, the Directorate undertook to cut advertisements and other bicycle related clippings out from papers. It compiled 27,080 inches of advertising, which had been placed in dealers' local newspapers, totaling an $18,956 investment in advertising.[35] Its research concluded that a majority of these advertisements were not of the type that could potentially create new business. "The vast majority undertook to sell wheels only to the man who was already in the market. Many featured the lowest priced wheels. Many were admittedly and self-evidently 'fake' advertisements quoting an outrageously low price in the hope of enticing the prospect into the store, when the dealer would attempt to sell him a higher priced wheel."[36] What the Directorate suggested in its findings and increasingly emphasized in directions to merchants was that they, as retailers, should busy themselves with cooperative tactics that could create new business, not steal customers away from their competitors. Trying to steal customers from one another signaled a sense that bicycle business was drying up and rather than try to create new business, something thought increasingly difficult because of competition from the automobile, merchants were racing to the bottom in terms of pricing.

The Directorate had learned from the mistake of price-cutting in the 1890s.[37] *Bicycling World* reminded industry members that "'the bicycle trade does not want a boom' like the last one, which had left a sour taste 'in the mouths of the survivors.'"[38] Clearly, they sought a profitable, yet reliable, market. An article in *MotorCycling and Bicycling* proclaimed, "Lack of Co-operative Competition and the Cut Price Boll Weevil Are the Chief Evils."[39] The author, T. J. Sullivan, a Directorate member, explained that "hole-in-the-wall" bicycle shops with a dealer who "waits like a spider for a customer," then pops out of the back of the shop to go get a part for the customer at another shop only to return and sell it at a fifty-cent profit were killing the business.[40] When Sullivan spoke of the "cut-price boll weevil," he was not talking about dealers undercutting one another. Rather, he suggested that dealers were using other dealers as their intermediaries—buying products from them and then selling it for profit. Sullivan used this example as a reason for the creation of a "hard-and-fast bicycle dealers' association" so that they could remedy this problem. The shop that had the product in stock and the "hole-in-the-wall shop" both made a profit on one item during separate transactions. The problem was, however, that when two merchants were making a profit on one product, they passed a higher cost on to the consumer. These exorbitantly priced tires and accessories could serve to contradict bicycle-marketing strategies, which suggested the bicycle was more economical than other forms of transportation.

The MBC and the Directorate not only encouraged the industry to work together and market utilitarian bicycles, they also saw benefit in promoting bicycle racing. The bicycle industry believed that increased interest in racing would boost the sales of all styles of bicycles, not just the competitive models. It encouraged dealers to take an active part in bicycle racing by promoting it or, if a town did not have races, to create them. For those new to race organization, the Directorate provided a bulletin to take them through the process, detailing how to advertise the races and how to procure prizes for the winners. For others, who had already organized races, the bulletin would help them build races that were more successful because they were backed by the Directorate, which had the support of "all the manufacturers and jobbers of bicycles and bicycle parts."[41] The Directorate's bulletin argued, "Everything that a dealer puts into a race, whether it be in the form of money or of energy expended in promoting the race, makes for an increased interest in the bicycle in *his immediate neighborhood*, which means more business and more profits for him at once."[42] The rationale was if the public could see bicycle races, they would also see how exciting and fast the bicycles could go, which would make them want to use bicycles themselves. The bulletin went on to explain that not only could the dealer be sure that those entering the race would visit his shop prior to the event to make sure their bicycle was in sound mechanical order; they might even buy a new bicycle. In addition, the dealer could expect to see more sales to recreational riders. It claimed, "Everyone who sees the race gets the importance of the bicycle thrust upon him in a most impressive manner."[43] It was expected that anyone young enough to potentially race would start to ask themselves if they could go as fast as the others and ultimately buy themselves a bicycle before the next race. Older men would find their interest in the bicycle renewed. After all, the bulletin posited, they were probably bicycle enthusiasts earlier in life anyway. Apparently, children who attended a bicycle race would get so caught up in bicycle fever that they would not let their father rest until he bought them one of their own.

Another way in which the MBC and Directorate strove for cooperative bicycle boosting was through the creation of "bicycle day," which grew into "bicycle week." Beginning in 1916, bicycle day was created in an attempt to achieve "the biggest year the bicycle business ever saw."[44] It was suggested that dealers all over the country should give their store a makeover. Some members believed, however, that not all dealers were doing everything they should to promote their trade because they were ashamed of it. This was one of the side effects of the rising popularity and excitement surrounding automobiles. One bicycle booster said of these shameful dealers, "he dislikes it to be known that he is a bicycle man, whereas it is one of the most enlightened businesses of the age and you, Mr. Dealer, should be proud of the fact that you are associated with it."[45] If dealers could feel embarrassed about selling bicycles then there was apparently some degree of stigma associated with the bicycle. Such a comment suggests that the bicycle was not as respected as it was during the 1890s—when bicycle shops were popping up in every town and entrepreneurs everywhere flocked to the bicycle industry. In fact, Denver had three times as many bicycle shops in 1898 as it did in 1895. In Providence, Rhode Island, the number had more than doubled.[46] There was added reassurance for the dealer, who should not feel ashamed because, "The bicycle is as necessary to our health as plumbing is to our homes and it is therefore as legitimate to offer a bicycle for sale as hardware or eatables."[47] With that comment, however, it seems that dealers may have felt more confident, or realistic, in selling bicycles as a means of exercise and recreation rather than a utilitarian vehicle.

During this era of vigorous bicycle promotion, there were also numerous articles in the trade journals giving tips to store owners on how to merchandise their goods more effectively. A key theme in these articles was the importance of providing a clean and well-lit storefront. One bicycle booster, Charles Gates, stressed, "If you have a pride in your business and add industry, neatness and politeness, success will have a hard job keeping out of your reach."[48] Storeowners were instructed to focus on marketing products in a bright and clean environment and to "Treat everyone who enter[ed] [their] place pleasantly, politely and with respect no matter how plainly or poorly they may be dressed."[49] Gates went on to suggest that the dealer always attempt to sell the most expensive product first and then work their way down from that point. He implored merchants to "not think because your customer looks poor that he wants the cheapest model, he may wish nothing but the best."[50] Lastly, he recommended that the dealer remain honest in all of their business. The logic was that tricking customers at the initial deal would only lead to a customer who never returned to the shop.

Aside from providing specific details on how storeowners could increase their sales, there were often pictures of "model" shops included in the pages of the trade journals so that dealers would know exactly what their shop should look like. One such picture shows the store owner in a bow tie and vest, standing behind one of his many glass display cases. Bicycles are in their own space across from him; tires, rims, and other accessories that are too big for the glass cases hang from the wall (see fig. 3).[51] All of this provided for a shop that was cleaner in appearance and easier to move around in. The focus on cleanliness, honesty, and equal treatment of all customers regardless of their outward appearance was not only a manifestation of popular attitudes of the era, but it was also an expression of where members of the bicycle industry felt their trade had gone wrong in the past. This was another call from industry leaders for merchants to help diversify the bicycle business. Treating all customers equally, regardless of their

3. A. W. Nourse in his bicycle shop. *MotorCycling and Bicycling*, September 13, 1915, 55.

appearance, reveals that there was a belief that merchants were ignoring potential customers who appeared poor. The emphasis on keeping stores clean was thought to make the shop more inviting to female customers who would be more likely to make a purchase if they were comfortable spending time in the store. Since the women that were thought to be most likely to buy bicycles were those of the middle and upper classes, cleanliness was very important. The call for honesty echoes T. J. Sullivan's comments about the "cut-price boll weevil," and suggests there were swindling dealers who were doing a disservice to their trade in their greedy attempts to make a profit. Industry leaders believed that all could have a profit, as long as individuals within the industry worked together in the prescribed manner.

In the spirt of cooperation, bicycle-parts manufacturers continued to provide free promotional materials to bicycle dealers. The Buffalo

Metal Goods Company informed dealers, "Our Service department is at your disposal—get action now and prepare for a Bumper Bicycle Season."[52] It added that its promotional materials were "full of convincing arguments to stimulate bicycle riding—the window transfers, pennants, pencil clips, price cards, display hubs, and wall hangers are just what you want."[53] All of these goods were available at no charge to the dealer. The ad also included examples of several posters and promotional materials they could make available. Just like the New Departure Manufacturing Company, the Buffalo Metal Goods Company produced coaster brakes. They, too, had much to gain from increased bicycle sales. Neither New Departure, Buffalo Metal Goods, nor any other parts manufacturer, however, created ads that were entirely without mention of their own product or company. In most of the posters and pennants the Buffalo Metal Goods Company provides in their advertisement, the distinctive name of their product, the Atherton, appears.

While dealers were encouraged to sell the most expensive products to customers first, no matter how they were dressed, they were also instructed to pay attention to each customer, in attempts to sell them the bicycle best suited for his or her needs. Dealers were cautioned against trying to sell lightweight bicycles built for speed to a "working man." They were also reminded, "probably 99 percent of all the bicyclists of the country, uses a heavier machine with 'effort-absorbing' roadster tires."[54] This was in contrast to the racers who rode the lightest bikes possible and therefore stripped of all luxuries. The recreational, or "working man," cyclist was thought of as not being physically trained. He would object "to being obliged to sweat and strain whenever he encounters any little rise of ground."[55] Common conceptions were that if cycling was not easy and relaxing than the average individual would want nothing to do with it. Apparently bicycle dealers knew this, but their problem was that bicycles were being shipped to them from factories with gear ratios that were too big. This made it more difficult for the average person to ride because of the strength it required. To remedy the problem, the trade magazine told dealers to take action and start requesting that factories send bicycles with smaller gears, informing them, "The factories have all sizes of sprockets. It costs them no more to put on a 64 than a 96 gear."[56]

There was confusion over whether the average cycling consumer wanted a product that could go fast or one that was easy to use. Dealers also needed to consider the particular topography in their own local market. Those dealers in Chicago or Minneapolis might find that the average rider accepted a larger gear, while those in hillier cities might find their customers would more readily enjoy their bicycles if the hills were not so difficult to ascend. As bicycles and accessories became increasingly complicated over the years, this would cease to be such a problem because riders could eventually buy bicycles that had multiple gears, which they could switch with the simple adjustment of a lever.

Gearing grew into an important issue by 1917. An article titled "The Importance of Gearing to the Trade" argued that factories sent out bicycles with a gear ratio that was too large because the factory heads and designers, whom the author did not consider "practical riders," had made an "error in judgment."[57] That error was due to factories receiving orders for bicycles that specifically requested larger gears. These came from younger riders and those who wanted to go fast but did not understand that the gears bicycle racers used were not suited for a novice.[58] The article contended that when dealers sold bicycles that were geared too highly it could result in injury to riders and the bicycle-boosting campaign underway because riders would think of cycling as hard work. One method the dealer could employ to overcome this problem was to practice a little bit of a deceptive tactic. Believing the boys who wanted a big gear mostly only paid attention to the front sprocket, the dealer could fix the bicycle with a larger front sprocket as well as a larger rear sprocket. This resulted in a more moderate gear ratio than that attained with a large front sprocket and smaller rear sprocket.

The real solution to the problem was for the public to be educated in bicycle gearing. W. T. Farwell Jr., a writer and field secretary for the Directorate, laid out the history of gearing and explained how different gears affected the bicycle and the rider.[59] Farwell was "well known as an authority on the mechanical end of the bicycle."[60] He gave reason to question the nature of bicycle racing's impact on other forms of cycling and argued that the problem of over-gearing began at the ground floor, where boys who are fans of racing ask dealers for those bigger gears. In these instances, boys were undoubtedly going to races, keeping up with the stars of the sport and paying close attention to all the specifics of their favorite racers' bicycles, which would seem to be good for the bicycle industry. At the same time, these young fans put too much faith in the idea that a lighter bike with bigger gears would make them faster. This resulted in them buying bikes that were beyond their muscular development. The same argument was made *MotorCycling and Bicycling*'s September 1917 issue.[61] Both articles emphasized selling the customer the bicycle best suited for his or her needs, but Farwell pointed out the misperceptions that resulted from watching experts and being told that much of what made them who they were was the bicycle they rode. Placing too much focus on the brand professionals rode and not the amount of training they did, made sense for bicycle manufacturers, from a publicity standpoint, but it also served to discourage newcomers who observed racers who made high speeds seem easy. Therefore, while industry leaders were telling dealers to organize and promote racing for better sales, some were also inadvertently suggesting that perhaps racing was a cause for dissatisfied customers.

This contradiction was not the only way in which industry leaders, and the trade journals they contributed to, led to dealers' confusion. Another problem was that during this era it was very common for one dealer to sell both motorcycles and bicycles because bicycle manufacturers also produced motorcycles—such was the case with Harley Davidson, the Westfield Manufacturing Company (formerly Pope), Miami Cycle, Excelsior, and others. In the instances that the motorcycle and bicycle manufacturer were one in the same, there was the potential for a conflict of interest if the dealer was forced to promote one form of movement over the other. In promotion of the bicycle, much of the emphasis was on the ease of use, leisure, enjoyment, convenience, and savings. Yet motorcycles were often promoted in much the same way, especially regarding leisure, thrills, and convenience. Dealers were told that the "health-bringing qualities of a motorcycle, to say nothing of its economical pleasure features, center his [a man's] interest in the machine immediately."[62]

One of the most popular trade journals even devoted equal attention to both motorcycles and bicycles. Because motorcycles and bicycles were in competition with each other, each were promoted as a means for transportation and a health restorative—dealers that carried both would undoubtedly have, on occasion, to choose to extol the virtues of one over the other.[63] If dealers promoted motorcycles as fast, efficient, and easy, there was an implication that they were superior to bicycles. One article suggested, "Go after the old men. Most of them used to ride a bike and can be persuaded to see the lightweight motor wheel or Cyclemotor, if afraid of the big boy. Make prospects of them, and if you don't catch 'em get their children for motorcycles and bikes and roller skates."[64] The illustration above the article pictured a sales clerk showing off his line to a well-dressed man and his son. A banner in the back suggested, "Buy the Boy a Bicycle."[65] Not only was the dealer potentially compromising himself by promoting the motorcycle over the bicycle to some customers and then the bicycle over the motorcycle to others, but he was also potentially damaging the image of the bicycle by suggesting the father buy a motorcycle for himself and a bicycle for his son. In this manner, the bicycle's status was demoted from something for adults to something for children. While the question of motorcycles for men and bikes for boys is one issue, the compromise that dealers had to make was just as important.

Because the entire bicycle-boosting campaign of the 1910s maintained that everyone was a potential customer, the industry's marketing campaign became convoluted and the bicycle's image became nebulous when compared to the image it enjoyed in the 1880s and 1890s. Formerly a luxury item for elites, the industry tried to broaden the bicycle's appeal as a cheap form of transportation for the working class, a practical and efficient means of carrying out business transactions, an object that could restore health, and a vehicle for women to not only complete errands but also as form of leisure and fashion. This was complicated further by the tendency of retailers who sold bicycles to offer motorcycles as well. Trade journals and bicycle advertisements too were trying to make such broad-based appeals that they were often marketing to one group at the expense of another. These attempts to broaden appeal, which ran in so many directions, could do little to clearly state or redefine what the bicycle was to represent. By trying to do too much, the bicycle industry achieved very little.

With the establishment of the MBC and then the Directorate, the industry was coming together as never before. Both organizations trained, or at least informed, small independent retailers how to sell more bicycles and what they needed to do to entice customers. They were not necessarily achieving their full potential, nor did they recreate the bicycle boom of the 1890s, but to a degree, they were surviving. At the war's end, as factories began to slow, foreign-made bicycles began to reappear prominently on sales floors.[66] The working class soon found that they too could afford automobiles. Now that society women and others were not expected to sacrifice, or be as frugal as they were during the war, who would the industry turn to for stability? How were they to maintain sales and relevancy at the end of the war? The industry was left to think about which part of its customer base was still intact and relatively unchanged after World War I.

The dawning of the automobile age and changing conceptions of mobility held great sway over the course of bicycle marketing. The industry tried to broaden the appeal of the bicycle by marketing it as a utilitarian vehicle for American workers, but it simultaneously held out hope that cycling would once again become a popular form of recreation for the upper classes. There was more confidence that elite women could be convinced to take up cycling than elite men, however. Elite men were preoccupied with automobiles, but the class distinction conferred by driving would lessen as cars became increasingly affordable over the course of the 1910s. Cars not only competed directly against bicycles in the market, they also widened the concept of mobility and gave impetus to the need to (re)define all other forms of movement. The car exacerbated the sense of desperation among members of the bicycle industry—as they saw sales unable to recover from the bust at the turn of the century—and led to an identity crisis for the bicycle industry. As a result, it was so desperate to broaden its consumer based beyond middle-class men that it tried to make cycling for everyone and therefore, no one in particular.

As the novelty of the bicycle wore off, so did the ideas that it necessitated great strength and agility to maneuver. With advancements in metallurgy and frame building technologies, smaller bicycles with smaller gears were finding their way into the homes and hearts of American children. The full-scale onslaught of the child market had not yet occurred, but by 1915 it was clear that the industry was considering American children as potential customers as it attempted to corner every part of the market. Curiously, even though the industry was now attentive to women, children, and individuals of all classes, there was still no discussion of the potential of marketing to nonwhites. First, the toy of elite men and then a means of liberation for women and a utilitarian device for all classes, the bicycle would ultimately become inextricably linked to childhood in the 1920s–1950s. The child was the bicycle's last hope. It was this sense of desperation and loss of a clear identity in the 1910s that would lead the industry to focus marketing on children in the decades that followed.

4

The Child Consumer

IN ITS BOOK *Fifty Years of Schwinn-Built Bicycles: The Story of the Bicycle and Its Contributions to Our Way of Life, 1895–1945*, Arnold, Schwinn & Company went into very little detail about the development of the children's bicycle market. Instead, it treated the occurrence as a natural result of forces beyond the industry's control. Recounting the bicycle industry's state at beginning of the twentieth century Schwinn wrote, "The heydey of the bicycle was over, and cheaper bicycles, if there were to be any at all; were the order of the day. Lower prices made the bicycle possible for older children, and gradually a new market for bicycles developed in America—a children's market."[1] This "children's market" was not created in a vacuum; bicycle manufacturers and merchants cultivated it to the best of their abilities. Their efforts were logical considering the increasing competition from cars, as well as the fact that the industry wanted to broaden its appeal. It was a move, however, that would have significant influence on bicycle consumption in the United States for many years to come.

The expansion of American consumerism is most often associated with growing affluence after World War II but that period represents the peak of developments that have their roots in the 1880s and 1890s. Richard Fox and T. J. Lears have argued that the genesis of that growth in American consumerism can be located within the preoccupations of white elite adults.[2] It would only be a matter of years, however, before those values of consumerism were imparted to American children. In fact, historian Steven Mintz shows how advertisements soon marketed toys directly to children but this development occurred even earlier than he suggests. Whereas Mintz locates it in the late 1920s, Lisa

Jacobson provides evidence that it had begun as early as 1911.[3] Paul Ringel argues that "children's active participation in commercial cultures of consumption and leisure was largely accepted in the United States by the eve of World War I."[4] Indeed, Jacobson shows that by the 1910s children's magazines such as *American Boy* "were trumpeting the untapped potential of the boy market and the dynamic salesmanship of the boy consumer in the advertising press. Children's magazine publishers continued to press their case during the interwar years, when the child consumer became the focus of numerous articles in the advertising trade press and the target of advertising campaigns for everything from breakfast cereal and toys to big ticket items such as radios and automobiles."[5] A close inspection of bicycle industry practices confirms that advertising's attempts to appeal directly to children were replete among its marketing strategies before the United States entered World War I.

Jacobson admits the 1920s were a "major turning point in the field" as even the advertising trade itself, not just children's magazines "s[a]ng the praises of the child consumer."[6] The bicycle industry followed a similar path, at first it seemed to experiment with children's advertisements in the first half of the 1910s. By the early 1920s, however, it was poised to go "all in" marketing to juvenile consumers. Jacobson argues that general marketing to boys marked a "privileging of boy culture" in a manner that offered psychic rewards to advertisers. Since advertising was primarily a male profession, "the boy consumer was an ideal spokesman for the progressive virtues of consumption and a "promoter of the new and improved," which reflected "advertisers' own self-image as the engineers of the nation's rising standard of living."[7] She also argues that the more overt appeals to boys' consumer appetites demonstrated "advertisers' new assessment of boy culture."[8] Along with the psychic rewards and new assessment of boy culture, however, it is clear that, at least for bicycle marketing, boys were also targeted because they were convenient. Not only were boys thought to be enterprising consumers who actively influenced their peers, thereby increasing sales, they also provided an opportunity for broadening appeals without reimaging the product. While the target demographic for bicycle marketing did in fact change, the ideals embraced by that marketing did not.

A key component of bicycle marketing was the idea of citizenship. Over time, the training of Americans to be good consumers, and therefore good citizens, occurred earlier in life. Building on the work of Benedict Anderson and Eric Hobsbawm, consumer historian Charles McGovern demonstrates how ideas of nationalism, which are founded on culture, have been significantly influenced by consumption.[9] In fact, McGovern argues that advertisers and consumer scientists "promoted consumption as citizenship and trained consumers to be citizens. In this sense, consumption became a core element of the American nation-state."[10] Bicycle advertisements reveal that goods were promoted to children in much the same way. In the process, certain ideals of masculinity were moved ahead in the life cycle, becoming traits that should be developed during childhood.

While the industry began to reconstitute the bicycle as a necessary part of the boyhood experience, it was also inadvertently transforming the bicycle into a child's toy. If the bicycle was encouraged as a part of childhood and the move to adulthood required a throwing off of those vestiges of childhood, then adults would certainly feel pressure to abandon the bicycle for something more grown-up, more exciting, and naturally, more expensive. By the 1920s, as the bicycle industry worked to expand its consumer base to include children, it faced two distinct problems: (1) how to appeal to a group that had no real income, and (2) how to convince parents to buy bicycles for that group—their children. The thought of creating advertisements directed specifically at children was a foreign concept for retailers since children did not have their own income and therefore would not be the ones to make the actual purchase. It was also true that many of the popular forms of advertising focused on describing the product, in contrast to more modern forms, which targeted the consumer.[11] Bicycles designed for children had been around since the 1890s but those "sidewalk bikes" did not command the same amount of attention from the industry as the children's models of the 1920s and 30s. This suggests they represented a smaller share of the market but census data and production numbers for the industry do not make it entirely clear what percentage they constituted exactly since they did not distinguish between models or even wheel sizes. Ads for these early versions of children's bicycles in the 1890s focused either specifically on the product or, in some instances, on children's parents. Manufacturers generally relegated such appeals to the pages of catalogs since there were no active advertising campaigns for the children's market. By the mid-1910s, however, this was clearly changing. As the bicycle industry encouraged merchants to "get after the boy," it also began creating advertisements with children in mind.[12] It did not decide to focus on younger consumers strictly out of desperation, although it was certainly doing anything it could to attract new customers. There were also cultural changes underway, changes that emphasized children's independence as well as their preparedness for adulthood. These changes were set in motion, in part, as a reaction to the perceived requirements for good citizens during World War I, which placed an increased emphasis on patriotic manhood and womanhood.[13] Simultaneously, there was a movement to reform children's education and play, which resulted in the growth of "activities for improving children's physical and moral characters" such as team sports and scouting. Paul Ringel explains further, "Reformers sought to prepare young Americans for modern citizenship by segregating youth from the rest of society, particularly urban, industrial environments."[14] Just as the bicycle helped men and women escape the debilitating effects of the industrialized city at the turn of the century, it was well-suited to do the same for children two decades later.

Thus, the 1910s were an opportune moment for bicycle marketing to make appeals to younger consumers—particularly boys. Girls were sometimes included in the calls to action but the emphasis was always on boys. When girls were mentioned, they were seemingly secondary. As early as 1917, leaders in the bicycle industry, such as W. P. Farrell, implored dealers and manufacturers to cater their stock to boys. He wrote, "Play to the kid all the time. If you don't you lose your best bet. The boy is the natural prospective customer for a bicycle. It comes along in his process of evolution as logically as the velocipede and roller skates. The bicycle is the next step. The bicycle is as much the expectation of every boy as an automobile is the expectation of every business man."[15] Farrell's suggestions give explicit insights into the formulation of a hierarchy of masculinity, consumption, and mobility. He did not create this hierarchy but it was recently overhauled, given the fact that automobile sales were only recently burgeoning.[16] Farrell was simply expressing what industry trends were increasingly revealing, that the bicycle would belong to boys. Any other groups who purchased bicycles were something of a windfall.

This turn to the juvenile marketing at the neglect of adults suggests that the bicycle industry was ceding way to the car. The fact that the bicycle industry seemed so ready to relinquish its share of the adult market was all the better for the automotive industry. As the bicycle industry began to devote more time and energy into marketing the bicycle to children, it helped to redefine and firmly entrench the bicycle as a lesser form of movement. In turn, American culture would come to associate manhood with the consumption of the automobile. This reveals a lot about the class ideals associated with consumer goods; those that were more expensive confirmed a higher status, but notions of class are also intrinsically linked to notions of gender. Furthermore, the manner in which Americans consumed the automobile to achieve these ideals also suggests something about mobility. Tim Cresswell's study of mobility in the United States argues, "The early history of the automobile was thoroughly entwined with the construction and defense of particular visions of masculinity. Mechanical prowess, the control of space, ideas of sexual conquest, and the feeling of power that comes from being in control of one's own destiny were all wrapped up in the automobile. This was reflected in ownership figures. In 1915 for instance, only 9.1 percent of car owners in the state of Maryland were women."[17] The fact that an automobile, which was becoming increasingly faster and able to go farther distances was more symbolic of masculinity than an object that required greater physical exertion to operate confirms that manhood was, in part, a function of one's freedom and ability to move.

Many of the bicycle industry's initial appeals to children surfaced during the Christmas season. Trade magazines also attempted to get dealers motivated to sell to children by running advertisements with joyous scenes, one of which included a boy standing by a Christmas tree, jubilant over his new bicycle, while his parents watched in the background, careful not to disturb the moment.[18] The "Dealers Department" section of *MotorCycling and Bicycling* magazine told dealers that when soliciting business during the Christmas season to not only get the children interested, but to engage their parents as well. Many of the suggestions sounded like ploys whereby the merchant and the child would conspire to convince their parents to buy a bicycle. "Pick out the one you like best and we'll help you get father to buy it."[19] Some ads simply encouraged parents to buy bicycles for their children, while others targeted the children directly.

As a consumer object, the bicycle had a clear advantage in its potential marketability as empowering for, rather than exploitative of, youth. Advertisements suggested that children save money to repay parents by using their new bicycles to earn revenue. They were not only encouraged to do chores or get jobs and become active consumers, but to take advantage of credit opportunities. Advertisements told parents that the purchase of a bicycle for their child was an investment. One such ad pictured a young boy smiling and holding up his bicycle in front of a Christmas tree. The copy explained, "He's happy because he has what he wanted most." It continued, "Any boy or girl can make his or her bicycle pay for itself by saving car fares, doing errands, etc. And best of all, this kind of work is fun."[20] Of course, the idea of children working for wages to help support the family predates 1915 but this was not a suggestion that parents send their child to work. Rather, it partially focused on the money parents could save and attempted to implant in children the idea that they could use bicycles to earn money. This manner of advertising bicycles was not just the marketing ploy of one company—it was part of the cooperative boosting plan initiated in 1915 by the New Departure Manufacturing Company, Goodyear, the Million Bicycles Committee, and then the United Cycle Trade Directorate—all of which held sway over the direction and nature of national advertising campaigns.[21]

Manufacturers, like the Davis Sewing Machine Company of Dayton, Ohio, began their Christmas advertisements by October, running ads in *American Boy*, *Boys' Life*, *Youth's Companion*, *Popular Mechanics*, and *Popular Science Monthly*.[22] An advertisement for Indian bicycles in *Popular Mechanics*' December 1917 issue told parents that a bicycle was the "best solution for the youngsters' Christmas gift problem."[23] The fact that this campaign was primarily directed at boys is demonstrated by the magazines companies chose to run advertisements in and more explicitly in statements about their intentions. The Davis Sewing Machine Company wanted Christmas season ads to "help Dayton dealers lengthen the bicycle buying season by calling the boys' attention to the fact that the fall is a great riding season."[24] Often it was the art that revealed who was targeted. An advertisement for United States Tires told readers that when asking for a bicycle for Christmas to insist that parents buy a bike equipped with US bike tires. The art showed a boy on his bike waving to his parents on the porch while his sister stood nearby holding a doll.[25] The advertising manager for the Davis Sewing Machine Company, S. H. Ankeney, believed more work of a similar nature needed to be done. He told members of the bicycle industry, "the reason more bicycles are not given for Christmas presents is that the attention of parents is not directed to the bicycle as a logical Christmas present for the boy."[26] This was precisely why advertisements directed at the juvenile market were run in adult, as well as children's, magazines.

The decision to market bicycles to children during the Christmas season was logical because it was the time of year for children to get relatively expensive gifts. *MotorCycling and Bicycling* proclaimed, "Every bicycle dealer should start a campaign to sell bicycles for Christmas at once. It is the universal testimony of the leading dealer in the country that Christmas is the best season between September and April to dispose of left-over bicycles."[27] In attracting the business of children during the Christmas season, industry leaders suggested that local merchants call on the help of the boys and girls who already had bicycles. They advised merchants to offer incentives to young customers who might come in for repair work—telling them that if they were to give the merchant a list of friends, neighbors, and classmates who might be prospective customers they would give them a bell or some other small accessory as a reward.[28]

After the merchant had the names and addresses of those prospects, they mailed a circular. An example letter was provided for merchants to use as a template. One proclaimed, "There's heaps of fun in a bicycle. You have envied your playmates who have them. Perhaps you have even learned to ride on a borrowed machine. It would be nice to have one of your own. Now is the time to get it. Just mention to father that you wish that Santa Claus would bring you one of those dandy bicycles you saw in the window of Jones Cyclery."[29] The circular implied that if they did not have a bicycle they were essentially being robbed of the childhood experience. As an umbrella organization for the entire bicycle industry, the Directorate assured merchants that it would do everything possible to help them move inventory during the Christmas season.

This increasing focus on children was not only apparent in advertising but also among bicycle retailers. Merchants were encouraged to adopt enterprising methods to get children into their store. Trade magazines told shop owners that the ability to plant a desire for a new bicycle in "the hearts of boys and girls" was a "psychological matter."[30] They were provided with examples of how other dealers had created plans that aroused such a desire. Specifically, the plan of one dealer in Ohio who had made an agreement with the local daily newspaper was included "whereby the newspaper offers a prize of a high-class bicycle for boys or girls or both who solicit subscriptions for the journal."[31] The newspaper publicized the competition while making sure to praise the local bike shop sponsor for its excellence and generosity. This part of the plan was designed to instill a sense of customer loyalty in the local community. Of course, only one or two—if a boy and girl won—could actually claim the bicycle, but the shop owner knew that even those who did not win would want a bicycle more than ever. In the case of the dealer in Ohio, the author informed others that "the boys of the community had been enthused to the highest pitch of hope and expectation and all had been working hard for subscriptions to the newspaper with the bicycle as an objective."[32] This technique would continue to be used over the years, and would take the form of essay contests and other such competitions where children could spend a few weeks working for, and daydreaming about, winning the grand prize of a brand new bicycle.[33] Bicycle boosters believed that the combination of seeing their children work to win a bicycle and the disappointment experienced if they did not win, would compel any parent to buy a bicycle for their child. Not only would they want to cheer that child up after losing the competition, they would also want to use the moment to teach them that hard work really did have a reward. At the root of such marketing tactics was a belief that children were an overwhelming force in the consumer choices their parents made. Marketing strategists told manufacturers and retailers if they sold to the boy they would have at their command a "progressive and loyal consumer, eager and able to influence family spending."[34]

The ultimate purpose of trade magazines was to insure the industry's success, and therefore increase sales. In those attempts, they reveal the thoughts and opinions of bicycle industry leaders. There were, however, also numerous articles, such as the one mentioned earlier, that unveiled the extent to which merchants followed industry leaders' prescriptions. In addition, they show merchants' own ideas on how to boost sales. One such revelation came from the story of a dealer in Toledo, Ohio, who believed the best way to increase sales was to start a club. His club welcomed "All white bicycle riders from the youngest to the oldest . . . without fear of initiation or any other kind of dues."[35] His desire to exclude nonwhites is unsurprising since bicycle races and clubs were segregated at that time. There was also a belief that the mere sight of African Americans participating in certain recreations would "disgus[t] white prospects."[36] The purpose of the club was to expand the age range of groups involved in cycling by teaching new riders the skills to ride their bicycles properly and "take care of themselves."[37] The dealer himself spoke of how he often went for rides with club members, and was interested in promoting a road race if he could get some other dealers to join him. He reported that these efforts resulted in the highest volume of sales his shop had ever experienced.[38]

It is noteworthy that the shop owner even specified that the club was for white riders, since that would have likely been assumed. It not only suggests that there were black cyclists in Toledo but that there were also some interested in using the bicycle for integrated social outings. This particular dealer also made it known that he did not extend credit, so his article offers some evidence of how concepts of race and class intertwined as well. What is surprising about this article is that other than starting a club for all ages, the merchant does not specifically mention advertising or marketing to children. However, the title of the article boldly proclaims, "Selling Cycles by Interesting Boys," and the editor added that the moral of the story was that "No bicycle dealer can make the worth-while success unless he succeeds in interesting boys and girls. But you can't interest them by sticking to your repair bench."[39] The conclusion of making sales by getting out and riding with patrons, or starting a club for them—not by relying on repairs—is a logical one to draw, but the use of this story as evidence that dealers must target boys was more of a leap. This spin that the editor, T. J. Sullivan, tried to put on the story gives insight into the specific agenda of this trade magazine and, by extension, leaders of the industry.[40]

Along with merchants, manufacturers were also extremely proactive in selling bicycles to boys. In fact, they often appeared to make more of an investment than retailers—due to their willingness to invest time and money into efforts to help dealers. Such was the case with the Buffalo Metal Goods Company's initiative to create lists of prospective buyers. The company's president, W. F. Emerson, explained, "First off, we write to boys asking them to send in the names of dealers in their towns. To the boys who send in dealers' names we give a souvenir. Then we get to work on the dealer by sending him three letters. If the dealer doesn't answer the third letter we mark him down as dead and cut him off the list."[41] For the boys who responded, the company gave away more than enough pencil holders or similar items, undoubtedly with the company's name embossed and the expectation that boys would share them with their friends. It also asked boys and, in turn, dealers, to send lists of boys who were prospective buyers. The company would then personally send letters to those on the list. Emerson bragged that through this method, the Buffalo Metal Goods Company had "hit up our sales to 100,000 Atherton coaster brakes this year, and our business this year has increased 60 per cent over last year."[42]

This was similar to the strategy bicycle dealers themselves would adopt in the future. An article titled "Going after the Bicycle Business" suggested, "Every boy in your community is a prospect for a bicycle and if the dealer can instill in the boy a desire strong enough for a bicycle he will sell a large proportion of the boys in his community."[43] The article instructed store owners in how to go after the juvenile market by giving examples of successful tactics that had been used by some of the more enterprising salesmen. It also revealed the bicycle industry's notions about boys' ambitions for consumer goods and their ability to persuade not only their parents but also their peers. One method of access to these ideal consumers used was to "secure a complete list of boys who are good live prospects" by mailing letters to schoolteachers and offering them a small amount of money for each boy for whom they could provide contact and other miscellaneous information. One such piece of information asked for was whether the boy had any means of earning his own spending money.[44]

As well as demonstrating emerging beliefs about the power of boy consumers, bicycle marketing also highlighted notions of American nationalism. Much like the Boy Scout movement and physical culture in general, the bicycle could instill in boys an appreciation for the beauty of their country while training their muscles and bodies to be ready for militaristic duties. Numerous advertisements showed boys developing themselves and coming of age in the countryside. Along with their bikes, they played in creeks and ponds. One advertisement for Harley Davidson bicycles pictured a boy holding a frog (fig. 4). The copy claimed that bicycles were great for the boy with "pent-up eagerness to get out into the country."[45] A similar ad for Columbia bicycles pictured a boy fishing (fig. 5). It told boys that spring was on the way and road conditions would be improving enough for them to visit their favorite patch of woods, lakes, and brooks.[46]

4. *Gee! It's a Hum-Dinger.* Harley-Davidson advertisement, *Boys' Life*, April 1918, 55.

Bicycle boosters told merchants to stress the health benefits of the bicycle and to promote it as a natural physical outlet for their customers' children. These strategies of selling bicycles were not only adopted in advertisements; merchants who mailed personal letters to prospective buyers' homes also used them. A letter from Jones Cyclery reminded a father who was recently in the store, "Nothing equals the

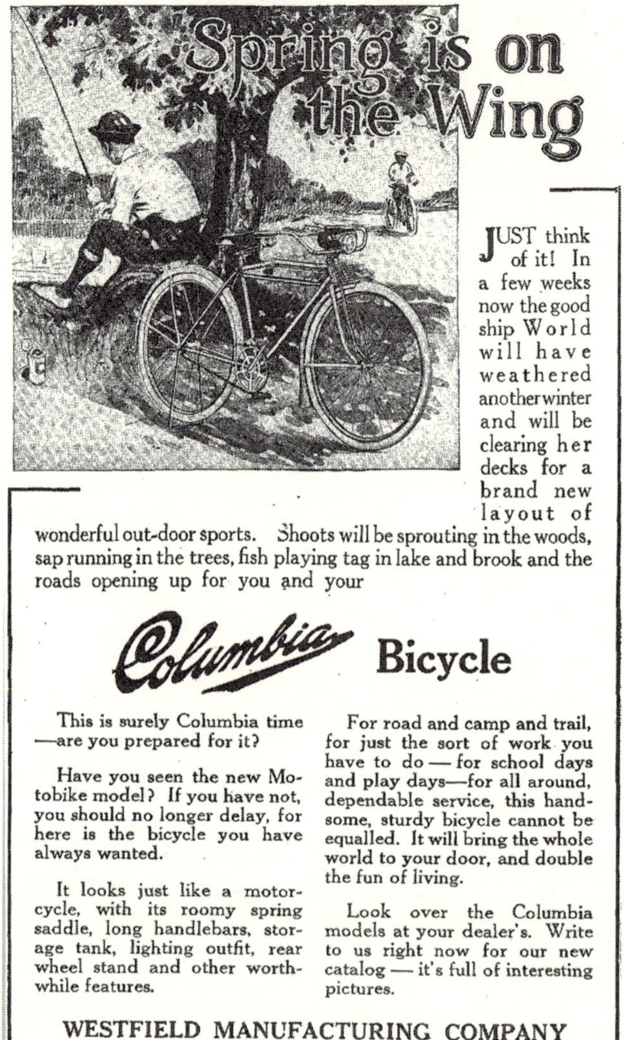

5. *Spring Is on the Wing*. Westfield Manufacturing Company advertisement, *Boys' Life*, April 1917, 39.

bicycle as a developer of sturdy bodies, strong lungs, ruddy cheeks, bright eyes, and self-reliance in your growing boy. You can buy your boy nothing that will give him more pleasure or do him more good."[47]

Bicycle promoters also continually employed health-care experts to help detail the virtues of their product. Martin A. Delaney, a "physical adviser for the city of Chicago," explained that bicycles were an ideal vehicle for boys' clubs and suggested "that the boys spend their vacations riding through the country on their bicycles. It appeals to me as the one best way to find real pleasure and at the same time improve physical condition. It is just the outing that should appeal to many who otherwise could not afford a vacation."[48] Delaney claimed to write the article for boy readers who had written to him to ask how they should spend their summer.

Boys were encouraged to ride bicycles, but only in moderation. Just as men had attempted to define the parameters of female participation in cycling, they also sought to restrict how much strength and health was appropriate for boys. Delaney was careful to point out the circumscribed masculinity of juvenile bicycles. Boys could work toward achieving manhood as long as they did not succeed or go too quickly. He cautioned boys not to overdo it imploring them, "Never ride after you become fatigued. I would also advise against crouching over the handlebars."[49] In 1890, men admonished women much the same way for riding with their "bodies bent well forward, knees up and down . . . struggling along with purple faces and hair awry."[50] Delaney's article was accompanied by updates on the progress of members of the boys' clubs, and other individuals, who were completing long adventurous rides over the summer. Boys were encouraged to go on multi-day trips as long as they paced themselves. Even though they were discouraged from exerting themselves too much, the acceptable amount of time spent on a bicycle was greater than it was for women or girls. No mention was made of girls even participating in multi-day bicycle trips. After all, these trips were meant to train boys to be men.

Now, instead of doctors telling adults to ride bicycles for health, they told children. Other trustworthy figures joined in to exalt the health benefits of bicycles. Even Santa Claus took part. One advertisement composed as if it were a letter from Santa proclaimed, "Every boy and girl who rides a bicycle is not as likely to have to be put to bed sick and have to take nasty medicine, because the bicycle makes them breathe more fresh air, makes their muscles strong and keeps colds, mumps and measles away."[51] While boys represented a wholesome—yet not fully developed—version of masculinity, they were also a convenient opportunity for the industry to maintain steady sales. Black Beauty Bicycles told potential consumers, "Physicians advise parents to get bicycles for their boys and girls . . . a health builder . . . that has made bicycle riding a fine form of exercise that stimulates the circulation of the blood, hardens the muscles and helps to develop every organ of the body. Besides being better than medicine it takes boys and girls out-of-doors, into God's own pure air and sunshine, where there are ever varying joys of sport, speed and sightseeing."[52] Rather than entirely redefining the bicycle, the industry was able to incorporate older, established marketing schemes to a younger audience. The bicycle maintained a certain image of masculinity. Instead of providing a means of affirming manhood, however, the bicycle became an initiating device in which boys attained adolescent forms of masculinity and thereby prepared for manhood.

Boys were also depicted using bicycles to perform tenets of American citizenship in advertisements that were overtly nationalistic. New Departure ran advertisements picturing a Boy Scout trying to sell something to a man in a suit in the foreground (fig.6). Images of tanks and explosions appeared overhead and in the background. The copy said, "Scouts of the U.S.A.—speeding from place to place on their trusty bikes—boosting the Red Cross, W.S.S., Liberty Loans—earning money to buy Thrift Stamps—are all helping put the 'punch' into America's soldiers in France."[53] Here, boys were told they could make a direct contribution to the war effort. A separate New Departure advertisement invoked a popular nationalistic symbol and told boys, "Ride a Bike for Uncle Sam."[54] In his study of American consumption and citizenship, Charles McGovern refers to such appeals as a part of "material nationalism." He shows that Uncle Sam was used in advertisements for a wide variety of consumer goods as well as other American symbols

6. *The Boys behind the Army*. New Departure Manufacturing Company advertisement, *Boys' Life*, April 1918, 49.

such as the Founding Fathers, Christopher Columbus, the Washington Monument, the Statue of Liberty, and bald eagles. *Printers' Ink* claimed that the use of national symbols, like Uncle Sam, were of double value. They provided a "decidedly likeable, lovable personality, plus the dignity of country-wide recognition. He [Uncle Sam] is a symbol of the whole United States; he is everybody rolled into one. . . . He is

America."[55] McGovern argues, "Uncle Sam's presence implied that the whole country used the product, and imaginative advertisers melded his image with that of the nation."[56] In essence, New Departure's advertisement that told boys to ride their bicycle for Uncle Sam was implying that they should ride bicycles for the good of their nation. Other advertisements used the imagery of war and bicycles together. The US Rubber Company commissioned advertisements with art that included soldiers in the background (fig. 7). The copy boldly proclaimed the boy of 1918 was more useful than the boy of 1914 because his work was "worth so much more to the country. He helps take the place of older chaps who have gone to war."[57] The B. F. Goodrich Rubber Company offered a booklet that boys could request titled "The Boy's Part in the Great War." It offered "Lots of pictures! Tells all about the war? How you can help your country win! How to use your bicycle in many new ways! How to make money to buy Thrift Stamps!"[58]

Outside of advertisements, there were also articles that tied notions of boys, bikes, and nation together. An article titled "How the Boy Scouts Help in War" was illustrated with a photo of two boys tacking a poster to a pole while a bicycle leaned nearby. The caption said, "They sometimes help the recruiting officers."[59] In fact, the Boy Scouts of America were trained for potential duties in the war in a more explicit and direct manner than they ever had been before. Here too, these boys would need a bicycle to do their part. A July 1917 article entitled "Getting after the Boy Scout Business" highlighted some of the "many patriotic services" that Boy Scouts were performing. Services such as, "carrying messages, collecting metal material, delivering mail, and in hundreds of devious ways they have taken the place of the men who were needed at the front."[60] Under the heading "Bicycles Aid Boy Scout Work," the article argued that "Were it not that these boys are sturdy cyclists, they would not be nearly so valuable to their country."[61]

Together, the advertisements and articles helped disseminate a juvenile version of masculinity in which boys exuded virtues of patriotism even without the ability to join American men at the war's front. More important for the bicycle industry was the notion that bicycles

7. *One Boy in 1918 Is Worth 3 Boys of 1914.* U.S. Rubber Company advertisement, *Boys' Life*, April 1918, 50.

were the ideal commodity for boys to buy because they aided the efforts of those who were anxious to get involved. The activities prescribed, however, were more similar to those suggested for wives and mothers, who were asked to do their part from the home front rather than the front lines.[62] Even while the expectation for boys was to play a supportive role, the imagery used suggested an eventual transition into actual physical service on the front lines. For instance, in the US Rubber Company advertisement (fig. 7) the boy on his bike looks toward soldiers marching to war and he is likened to a soldier on a motorcycle riding alongside the infantry.

During World War I, there was decidedly more attention given to the maintenance of the population's physical strength and mental determination. Training boys would help ensure that they grew to be stronger, abler-bodied, men. Bill Brown points out how this may have helped sooth nationalistic fears of decline because "producing the boy" was seen as "part and parcel of preserving the nation."[63] Articles instructed bicycle merchants, "Arrange to have the boys with bicycles meet one day a week at [your] store and then have a trip arranged for them and take them on a scout through the country, stopping at dinner time and cooking their dinner in the open."[64] Merchants were told that the war offered a great opportunity for sales suggesting, "He [the boy] likes to feel that while he is not old enough to carry a gun and go to the front, he can do the next best thing and work for his country in such a way that his work will count. It is certain that many bicycles will be sold to Boy Scouts for this very reason."[65] Dealers were also told that they would "have little difficulty in disposing of their bicycle stocks if they go after the Bicycle Boy Scout business properly."[66] They could do this by setting up window displays with a wax dummy dressed as a Boy Scout, and also by getting the name of the chief Boy Scout in their community, a name they should have on their prospect list anyway.

Even though the industry was focusing on a younger demographic, there was still an underlying assumption that boys would enjoy their bikes more if they were used in a manner that simulated manhood. The bicycle was thereby capable of indoctrinating boys to manhood early on—by getting them back to their rustic heritage out in nature, cooking and eating by a campfire, and by training them in business, or by aiding their contributions to the war effort. When it came to paying for the bicycles, dealers could "suggest a campaign among parents of the Boy Scouts and business men to raise a fund to mount Boy Scouts on bicycles."[67] In other articles, merchants were also informed that some Boy Scout groups, such as those in Rochester, New York, were preparing for messenger duties in the war effort by practicing message relays. Bicycle boosters made sure that merchants knew to concentrate on the boy and to take advantage of patriotic sentiments during the war effort, reflected by the growing Boy Scout movement. They told merchants, "Several bicycle troops are now being formed in the various divisions in anticipation of doing war-time duty."[68]

The bicycle industry continued to use ideals of adolescent masculinity to promote bicycles after World War I with considerable success. It was the war itself, however, that first provided the sense of urgency that convinced parents that it was never too early for their boys to begin preparing for manhood, or to train to become better citizens. Bicycles could help boys do both in the same ways it helped men of the 1880s and 1890s improve themselves—by granting them independence and the ability to convene with nature. As a result, the image of the bicycle became younger, but its qualities remained the same. That younger image, while good for stable sales, was founded in part on alterations in ideals of masculinity and mobility. Bicycles were ideal for boys because they taught self-reliance but not total independence; they built strength but did not overdevelop the body, and unlike the car they increased one's mobility but maintained limits. Just as juvenile masculinity was the intermediate step between childhood and manhood, bicycles became the intermediate step between pedestrianism and automobility.

Clearly, the bicycle industry was experimenting with methods for developing a juvenile market before the United States entered World War I, but it had yet to make the full transition to concentrating solely on children that would come in the 1920s. In part, this was due to the war itself, which provided forces that maintained adequate sales of adult models. The emphasis on economy, scarcity of fuel, expanded foreign markets, and use of bicycles in governmental duties domestically and abroad all served the bicycle industry well, even if sales did not hit the one million mark attained in the 1890s. By giving greater attention to the Christmas season and beginning to reconfigure the bicycle as a boy's—no longer a man's—ideal means of becoming an independent consumer and therefore citizen, bicycle marketing appeared to be more self-conscious and more advanced as it attempted to broaden the bicycle's appeal. While World War I did provide the impetus for some stability in terms of sales, the industry would be left with some very big questions in terms of sales and marketing strategies at the war's end. Its impact on ideals of childhood and citizenship, however, proved long lasting and would dictate the course of bicycle marketing for the decades to follow.

5

The Postwar Slump

AS THOSE IN THE INDUSTRY who were aware of the benefits of World War I for bicycle marketing might have nervously anticipated, the end of the war meant there was a very real chance that sales would decline. Indeed, there was a decided "slacking up" soon after the war was over—as adult consumption of the bicycle began to decline once again. Still, the years 1916–20 were relatively good for the bicycle industry. The total US market "apparent consumption" topped 475,000 units per year for all five years. The best year by far was 1920, in which 750,000 bicycles were produced. Numbers in 1921 and 1922, however, fell drastically to around 150,000.[1]

Photos in the trade magazines demonstrated that as late as 1919, even adults were consuming the bicycle at a higher level than they had immediately before the war. Bicycle boosters argued that changes occurred because public transportation was too expensive and inefficient. In an attempt to exploit potential frustrations with public transportation, boosters suggested workers ride a bicycle by explaining that it was faster for shorter distances and healthier. They argued that bicycle riders would not only feel better than average workers because of the vigor of exercise but also because "the car is full of all kinds of odors which have a tendency to make us feel stuffy and not up to our usual selves."[2] There was also some quick math to show readers that if they took the car three hundred days a year at ten cents per day, they would be spending at least $30 a year, and that a bicycle would be more cost effective. After one year, it would have paid for itself. Cyclists were also told, "You will also find that you have been many more places than you would have been had you depended on the cars."[3] This point made note of the liberation that could come with a bicycle. Cyclists were free to choose their own routes, whether they wanted to take the fastest route or the scenic route. Riding on a car presented workers with the same route, sights, and experience every day, making their lives feel just as limited and mechanized as the industries in which they worked.

While sales seemed good in the first two quarters of 1919, leaders of the bicycle industry were aware that they were going to have to work together to maintain a similar level of output once the nation returned to "normalcy." By July 1919, *Motorcycle & Bicycle Illustrated* was entreating members of the industry to attend the upcoming annual convention. A full-page ad in the magazine read, "Most important convention in years—big problems affecting reconstruction of the industry following peace are pressing for quick and practical solution. Now is the time to Get Business."[4] The primary objective of the convention was to find ways to boost sales for the entire industry. At the convention's end, the industry was certain it had done just that. An announcement following the cycling convention touted the promise of a new era in bicycle marketing. The headline read, "The Cycle Trades under One Big Tent: How the League of Nations Idea Has Been Worked Out in the Cycle Trades of America."[5] The article triumphantly continued, "The Cycle Trades of America is the title of the Cycle League of Nations . . . a real governing constructive force, made up of all members who belong to the various associated bodies . . . empowered and equipped to do big things for the cycle and allied industries."[6] A representative group of 283 tradesmen who attended the convention made this decision, which marked a renewed concentration on stimulating the sales of bicycles, parts, and accessories.[7] Under this umbrella organization—like its predecessors, the Million Bicycles Committee and the Directorate—the industry could move in a relatively unified manner and take aim at reworking marketing schemes.

A collective decision in the industry to create the Cycle Trades of America (CTA) added some energy to the cooperative boosting effort as it strove toward better organization than that of its predecessors. Its chief objectives were to establish official headquarters in New York City with a paid secretary to preside over the association and "execute the will of the C.T. of A. directors along the lines of cycle promotion and propaganda."[8] More importantly, the CTA was responsible for overseeing and directing the advertising campaign to promote bicycles. They would do so with money contributed from bicycle manufacturers and parts makers.[9] The association voted that funds for the "national publicity campaign" would be raised through a 1 percent levy on the business of all bicycle, parts, and accessory manufacturers. This reportedly gave the association an initial budget of around $150,000 as of September 1, 1919.[10] The CTA, more than any other organization or individual, was a conglomerate that had a powerful influence over the direction of bicycle marketing, but its marketing reflected greater trends in the industry.

The bicycle industry had recently began working to raise awareness of the opportunities to sell bicycles to adults for utilitarian purposes and the CTA would continue those efforts. The August 6, 1919, issue of *MotorCycling and Bicycling* included an article entitled "Bicycles in Industrial Transportation," which contended, "An early morning ride for a mile or two in the fresh air and at the same time with sufficient exercise to exhilarate without tiring, is bound to bring the worker to the factory with a zest for work."[11] Factory owners, who were suggested to have come to the same conclusion, had already "bought quantities of bicycles, in turn selling them to their employees on the installment plan."[12] The industry now apparently saw value in creating more advertisements that would speak to the laboring classes whereas it previously favored the middle and upper classes. Dealers were told to take advantage of industrial workers' increasing use of bicycles by talking to local factory owners to see if some kind of plan or agreement could be worked out. Quotes from several factory representatives who favored workers' use of bicycles were included in articles. A representative from the Underwood Typewriter Company said that his factory provided accommodations for 850 bicycles, adding that most of that space was indeed used by the employees.[13] The president of the American Rolling Mill Company said, "You may be interested to know that no less than 1,600 of our men depend absolutely upon the bicycle as a means of transportation." The Pierce-Arrow Motor Car Company estimated that 850 men rode bicycles to work and National Cash Register Company simply said "hundreds" of their employees used bicycles.[14] The article was accompanied by a number of pictures showing large bicycle sheds, numerous racks, and rows of bicycles outside and around various factories. Some pictures also showed employees leaving work on their bicycles. Each picture had a caption explaining where it was taken. Companies such as the US Armory and the Boston and Albany Railroad shops, United Shoe Machinery Company, Dayton Steel Foundry Company, Pierce-Arrow Motor Car Company, Underwood Typewriter Company, National Cash Register Company, Smith & Wesson, and the Gilbert & Barker Company were all showcased throughout the magazine's August 6 and August 13 issues. More than a simple suggestion that they market bicycles as transportation, these articles showed that adult workers and their employers already saw the value of bicycles. All manufacturers and merchants needed to do was be sure to supply the demand. The fact that employees were riding bicycles to work in such great numbers was also intended to serve as a source of encouragement and pride for bicycle merchants. Merchants and manufacturers could be proud that their product was so valuable in aiding workers' commute to work and the bicycle's important role in the manufacturing boom, which was vital in supplying Europe during, and shortly after, World War I.

"Bicycles in Industrial Transportation" argued that industrial workers were increasingly turning to bicycles because of the cost and uncertainty of "ordinary means of transportation." This included what the author described as a "shortage of cars."[15] Continuing a key rationale for support of the bicycle in the 1890s, it claimed that bicycles were preferable to other forms of transportation because employees who used them to get to work arrived feeling refreshed and more prepared to put their energy into their work. An advertisement showcased in *Printers' Ink* made a similar point. It told workers, "Make your trips to and from work a pleasure instead of a mean ride on a hot, crowded car. Ride a bicycle. . . . The bicycle is the most economical mode of transportation."[16] The artwork featured two men on bicycles, wearing jackets and ties, passing a crowded streetcar with other men struggling to get on and off. This ad was extremely reminiscent of advertisements from the turn of the century that employed idealistic notions of manliness as a means of selling bicycles. In the pursuit of this goal, the ad stressed that the bicycle provided "the exhilarating tonic of fresh air and . . . the open country." The bicycle was not only liberating, but also a healthy activity. The copy continued, "My, how good you feel! The red blood sings thru your veins, driving away those mean morning headaches and that old sluggish feeling! You get to work feeling like taking that old job and fairly 'eating it up!' Health and a clear brain go a long way towards making a successful man. A bicycle goes nearly all the way towards making a healthy man!"[17] Much like advertisements from the 1890s, one of which claimed, "Save $60 a year—have elegant time doing it—never felt so well—can do ten hours' work in seven—salary raised yesterday—employers like healthful men," these advertisements continued an old tactic to an entirely different generation as well as a slightly lower class of consumers.[18] The advertisement of the 1890s mentioned salary, which suggests it was targeting middle-class managerial types. The 1920 advertisement, while picturing a man in a hat and tie did not make it as clear if he was of the working class or middle class. Also, this was part of a series of advertisements that stressed the economy of riding a bicycle rather than the streetcar.

This line of marketing, however, was somewhat short-lived and centered around 1919 and early 1920. Judging by how quickly such advertisements disappeared from magazines and newspapers, the CTA soon gave up on the tactic. It was apparently ineffective at achieving the kind of returns the association sought. Bicycle historian David Herlihy argues that at this moment, the CTA conceded defeat and "shifted its focus back to the faithful juvenile market" due mostly to the increasingly affordable automobile.[19] This does appear to be true, but there were other factors that contributed to the bicycle industry's focus on juveniles. Indeed, numerous industries were making a move toward marketing to children and taking advantage of the growth of childhood consumerism in general. Additionally, the bicycle industry would direct their attention to boys not only because adults were buying cars—there was also a belief that children's consumer habits could be controlled.[20] This aspect was crucial for an industry that wanted stable growth most of all.

As they entered the first quarter of 1920, there was a degree of pessimism among members of the bicycle industry apparent in the fact that boosters were increasingly calling on industry members to remain optimistic. In 1920 the number of bicycles sold was 750,000, but in 1921 they plummeted to 149,192.[21] By the last quarter of 1920, the sense that 1921 was going to be a lean year was setting in. *MotorCycling and Bicycling* called for opinions on the state of the industry in December, asking whether the "slump" would continue. Without much detail, one manager responded that 1921 would be a good year because people were in the bicycle-riding habit and were not likely to forget it. He clarified that he did not necessarily believe a lot of bicycles would be sold in 1921, in comparison to years past, but it would be a good year for the sales of tires and accessories.[22] Edward Arnhem, the general manager of Arnold, Schwinn & Company, offered a similar argument. He believed that bicycle sales would stabilize in 1921 because the public's taste had not changed. He argued that human nature never changed—boys, girls, men, and women would all desire bicycles in 1921 just the same as they had in 1920.[23] Arnhem's suggestion that "human nature never changes" was rather shortsighted and overly simplistic.[24] While the basic principles of consumption and human need, or desire for the consumption of goods may stay relatively constant, the items that consumers choose to buy and their rationale for those purchases certainly changes over time. Rather than serving as an informative article, Arnhem's views were more than likely included simply because he provided yet another respected voice in the industry, which encouraged everyone to remain optimistic.

Another attempt to inspire optimism, spoke of how the industry had experienced slumps before, such as "the slump of 1907 . . . and then again, in 1914."[25] The "slump of 1907" was more of a banking panic in which business experienced a brief yet severe contraction. It resulted in a significant decline in output and employment and ultimately led to the creation of the Federal Reserve System to protect against potential banking failures in the future.[26] During 1913 and 1914 there was a minor economic depression, "which was accentuated by the economic disorganization of the first few months of the European conflict."[27] Allied funds were liquidated and quickly exhausted, leaving the United States to confront the question of whether to allow "the Allies to borrow funds from American bankers or of allowing purchases to fall off sharply with the probable consequence of a serious depression."[28] At first, preferring a strict definition of isolationism, the Wilson administration and Secretary of State William Jennings Bryan banned American loans. By March 1915, however, they both relented proving the panic to be short-lived as it was soon corrected by a "five-year period of enormous industrial and agricultural expansion caused in the first instance by increased European needs and later augmented by American participation in the war."[29] That expansion, however, ended shortly after the war came to a close. At the same time, bicycle sales began to plummet.

The postwar depression was not immediate. There was actually a small boom in the last quarter of 1919 that lasted until the second quarter of 1920, which explains why the bicycle industry was still somewhat optimistic even months after the war's conclusion. The economic historian W. Elliot Brownlee argues that while it is tempting to credit pent-up demand for consumer durables, it was actually the continued market for American exports as well as an "inflationary psychology that pervaded the American buying public" (table 5).[30] Even the Mead Cycle Company, who sold bicycles at extremely low wholesale prices, raised its prices significantly during this time. Offering new models for as low as $10 in 1914, their prices increased to $15.75 by 1917.[31] Because of their experiences seeing prices jump so drastically during the war, Americas who expected further hikes attempted to preempt increasing sales prices.

One bicycle booster, Sam Fetter, hoped to inspire confidence among members of the bicycle industry by suggesting the dips in sales they experienced in 1907 and 1914 were not as bad as most seemed to remember since they were over so quickly. In fact, he claimed the slump of 1920 would be short as well and his company knew precisely when it would end. Yet after giving it more consideration, he stated that

TABLE 5: Foreign Trade in the United States, 1914–21 (in millions of dollars)

Year	Exports of domestic goods	Imports of goods
1914	2,329.7	1,893.9
1915	2,716.2	1,674.2
1916	4,272.2	2,197.9
1917	6,227.2	2,659.4
1918	5,838.7	2,945.7
1919	7,749.8	3,904.4
1920	8,080.5	5,278.5
1921	4,378.9	2,509.1

Source: Harold Underwood Faulkner, *American Economic History* (New York: Harper & Row, 1960), 585.

a decision was made not to share that knowledge with other members of the industry since it was such a great advantage for his company. He suggested that he would be willing to share the information with select members of the industry provided they send him a request.[32] This could have merely been a gimmick to procure business contacts, or a ploy to inspire merchants to go after business with the same vigor and confidence they had when sales were good. Either way, his comments seemed to contradict the spirit of coöperative boosting other members of the bicycle industry had worked so hard to promote in years prior.

Responses from those involved in the motorcycle industry made it apparent that the slump was curtailing their business as well. They too conveyed concern about motorcycle sales in spite of attempts to sound optimistic. Hugh Weed, vice president of the Carter Carburetor Company, commented that at least the motorcycle and bicycle industry was not hit as hard as the automobile industry.[33] Weed, however, had no way of knowing just how drastically sales would drop in 1921 and 1922. His comments reveal a general sense of confusion that both the bicycle and motorcycle industry suffered regarding the cause of slumping sales. He posited, "the present depression is more psychological than real" because there are no instances of "bad crops" or "other fundamental causes of real panics."[34] He failed to consider the sharp curtailment in exports. He explained, "What depression there is is due more to buyer's timidity in the face of a general falling market than anything else."[35] Another member of the bicycle industry, A. H. Bartsch, argued that a slump in sales would actually be good for the bicycle industry. He advocated a free-market view of the industry, and suggested that the slump would foster a necessary "weeding out process."[36] He wrote, "Those who have a substantial organization—an efficient selling organization—and economical production organization and an advertising department headed by a man of equal common sense should have no difficulty in weathering the battle of sales that opens the year 1921."[37] This "battle of sales" would force members in the industry to be smarter and more efficient in their production and marketing techniques. Bartsch believed that sales would begin to pick up in the spring and general prosperity in the industry could be expected to last possibly into 1925. That is, if many of the competitors "who have been pulling on [the] 'business skirts' . . ." of others in the industry were eliminated.[38]

The only contributors to the debate who were specific about problems their industry faced were Irving Beck and A. E. McGavin. Beck predicted a bright future and argued, "banks and Federal Reserve system have shown their ability to cope with the most drastic financial situation that has ever occurred in the history of the world."[39] He proclaimed, "the unemployment situation has seen its worst days during the present depression and will take a strong turn in favor of reemployment after the first of the year."[40] As it would turn out, Beck was right. Unemployment rose from 5.2 percent in 1920 to 11.7 percent in 1921 but fell back to 6.7 percent in 1922.[41] McGavin believed that the industry was actually doing better than in years past, aside from the fall of 1919, "when the demand far exceeded normal supply."[42] His comments suggest much of the fluctuation was due to a market trying to correct itself. The inability to meet demand in 1919 led to uncharacteristically high sales during the first part of 1920, which led to a dry spell in 1921. Economic historian W. Elliot Brownlee argues that there was a general overexpansion of inventories across American industries. The boom peaked in January 1920 and the lowest point of the depression came in July 1921. The major problem during this period, in his opinion, was inflation.[43] As the economy encountered a period of deflation to correct the inflation that occurred during and immediately after World War I, the bicycle industry similarly faced a period of drastically lowered production in 1921 and 1922 to stabilize the uncharacteristically high level of production during the first three quarters of 1920.

In discussing some of the particular causes for stifled sales, McGavin explained, "The export situation has of course, been greatly handicapped on account of the attitude of banking institutions all over the world. In fact, this has been our greatest handicap during the past two and a half months, prior to which time we operated our maximum production."[44] If wartime was good for the bicycle industry because of increased laxity of regulations on exports and therefore the American bicycle industry was fulfilling much of the need for bicycles in Europe, then it was also true that peace had put an end to much of that, particularly after European countries recovered from the war. More importantly, the working class, which took to bicycles en masse during the war, was now feeling increasingly insecure about their own economic prospects. McGavin detailed the state of the industry in the United States, writing that they had not necessarily laid workers off, but they had cut their hours by 15 percent.[45] In his opinion, the saving grace of the bicycle industry was the fact that they had been steadfast in "underproducing in comparison to the demand."[46] This was a vestige of lessons learned from the bicycle boom of the 1890s, when production went well beyond demand—driving down the price of bicycles and arguably diminishing consumer desire for bicycles.[47] The sales figures for 1919–22 suggest that the industry did not actually under-produce as much as it needed to as sales rose from 479,000 in 1919 to 750,000 in 1920, but then dropped drastically in 1921 and 1922 to 149,192 and 150,000 respectively.[48]

W. D. Callender—publisher of *MotorCycling and Bicycling*—described the first few months of 1921 as a period of readjustment. He implored dealers to place their orders immediately, arguing that manufacturers did not have enough volume in orders to keep the prices down. He wrote, "BUY IT NOW, Mr. Dealer, Mr. Jobber, Mr. Consumer. Buy it now because it probably won't be less, and may be more. Buy it now because it is your duty to do your share in equilibrizing the present trade situation."[49] He went on to suggest it was a "civic duty" to buy what they could during the "period of readjustment."[50] Callender also employed a quote by Henry Ford, "the sage of Detroit," to inspire dealers and jobbers.[51] "Our cars, and trucks and tractors are now as low as they can be, but we are not getting orders enough. If we don't get more orders, we will be forced to increase our prices."[52] Like Ford, Callender was writing on behalf of manufacturers and making an argument that the hesitancy to buy was bad business for everyone in the industry. Low-volume production would increase the cost manufacturers had to invest in each unit. Those costs were then passed on to the merchants and jobbers. The year 1921 was clearly a year in which the industry struggled to adjust to a contracting economy after World War I. It also marked a new phase of bicycle marketing in which adults received less and less attention while children received decidedly more.

As industry marketing moved away from adults, it renewed its commitment to the type of juvenile advertising employed before the war. Even though the war was now over, ideas of citizenship, health, and manhood remained the subject of ads directed at boys. The specter of world war had, no doubt, put the United States on notice that the pride and enjoyment they took in their country could not be guaranteed unless there were future generations of strong, patriotic citizens at the helm. The bicycle, much like the Boy Scouts, was a tool to help young Americans develop their bodies and minds. In fact, the bicycle and Boy Scouts were often promoted together as a means of instilling confidence, strength, and self-reliance in American boys.[53] In this manner, the bicycle was still promoted on the basis of masculinity except now it was more focused on ideals of adolescent masculinity rather than adult masculinity. Many of the ideals expressed shared much in common with those that were used to promote the bicycle at the turn of the century. It was as if those ideals had become so natural and commonplace that expectations for attaining them were moved forward in time for citizens who were younger in age. At the same time, the possession of a certain amount of boyhood exuberance came to be expected of adult males. Historian Woody Register refers to this as "Peter Pan Manhood." In accordance with the idea "a man, in order to achieve and enjoy the full benefits of American life should never stop playing or being a boy."[54] Once all vestiges of this boyish nature, which was now controlled, were lost, so too was the ideal man.[55] He then moved on into the realm of old manhood; a decidedly weaker and less virile stage of masculinity.

The CTA was instrumental in the continued use of ideals of patriotism and citizenship to market bicycles to boys. It created art and copy for distribution to merchants who agreed to use it in their own personalized advertisements, which appeared in local newspapers.[56] It also created national advertisements. One such ad in the *Saturday Evening Post* pictured a group of boys who appeared to be scouts mounting their bicycles (fig. 8). It asked, "Does Your Boy Have This Opportunity? Does he have the glorious chance to develop himself physically and mentally in the happy way a bicycle brings?" One of the ways in which ideals of physical and mental development were combined was by leading boys on bicycle rides to places of "historical and civic interest." The boys shown in the advertisement are at Washington's headquarters at Valley Forge. It informed readers, "The Bicycle Clubs all over this country are contributing more to the young manhood of America than almost anything else. . . . The clear steady eye—active, alert mind and clean, healthful body of a bicycle boy or girl are beyond valuation."[57] The girls were tacked on as an afterthought. By 1920 it is estimated that there were more than seventy thousand Girl Scouts nationwide, yet no mention was made of the Girl Scouts, nor was there any attention directed at girls specifically.[58] Whereas boys were often the sole group mentioned in advertisements and marketing schemes, girls were only mentioned in conjunction with boys and they were always second. Girls could be included but boys were the focus. Advertisements also encouraged a grassroots movement among American youth to start their own bicycle clubs. "Give your boy a bicycle. If there

8. *Does Your Boy Have This Opportunity?* Cycle Trades of America advertisement, *Motorcycle and Bicycle Illustrated*, February 24, 1921, 31.

isn't a club in his neighborhood, inspire him to be the organizer."[59] The advertisement was included in *Motorcycle and Bicycle Illustrated* as an example of how the CTA was attempting to increase bicycle sales among boys. Members of the industry were expected to see this sample advertisement and follow the example by appealing to the "young manhood of America."

Even though the industry's focus was clearly shifting to boys, other sections of the market were not to be entirely forsaken. This was especially true for merchants who were reminded that *anyone* was a potential customer, including women, men, and girls. One article proclaimed, "The object of promoters is to interest every man, woman, girl and boy who is attracted to the bicycle, first of all, but there are not restrictions."[60] A separate article reminded salesmen, "don't overlook the girls. Trade among the girls may be stimulated in the same manner as the boys and a great deal of business would result."[61] While the industry seemed desperate in reiterating that *every* individual represented a potential sale, as far as advertising dollars were concerned, there was clearly a more concerted effort to sell bicycles to boys. One store owner explained, "In my advertising budget I direct 90 percent of my advertising toward the boy."[62]

The CTA led the charge in concentrating bicycle marketing on boys but other industries were noticing the power of juvenile consumerism as well. An advertisement for *Boys' World* told advertising professionals, "Boyhood recollections are the ones remembered best. The sound commercial importance of this fact is being successfully applied by a growing number of national advertisers."[63] An example was given of how a cereal company was focusing their entire campaign on boys. *Boys' World* claimed, "the advertising campaign in the boy field" was doubly effective because it produced immediate results and inspired "future goodwill that insures tomorrow's market."[64]

Another business that quickly realized the value of advertising to boys was the Sprague Publishing Company. Sprague ran advertisements in bicycle trade magazines that reminded bicycle and parts manufacturers that their juvenile magazine, *American Boy*, was the perfect means of reaching their new audience. One advertisement called attention to the disproportionate share of the market that boys represented (fig. 9). It claimed that based on the statistical data provided by surveying 288 dealers from across the United States, "71 percent of bicycles are bought by persons under 21 years of age."[65] Curiously, even though the statistical data do not account for the gender of these consumers, the advertisement assumes they were boys.

9. *How the Boy Market Stacks Up for Size.* Sprague Publishing Company advertisement, *Motorcycle and Bicycle Illustrated*, February 17, 1921, 24.

As a magazine with a predominantly juvenile audience, *American Boy* was better served by an exaggeration of the survey's conclusions. Sprague's ad compared, "How the boy market stacks up for size!" It told manufacturers and merchants, "the boy market is both your most reliable market for steady volume of sales—*and your greatest source of sales.*" It went on to discuss the virtues of the boy market as "a great, natural demand that responds most readily to your own efforts to develop it."[66] Not only was there an appeal to manhood in the manner bicycles were advertised to boys, but there was also an appeal to manufacturers' inherent paternalism. The boy market represented a section that was loyal, virtuous and, more importantly, it was a group that could easily be molded and manipulated by marketing and clever sales tactics. Companies would obviously want to try to reach this ideal market.[67]

American Boy told readers, "Out of recent buyers of Harley-Davidson Bicycles who stated their ages on registration cards, 58.1% were 16 years old and younger. There's no getting way from the fact that the bicycle dealer who goes after the boy trade gets the biggest share of the pie."[68] Echoing the extolment of the boy market, the ad continued, "Boys are natural prospects for bicycles. And the great volume of advertising for bicycles and accessories to boys in THE AMERICAN BOY makes his going still easier."[69] Boys were valued as consumers not only because they were thought to be loyal and easily swayed by advertising, but also because they were considered highly susceptible to peer pressure and jealousy. Dealers were encouraged to go for group rides with their boy customers and told that "if the kids have good times they'll tell all the other lads and get them to buy bikes from your store."[70] There was a picture accompanying the message, which showed four boys who had stopped along the road to climb and sit on a downed tree, where they could talk and enjoy nature. C. B. T. Hamilton, a Wichita, Kansas, dealer, recounted how he used child envy to sell bicycles by targeting the children of a "well-to-do oil man."[71] He began with appeals to the father but then had his own wife talk to their mother and finally, he sold a bicycle to a boy on the same block. While delivering the bike, he stopped by the oil man's house to show his sons the bike and to let them know where he was taking it. Once delivered, he then encouraged the new owner to make sure to show it off to all his friends in the neighborhood. By Christmas, the oil man had visited the shop and the negotiations for two bicycles began.[72] This revealed that advertising and marketing professionals were still guided by the rationale that if they could sell the boys of the wealthiest families first, they could then sell the rest of the neighborhood—even if it was done passively.

The Sprague Publishing Company continued the tactic of exalting the virtues of the boy market in their advertisements directed at manufacturers, yet their claims became increasingly bold. One of their ads featured a letter from the Miami Cycle and Manufacturing Company in which the sales manager applauded the Sprague Company's marketing scheme writing, "The boy market should always be foremost in our minds."[73] Sprague argued, "The boy market is a natural demand. Every boy expects a bicycle as his birthright. All effort spent in developing boy prospects brings the big, immediate sales, the volume of dependable business on which you can bank. The basic soundness of the bicycle trade for years has rested in the boy market. It is no question with the boy as to whether he shall have a bicycle. The big question to him is 'which bicycle?'"[74] This sentiment came to be widely accepted by industry leaders and was echoed by a photo included in the February 9, 1921, issue of *MotorCycling and Bicycling*. The caption read, "A bike is the birthright of every American Boy." In it, a young man posed with one hand on the seat of his bicycle amidst a lush valley.

Simultaneously, the CTA worked to make the promotion of boyhood and bicycles synonymous by moving the celebration of bicycle week to coincide with the celebration of National Boys' Week.[75] Even bicycle week changed as the industry concentrated more fully on boys after the slump in 1921. In years prior, the bicycle industry celebrated Bicycle Day—subsequently Bicycle Week—at different months of the year depending on the state's location. Southern and western states often celebrated a little sooner than the rest of the country, which waited until May, a time when the weather was more suitable for promoting and riding bicycles. The CTA, however, decided to make the late April/early May date official for the entire country to cut down on confusion and, more importantly, because members wanted to combine Bicycle Week with National Boys' Week.[76] The New Departure Manufacturing Company made sure that *Boys' Life* readers knew about the event with a notice that said, "Bicycle week is only another way of saying 'Boys week.' Boyhood without a bicycle is like a summer without flowers. This week is yours."[77] The campaign was reportedly a great success as "many bicycles are sold to children prior to the close of school."[78] Members were informed that "Newspapers in several cities ran races and parades in co-operation with the local dealers; authorities, Y.M.C.A.s, Boy Scouts, Rotary Clubs, and other civic organizations fostered exclusive bicycle activities or had bicycle events as leading features of programs."[79]

By 1923 the Christmas campaign was another staple of bicycle marketing. The CTA gave detailed information about the campaign in their yearbook, stating that 1924 was their "second attempt at advertising bicycles at Christmas time, and while the result showed fewer complete pages of dealer advertising than in the previous year, there was quite an increase in the number of half pages and less."[80] In general, the only other annual opportunity for children to get such a relatively expensive toy would be on their birthday. Implicit in many of these advertisements was the idea that if parents had not, or would not, buy their child a bicycle, they were somehow failing them. The guilt that a parent would feel in depriving their child of something that other kids had would be a strong motivation for buying. Bicycle retailers also made sure to relieve parents of the burden of such an expensive gift by establishing payment plans. The Mead Cycle Company ran advertisements for its Ranger bicycle in numerous magazines calling attention to its thirty-day free trial and twelve-month period in which to pay.[81] A report from Akron, Ohio, attested to the success of the Christmas campaign claiming to have "unprecedented bicycle sales . . . with the near advent of the Christmas season. Survey of the several dealers in the greater Akron area the past week disclosed sales are far ahead of last year at this time and almost double those of years previous. Even prewar days failed to give dealers such a volume of bicycle business."[82] One dealer reported to not only sell more bikes—sixty bikes sold with two weeks until Christmas and expectations of selling over one hundred—but selling bikes of a higher price on average than the year before.[83]

Other bicycle sales methods combined the benefits of a greater emphasis on consumerism during Christmas with year-round appeals targeting desires for strong healthy children. Industry leaders suggested that dealers try another circular intended for parents to read their children at bedtime. This way, the sale could be made to the child and parent simultaneously. In this particular story, Santa asks children to remember to send him letters to let him know what they want for Christmas. He goes on to tell them, "I am always especially glad to receive letters from children telling me that they want bicycles and wheel toys because I know that they are the most useful things in my whole shop. They last always, they make it easy and jolly for children to go anywhere, to do errands for papa and mama, to have fun in races and cross-tag, and above all they keep children who ride them strong and healthy."[84] These ideas were continually reiterated in advertisements and marketing directed at the children, but coming from Santa, an omniscient entity, they could be trusted, at least in the children's eyes. Of course, Santa mentioned the specific store that he wanted the child to visit in order to pick out the exact make and model he or she wanted. While the probability that merchants took the time to mail out circulars such as these and that parents would go so far as to read the stories to their child—telling them to ask for a bicycle—was slight, the point is not that this is how the industry sold bicycles. Rather, it is a story of the adaptations made by the industry to *try* to sell bicycles.

Regardless of specific advertisements or circulars, the bicycle industry's increasing emphasis on selling their products during the Christmas season appeared effective precisely because it became a staple of bicycle marketing. In this manner, the industry took advantage of cultural changes that made childhood consumerism more common. It also helped to reshape the image of the bicycle as a toy rather than a means of transportation for adults. It was something to be given as a gift for pleasure, not like a necessity that is bought when it is needed.

World War I had inspired a heightened focus on patriotism and stressed a need for strong, healthy children who represented the future of the country. Bicycles offered a chance to fortify children and prepare them for adulthood by providing healthy exercise and independence. Members of the bicycle industry seized the opportunity to market bicycles to boys as a means to become healthy citizens. By 1922 it seemed marketing efforts were paying off as the Boy Scouts of America began to readily use the bicycle in their activities. Articles written by scout leaders, including the organization's founder, Dan Beard, titled "Hiking and Camping with a Bicycle," and similarly, "Bike Hiking" by W. C. Wessel, offered information on how Boy Scouts could use their bicycles during scouting excursions.[85] Boys' magazines also included stories about young male protagonists whose dreams came true when they got their first bicycle and others about boys who used bicycles for adventure. A story in *St. Nicholas* told of a boy who saved up his money for a bicycle he really wanted but then he unselfishly uses the money to buy his mother a birthday present instead. He soon won a $50 prize along with a blue ribbon for a tomato he grew, but when he returned to the bicycle shop he found that the bicycle he wanted most was already sold. After arriving home disappointed, his mother told him to go feed the chickens, and he suddenly saw that his own mother bought the bicycle for him as a reward for being such a good son.[86] *Boys' Life* included adventure stories involving bicycles. One in particular was about a young detective who rode his bicycle all the time and because of that he knew "more about the surrounding country than anyone in his class."[87] He then uses that knowledge and his bicycle to save the day.

There were also real stories or testimonials from children themselves in magazine pages. When *St. Nicholas* invited readers to participate in a writing contest describing their happiest moment, William Biscoe (age eleven) described feelings that seemed straight out of an industry advertisement. "When I was a very small boy, I wished very much for a bicycle. If I could only have one, like my companions, for my very own! That was my only thought day and night."[88] Biscoe goes on to recount how he received his first bicycle as a surprise and how it was the happiest moment of his life. Another reader submitted story by thirteen-year-old Louise Corcoran recounted waking up on her eleventh birthday only to be disappointed to find that none of her birthday presents were "special." Once she got home from school, however, she found a new bicycle waiting for her in the garage. She wrote, "I was so surprised and happy that for a moment I couldn't say a word, for this was the thing I had wanted the most but had least expected to have. . . . This was my very happiest memory."[89] The inclusion of such stories in children's magazines made it seem that a bicycle was indeed a very important, if not crucial, part of the American childhood experience. These stories validated much of the bicycle industry's marketing strategy.

The success of the Christmas campaign and general marketing to children was made clear by a bicycle industry report to President Roosevelt over a decade later. The industry admitted that by 1923, their product had clearly begun to change from a means of transportation to a "plaything for children."[90] That same report revealed that by 1928 the industry had become "highly seasonal . . . due to the fact that bicycles are so largely used as Christmas presents for children."[91] By the late 1920s sales had recovered somewhat from the slumps in 1921 and 1922 but the industry was still far from the output experienced at the end of the nineteenth century. Disappointed and lacking confidence in its ability to sell adult models after 1920, the industry seemed to give up on consumers who were old enough to drive a car. Its marketing goals had clearly changed. Those changes helped transform bicycle consumption and alienated adult consumers by catering to children. The bicycle industry enacted these tactics in the pursuit of increased sales, but it inadvertently helped alter the image of the bicycle—inextricably linking it to childhood.

Throughout the 1910s, the bicycle industry continued to make appeals to adults. In the first half of the decade the industry busied itself trying to increase business, most noticeably by trying to expand the bicycles' appeal first to women and then to children. Initial attempts at selling to children were apparent in the Christmas campaign but by 1917 the bicycle industry was clearly employing ideals of citizenship and consumerism to market their product to boys. As World War I progressed, the industry experienced a boost in sales as industrial workers took up cycling for utilitarian purposes and exports to Europe rose significantly.

After the brief attempt to step up marketing to adults in 1919–20, the bicycle industry—finding success in their advertising campaign to children during the war—began to focus on children. While the industry clearly began marketing to children as early as 1915, by 1922 boys were the primary target of bicycle marketing strategies. This focus on juveniles would grow tighter over the following decades. As the bicycle and childhood became more closely linked and expectations of consumerism increased, children grew noticeably more sophisticated, savvy, and independent.

For a moment, the industry was encouraged by the increased number of adults using bicycles. Patriotic notions of sacrificing luxuries for the war effort and restrictions on gasoline usage, as well as rising public transportation costs, all played a role in increased bicycle usage among adults. However, the fact that bicycle ads targeted industrial workers shows that the availability of work, which now enabled the lower classes to afford bicycles, was more significant than consumers from the middle and upper classes who came back to cycling to conserve war materials. The slumping economy, which led to increased unemployment and even the return to prewar levels of production meant that the lower class could no longer easily afford luxuries like bicycles, and the middle and upper classes had no need for them. As a result, the bicycle industry, realizing it had little hope of selling adults without the help of outside forces, renewed its commitment to children. The growing support of childhood consumerism across numerous industries was also encouraging. *Printers' Ink* and advertising experts all argued that boys were ideal consumers who influenced their whole family and peers. As a relatively new consumer group, they offered a new opportunity for the industry to boost sales. After the industry switched its focus to children, its tactics remained relatively unchanged from those of the 1890s. The success the bicycle industry would find among juveniles was somewhat slow in coming but it did come and it proved worthwhile.

6

The Safety of Cycling

SUCCESS, for the bicycle industry, did not happen overnight. The 1920s and early 1930s were an extended period of limited sales—hovering between 250,000 to 350,000. During this period, changes in American culture had a pivotal impact on marketing and consumption of the bicycle. A key ingredient in those alterations to American society during the interwar years was the booming automotive industry. The bicycle industry not only addressed concerns about safety issues regarding the prospect of automobile and bicycle traffic on the same roads, but it was simultaneously affected and inspired by its competition. The challenge was to find a way to survive and thrive in a world with automobiles, rather than in place of them.

Americans' move to suburban communities was one way in which changing cultural ideals manifested. This, in turn, had a significant impact on transportation and recreation. As the 1920s progressed, the automobile became an increasingly important part of consumer culture in the United States. While automotive culture in the United States was indeed waxing, the popularity of the bicycle was waning, at least for adults. Previous studies have posited that the bicycle was replaced by the car, but few have elaborated on how this happened. David Herlihy points out that by the late 1930s the industry was shifting from marketing bicycles as affordable transportation for adults to a fun and practical commodity for children.[1] Steven Riess argues, "While in other parts of the world the bicycle remained an important mode of transportation and a major sporting device, Americans increasingly regarded it as a child's toy. The car replaced the bicycle in the hearts of Americans because it was more exciting and ownership conferred greater prestige."[2] Both of these points have merit. Examining the changing social conditions of the 1920s provides a clearer understanding of why the bicycle industry allowed, even encouraged, this transformation of the symbolic nature of the bicycle to occur.

By 1925 many Americans had abandoned cycling not necessarily because they preferred cars, but also because automobiles had become so pervasive and were moving at such high speeds that people began to see cycling as increasingly dangerous.[3] The annual number of fatalities involving automobiles had risen from around five hundred in 1907 to over fifteen thousand in 1923.[4] Unlike the dangers that the ordinary (high-wheeled) bicycle presented—dangers that could be overcome with courage and athletic ability—the dangers of riding a bicycle in light of increased automobile traffic were much more difficult to spin into a positive for bicycle consumers. Simultaneously, with the children's marketing campaign well under way, the bicycle was quickly becoming associated with childhood and seen as something that adults seldom used, and then only for fun. Adults who employed bicycles for transportation, or for utilitarian purposes, were either seen as old-fashioned, eccentric, or simply unable to afford other means of transportation. The bicycle industry's marketing decisions, along with rising usage of the automobile, worked together to redefine the bicycle in America. These developments were spurred on by Americans' changing notions of progress and success, both of which were imbedded in the American dream—a pursuit founded on consumption. They were also encouraged by increasing suburbanization.

Suburbanization was good for the bicycle's juvenile market, given the growing concern for safety on public roads, but it was less positive for adult models. Most suburban adults seemed unwilling to use a bicycle to commute to jobs in the city. Not only would their commute require physical exertion, but it would also be rife with the dangers that came in sharing the road with automobiles. Awareness of this resulted in a bicycle industry that was even less active in pursuing adult consumers in the 1930s and in the following decades. This had a detrimental impact on the image of the bicycle as well. A report to President Franklin Roosevelt on behalf of the Bicycle Manufacturers

Association, "an incorporated membership society organized in 1910 representing in excess of 87.5% of the known members of Industry and 97% of the volume of production," called attention to the transformation taking place. Regarding bicycle production, it explained, "From 1923 to 1932 the decline in production, except for 1929, has been consistent. It was during this period that the demand for the bicycle as a means of transportation became secondary to its demand as a plaything for children."[5] American adults were driving cars more and riding bikes less. Children, on the other hand, were increasingly encouraged to ride bicycles. While the automobile was integral to the white middle-class adult experience, the bicycle was just as integral to the experience of white middle-class children. Both parent and child would think about the bicycle in new ways as the automobile age came into being, but this was not a simple result of the emergence of the car. The bicycle industry's reaction to the car also had a crucial impact.

Cyclists were wary of motorists from the very start and those concerns would give way to outright fear as automobile traffic increased throughout the 1920s and 1930s. The booming popularity of the automobile changed not only the streets and conceptions of what was safe to do in those streets, but also the landscape.[6] The automobile gave impetus to sprawling American suburbs.[7] Middle- and upper-class American families could move out of the city into suburbs, where they could have their own yards and homes, separate from their neighbors.

As the automobile and public transportation increasingly affected the utilitarian portion of the bicycle market, the United States' cultural divergence from France, Belgium, Germany, the United Kingdom, and other European countries—where the bicycle remained significantly more competitive with automobiles—became more pronounced. In his book on the history of the bicycle, David Herlihy writes, "The number of bicycles circulating in the United States climbed to about two or three million by the mid-1930s, but that figure paled in comparison to the European fleets. Germany, which had half the American population, counted fifteen million bicycles. Great Britain and France each had about seven million cycles, followed by Italy with four million. Even the tiny Netherlands had three million: one for almost every other citizen. Every working day, some 40,000 cyclists commuted in and out of Amsterdam alone."[8] Sociologist Thomas Burr attempts to answer how this could happen with his comparative study of the bicycle market in France and the United States. Burr argues, "Bicycles lost social legitimacy in the United States and retained it in France" because of the overproduction of bicycles in the United States in the 1890s. This, he suggests, caused bicycle prices to decrease dramatically and allowed members of lower classes the opportunity to enjoy cycling, which negated the status that bicycle ownership conferred.[9]

An article from the *New York Times* in 1925 seems to agree with Burr, arguing, "The bicycle was handicapped by its failure to appeal to snobbishness in those early days of motoring. It was the cheapest means of transportation and had to take the consequences."[10] The *New York Times* further predicted a revival of the bicycle and contradictorily argued that both the reduction in price of bicycles, as well as encouraging the wealthy to take up bicycle riding, would cure dwindling sales—the sentiment being that in order for the bicycle to survive it would need to appeal to all classes. Others believed that simply getting middle- and upper-class Americans on bicycles was good enough. The president of the Cycle Tradesmen of Dayton said, "What a curiosity it would be to see our socially prominent men and women riding the two-wheeled vehicles."[11] Were this to occur, they assumed the lower class would also buy bicycles, as they sought to mimic the social elites. In 1922, however, bicycle manufacturers did indeed reduce the retail price of bikes by 40 percent. While it may have temporarily increased sales, it did not bring the bicycle back into vogue.[12] What the industry really wanted, after all, was not another cycling fad that would play out in a matter of years—it wanted sustained sales growth. The price reduction was yet another failed attempt at attracting adult consumers, which would, in turn, influence the industry's continued move toward younger consumers.

Thomas Burr points to the impact of automobile production, suggesting that the automotive industry created two distinctive markets in France and the United States. He argues, "Leisure use [of bicycles] collapsed in the United States, but adjusted itself to a new class of riders in France and continued to be a major factor in the market."[13] He contends that another reason for the bicycle's continued success in France was because it was substantially more difficult to procure and maintain an automobile there than it was in the United States. This was due, in part, to "political factors," such as strict driving tests, the early establishment of license requirements, and high gasoline taxes.[14] Frank Bowden, head of the Raleigh Cycle Company echoed the sentiment, writing, "'It is remarkable that with a population of 110 million, the output of [American] bicycles is not greater than in England.' He attributed the weak demand to the 'astounding' prominence of the increasingly affordable American automobile. 'Everyone's Ambition in the States,' he concluded, 'seems to be to have a motorcar.'"[15] While bicycling was less popular than it was in Europe, even by the late 1930s, bicycle merchants were convinced that rising sales meant the American automotive boom had ended. As a result, they believed that adults were coming back to the bike. Leisure usage of the bicycle did not collapse—as Burr suggests—so much as it sputtered out of fashion among adults, with a fast and fleeting increase in cycling beginning around 1934. Otherwise, leisure use continued to transform as the bicycle industry catered to, and therefore made their product emblematic of, youth.

In 1925 an ex-amateur bicycle racer from the United States, Hans Ohrt, called attention to the trends in American bicycle design in comparison to those of France. Ohrt claimed that France led the world in bicycle manufacturing, even in spite of the fact that it was also a world leader in automobile usage, simply because it had remained optimistic in bicycle production.[16] To say France was a "world leader" in automobile usage is vague and somewhat misleading. In 1920 it was still behind the United Kingdom and well behind the United States when it came to the number of inhabitants per registered passenger vehicle. Although France would surpass the United Kingdom by 1930, it appears to have never surpassed the United States.[17] Regardless of whether France led the world in automobile usage, Ohrt's claim about dwindling bicycle sales in the United States is worth considering. Contrary to Burr's insinuation that bicycles continued to do well, in part, because cars were harder to procure and license in France, Ohrt believed problems with bicycle sales in the United States were entirely unconnected to automobile sales. He argued that the reason why "thousands of bicycles are used by all classes . . . old men and women as well as boys and girls," in France was a matter of design.[18] In comparison to American bicycles, he explained, European models were more desirable in France because they minimized "unnecessary weight."[19]

In 1923 an article in the same magazine—*Motorcycling (Including the Bicycling World)*—informed readers, "Bicycles enjoy far greater popularity in the European countries than they do in the United States."[20] This was especially true in the cities where German workers were much more likely to use bicycles as transportation than Americans. In spite of the fact that the number of adults commuting via bicycle had supposedly declined because of cheaper public transit options, Germany still "ha[d] about ten million bicycle riders, both male and female and of all ages."[21] The article focused on the problems that arose out of the growing congestion in the city streets, especially with automobiles, public transit, and bicycles all fighting to ensure their right of way. This led to a need for city officials and city planners to take more caution to "regulate traffic conditions and to design streets and roads in such a way, that the bicycle rider will find it safe and a pleasure to ride his bicycle and that he will not obstruct the traffic."[22] It was clear that the bicycle's lack of speed was becoming a major issue for the growing number of cars on the road. The article also insinuated that motorists were annoyed with cyclists who were in their way. Even public transportation officials seemed to express dissatisfaction with cyclists occupying their stops. It is also apparent that these problems were not unique to the United States. Still, the bicycle remained popular elsewhere. The decline in bicycle consumption among American adults suggests that American cyclists were, at least momentarily, more willing to give up their right to the road than to take a chance of insult or injury while riding a bicycle.

Bicycle sales averaged around 585,000 per year from 1916 to 1920 but the average number of sales for the next thirteen years was approximately 288,000.[23] Aware that sales were well below expectations, members of the bicycle industry set to work trying to figure out the precise cause of the slump and a means to overcome it. In 1925 *Motorcycling (Including the Bicycling World)* surveyed bicycle dealers on how to improve their sales. The magazine then published a selection of the responses it received in July, but prefaced those with the statement, "Before analyzing the replies, however, it behooves us to state that the number of replies to the questionnaire seem to indicate that bicycle dealers as a class are not very articulate."[24] Still, it claimed the "replies represent a fair cross-section of the trade from the Atlantic Ocean to the Pacific, and from Maine to the Gulf of Mexico, covering 12 states and as such are of some value as an indication of the trend of dealer thought."[25] Regarding obstacles to bicycle sales, among various concerns, dealers listed automobile traffic (particularly Fords), lack of a set price, mail-order businesses and department stores, lack of publicity, and hard times.[26] According to the report, most dealers believed "aggressive action" needed to be taken to cure the ailments of the retail bicycle business. Specifically, dealers recommended:

> Take action to put the bicycle before the people, to make them see the economy of bicycles as compared to automobile . . . show the customer that it pays to ride a bicycle . . . the bicycle will be used more; people are finding out that they can't afford cars; notice more men riding bicycles lately . . . more national advertising . . . as long as cheap second-hand cars can be sold on easy terms to folks who cannot afford them, these same cannot and will not buy bicycles . . . [and] raise funds to repeal the Volstead Law that caused hard times.[27]

Most of the responses sought relief through advertising and publicity but the type of advertising called for was varied. While some called for advertising that was general in nature—playing on the benefits of using a bicycle—others believed the advertising should target the automobile directly by talking about the advantages of bicycles over cars. The one reply concerning the Volstead Act was prefaced as "very original," but what the respondent, A. L. Deninger, was talking about in general terms was the economy. He believed it was simply hard times that caused the bicycle business to suffer. At another point in the survey Deninger expounded on his point about the Volstead Act, writing, "The dry law keeps 200,000,000 (?) men out of employment. This alone ruins our business."[28] The editor included the question mark because the number quoted surpassed the total US population at the time—another, subtler, reminder that the dealers had no clue. In fact, the piece made an effort to show that dealers were all over the board when it came to stimulating sales, demonstrated beautifully by the seemingly random response of the Volstead Act. What is curious about the returned surveys is that many of the merchants who responded were apparently most concerned with adult consumers. None of the responses directly mentioned a need to do more to entice children, nor did they explicitly address concerns about safety.

In spite of that, addressing safety issues and continuing a pattern of increased marketing to children was precisely the direction the bicycle industry would take over the next few years. There was an apparent disconnect between industry elites and retailers. The claim that dealers were "inarticulate" highlights some condescension and mistrust of merchants' opinions. To be sure, industry leaders were concerned with the loss of sales to American adults but their solutions were somewhat varied and often overly ambitious, or flat out delusional. In 1925 it was hard to predict the long-term continued growth of automobile sales but many of the changes that would make the car such an important part of American life were already under way. While some wondered what ailed the bicycle retail business, others were more specific in addressing the issue of why adults were abandoning the bicycle.

In the Cycling Notes and Comment section of *Motorcycling (Including the Bicycling World)*, one of the industry's leaders, W. T. Farwell, asked, "Well, Why Don't They?" Entertaining the question of why more adults did not ride bicycles, his answer was, "fear." He argued that grown-ups were consumed by a "Fear of traffic, fear of what the neighbors will say, and fear of a little leg work."[29] Farwell described America as a nation of "automobile riders" explaining, "Everybody—almost—owns a car, and to ride a bicycle is considered out of date. It's all right for the kids, but just a' bit beneath the dignity of the kids' parents."[30] His comment contained implications about the changing gender, age, and class ideals embodied in the bicycle. By the 1920s, in light of the growing popularity of automobiles, the bicycle was not the first choice for the purposes of conspicuous consumption, nor was it the most popular way to display gendered ideals of manhood and womanhood. Farwell argued that to continue riding a bicycle was seen as holding on to relics of the past. Accordingly, the car was attractive, in part, because it provided an opportunity to demonstrate financial means and modernity, just as the bicycle once had in the 1870s and 1880s.[31]

The growing number of cars on the road arising out of changing patterns of consumption led to proliferating traffic problems, particularly on the city streets. In their booklet, *Cycle-Logical Ways to Happier Days*, the Cycle Trades of America (CTA) suggested that the growing automobile culture was bad for manhood. A physician, Dr. E. Parker Sanborn said, "It wouldn't hurt the daddies a bit to take regular exercise on a bike. Riding so much in automobiles is responsible for soft, flabby muscles, sluggish circulation and a lot of things cycling chases out of a man."[32] Farwell, a field representative for the CTA, suggested that the growing popularity of cars was detrimental to even those who preferred riding a bicycle. As America entered the age of automobiles, the bicycle industry was forced into a defensive position—faced with the task of proving that their product was not dangerous. Farwell argued, "The dangers of riding a bicycle are more apparent than real. With ordinary care—watching traffic signals and keeping close to the edge of the street or road—the cyclist is just as safe as any other road user."[33] Obviously, this is an embellishment since the contest between two cars in an accident was quite different than that of a car against a bicyclist—family cars could weigh over 2,700 pounds and exceed 70 miles per hour.[34] Farwell's intended point—that a person has just as much chance being struck by a motorist whether they were walking, cycling, or driving—was unlikely to console cyclists since they would have understood the disadvantages of the physics in a car versus bicycle scenario. His point that adults were not riding bicycles as much in the 1920s due to fear, however, is more credible. At a time when bicycle-related accidents had risen, with over five hundred fatalities and fourteen thousand injuries per year, bicycle ads and promotions paid keen attention to bicycle safety.[35]

Whether the bicycle was less safe, given the increasing amount of automobiles on the road, was indeed important for the bicycle industry to consider. Not only did it need to give attention to issues of safety in advertisements, but it would also take safety into consideration when designing and producing bicycles. At the same time, if the public could not be convinced that the bicycle was safe, in light of automobiles, the industry could focus instead on models that were not necessarily designed for commuting, such as children's bicycles and leisure models. These models were relatively heavy and inefficient yet stylish and ornamental in design. Conveniently for the bicycle industry, rising suburbanization in America provided an arguably safer environment for children to ride their bicycles—among their own neighborhood streets.

A *New York Times* columnist echoed the fears of growing automotive traffic and argued that cycling was simply less popular because of the increasing danger of riding a bicycle on public roads. "In the United States, with its 20,000,000 motor vehicles, bicycle riding has become too dangerous to be indulged in as a recreation. There was not better exercise in its prime. . . . A great sport went out in the United States when cycling was abandoned."[36] While it is clear that cycling was not completely abandoned at the time this article was written, it had most definitely experienced a great loss in popularity. In spite of dwindling numbers, cycling for leisure and sport both survived. Even by 1924, six-day races were still able to set attendance records. A race at Madison Square Garden in December 1924 made headlines for drawing over eighty thousand spectators with more than $200,000 in gate receipts—promoters were expected to have made nearly $150,000 in profit.[37]

If some gave up cycling due to fear, others sought solutions. In larger cities, cyclists called on public officials to support the development of cycling paths. In some instances, those petitioning for bicycle paths tied their demands to ideals of patriotism and paternalism, claiming that cycling paths were important for youth. A bicycle dealer in Kenosha, Wisconsin, teamed up with a local bicycle racing legend to appear before the city council where they "convinced them that in order to preserve our future democratic and republican possibilities—the younger generation of today, it was going to be necessary to set aside a tract of land for them to ride their bicycles on in safety . . . instead of in the streets which are becoming more crowded daily with insipid motorists who have no regard for life or limb."[38] According to the article, "the city agreed to set aside a plot and to assist in every manner possible, the planning and constructing of an oval, to be used exclusively by the bike riders."[39] The track was popular among the children of the community, with over nine thousand people showing up for the grand opening, many of them the fathers and mothers "who crowded the natural amphitheater that they might see and cheer their boy or girl to victory."[40] The author excoriated the "dealers who claim that the game is not what it used to be, that it is dying out, and that no one is interested in bicycles since second-hand Fords are so cheap."[41] In fact, many dealers believed the future of the bicycle was bleak; this is precisely why there was so much encouragement in the pages of trade magazines.

Industry leaders continued their efforts to combat the growing belief that bicycling on the streets was unsafe, particularly for children. Ultimately, though, they had to convince the public, but that could only occur after first convincing merchants. Throughout the next few issues of *Motorcycling (Including the Bicycling World)*, the editor, T. J. Sullivan, who was also a member of the CTA, would publish several articles stressing the burden on merchants to reassure concerned parents and to disprove the common misconception that the bicycle was unsafe. Sullivan said, "bicycle dealers, themselves, are the worst offenders in spreading the 'dangerous' bicycle propaganda. They have heard so much about bicycles being unsafe for children to ride in the public streets that they have come to believe it."[42] As this was a trade magazine and a big portion of Sullivan's audience was the very merchants he was scolding, he implored dealers to check the facts. He claimed, "If they did, they would be able to convince themselves first, and then the public, that the hue and cry about bicycles being unsafe to ride is based absolutely on pure imagination."[43] He also believed they would find that many of the children who were killed by automobiles died while running out into the street for various reasons, not riding a bicycle. He cited Chicago coroner records, which "show that not more than two or three in any year were killed or injured while riding bicycles. Playing baseball or football or tag in the streets, roller-skating, or merely running from behind one vehicle into the path of another going in the opposite direction" was what actually caused automobiles to accidentally kill children.[44] This information was provided so that bicycle dealers might combat the misconception that bicycles were dangerous. It also gave them an argument to make when trying to convince parents to buy their kids a bicycle, rather than a football, baseball equipment, or roller skates. Sullivan even went so far as to claim the bicycle was safer than shoes; however, this article was written for bicycle dealers and other members of the industry, not the general public, so this level of bias was unsurprising. The articles he published subsequently would employ the same line of reasoning.

Historian Peter Norton explains how the growth in child fatalities caused by automobiles—there were approximately seven thousand in 1925 alone—"contributed to widespread hostility towards automobiles and motorists among city people."[45] Indeed, one article, possibly written by Sullivan, sought to persuade bicycle merchants that motorists were the real problem. It suggested:

> Children with bicycles are not forced to play in the streets. The bicycle transports them quickly and safely to protected enclosures where they are safe from the careless motor moron. And on their bicycles while going to and from the parks and playgrounds they are safer than afoot. Every automobile driver is on the alert when he sees a boy or a girl on a bicycle ahead of him. It is easier for the car driver to avoid the cyclist for the reason that the boy or girl awheel is not so likely to make sudden swerves into the path of the machine as the boy or girl afoot is. Besides, the bicycle rider is more visible than a boy or girl afoot.[46]

The article went so far as to make the argument that dealers were actually ensuring children's safety when they sold them bicycles. Otherwise the child might walk to the park or playground, whereas on their bicycle they would be much more visible and safe. It boldly proclaimed, "The only safety precaution to avoid the 'slaughter of the innocents' is to provide them with some means of transportation between their homes and the public parks and playgrounds, and what is so ideal for this as the bicycle?"[47] This was a point that would hopefully inspire merchants, but at the same time a point that merchants could disseminate to the public when appealing to parents.

This sentiment was reiterated by Sullivan in an article that blamed decreased sales solely on misconceptions about safety. He wrote, "Bicycle dealers, you have been on the defensive too long in the poison gas attack upon your business through the insidious propaganda that children on bicycles are in danger when using the public street and highways. That poison gas is not only entering the homes where your best customers, children from 8 to 16 years live, but also in your shops where you have 'dug in' while it is destroying your salesmanship and gradually asphyxiating your business."[48] He reassured dealers, "The facts of the situation are that more children have been killed by the lack of bicycles than by those using them."[49] The article included excerpted stories from the *Chicago Tribune* of children who had been killed by automobiles while playing in the street. Sullivan contended that the children would not have died if they had bicycles because they would have been playing at a public park or playground instead of in the street.[50] He concluded the article writing, "ASK PARENTS 'CAN YOU AFFORD TO RISK YOUR CHILDREN'S LIVES BY DENYING THEM BICYCLES?'"[51] Sullivan was attempting to spin fears of cars killing children. Rather than deny that cars were a threat, he insisted they were, but that the bicycle was the best way to make things safer. In this slight twist of description, the automobile became the negative and the bicycle the positive.

Other concerns about the safety of cycling manifested in calls for bicycle paths and tracks that were located safely away from automobile traffic. These calls did not come solely from enterprising bicycle dealers; however, there were many "cyclists . . . urging more cycle paths." The number of people making these calls picked up momentum over time. By 1938 it had snowballed into what was described as countless "groups, organizations and individuals . . . clamoring and petitioning for bicycle tracks, exclusive lanes marked off," and so on.[52] One writer, Fairfax Downey, noted ironically, "The bicycle was on the other end of the controversy in 1899, when the buggy interest brought suit to have those horse-scaring bikes ruled off the road. But the Supreme Court was moved to declare that the bicycle was a vehicle and as such had the same rights as other vehicles."[53] It is true that bicycles faced legal action from the horse and buggy riders of the 1890s, but in that instance, cyclists had to fight a legal battle for their right to the road. By the 1920s, rather than trying to get automobiles outlawed from public streets—the action carriage drivers took against cyclists—bicycle proponents were more interested in the creation of their own paths. Nineteenth-century bicycle proponents had successfully advocated for safer and smoother roads as early as the 1880s with the good-roads movement led by the League of American Wheelmen.[54] Whereas early efforts were more concerned that roads be navigable, the bigger battle, beginning in the 1920s, focused on safe access to the roads or newly constructed paths separate from streets and automobiles. In a twist of fate, advocates now feared being crowded out of the smooth surfaces their predecessors had worked so hard to create.

The CTA downplayed the safety concerns all together. Instead, it instructed their two touring bicycle advocates—whose primary job was to visit schools and talk to children about bicycles—to refrain from talking about safety issues for fear that it would become the focus of the conversation. In a similar manner, merchants were instructed to limit discussions about safety to private conversations with parents. It was not an ideal point to highlight in advertisements and marketing.[55] Still, some companies did allude to safety issues in their advertisements, but only in a general sense. This was most apparent in the advertisements for coaster brakes, tires, and rims. The Lobdell-Emery Manufacturing Company, for instance, ran an advertisement for their chromium-plated bike rims that said, "More riding miles of comfort, safety and speedy performance boys!"[56] Tire and brake manufacturers were also sure to mention that their products could add to the safety of the bicycle by helping riders stop more quickly. Dealers played up these safety features as well. T. J. Sullivan publicly applauded "one wise dealer" who reportedly sold "upward of 800 bicycles a year us[ing] the coaster-brake as an argument for convincing parents that bicycles are safer than walking."[57] He told parents, "Now look at this bicycle. You see this brake? Notice how quick the bicycle stops by pressing back on the pedal. Much quicker than a child can stop when running."[58] Manufacturers also made connections between the advancements in their product and the automobile industry. The New Departure Company promoted their brakes in *Boys' Life* magazine, proclaiming, "And that New Departure coaster brake, Boy! How smooth it works. Has 24 braking surfaces on the multiple discs—works just like Dad's automobile clutch. It sure is a dandy. You should get one laced into your bicycle—any dealer can do it for you, and it doesn't cost much."[59]

While the trade magazines and industry leaders focused on the issue of bicycle safety regarding children, merchants and adult cyclists advocated for safer conditions for adults. Much like the survey sent out to dealers in which their concerns about the adult market were largely ignored, merchant's ideas and goals differed from those advocated by trade magazines, industry leaders, and manufacturers—who were more interested in children. If there was any debate to be had, things would certainly fall in the direction of industry leaders and manufacturers who had more power over production and design. In looking to their future, however, both sides could agree that the growing number of cars on the road was not the only factor affecting consumption of the bicycle. As the United States' population continued to grow and consumption of vehicles shifted, so did residential patterns.

The *New York Times* predicted the bicycle's comeback, explaining that one of the reasons for the recovery of bicycle sales from the abysmal numbers in 1921 and 1922 was the increasing prevalence of suburban living.[60] Retailers believed that suburban life—made possible by the automobile—created an environment in which "children [could] use bicycles with safety."[61] The article's headline boldly claimed, "Youth Exhausts Thrill of Auto and Roller Skate and Goes in for the Old-Time Fun of Pedaling."[62] General Motors' vice president and committee member of the CTA, DeWitt Page, told crowds at the convention of cycle trades in Atlantic City, "The automobile . . . has made possible the development of suburban life, and in the suburbs children can use bicycles with safety."[63] Conversely, suburbanization had adverse effects for bicycle usage among adults since it complicated commuting to work. Still, there was a way for the bicycle industry to try to make a positive out of this cultural development that was beyond its control.

Bicycle boosters promoted their product by proclaiming, "Bicycles Take Children off the Streets." Along with making a point about how children's bicycles increased safety, the article also made some implications about the virtues of suburbanization and the dangers of big cities. It argued that children killed by automobiles were usually from "big apartment house districts [who] are forced to use the streets" because there was no neighborhood playground or park. The bicycle was valuable because it would make playgrounds and parks, which may be some distance from the child's home, more accessible.[64] As much as a statement about the safety of bicycles in the city, this perspective also offers insights into the way in which class affected bicycle consumption. For the children who grew up in these "big apartment house districts," a bicycle was not as likely of a gift to be found under the Christmas tree as it was for children growing up in the suburbs. Not only would the bicycle be a relatively expensive item for lower-class parents to buy, but in the cases that they may also be living in urban apartment complexes, the bicycle would also be impractical. This was especially true if the complex did not provide bike racks or at least have an elevator.

Dealers certainly noticed the important opportunity that growing suburbs created. In 1928, Howard Jefferis, a bicycle dealer in Louisville, Kentucky, who had been in the business for thirty-eight years, made the decision to move from his downtown location to the suburbs. Recounting his decision, a story told merchants, "Mr. Jefferis advises the bicycle dealer to pull up stakes and push into the suburban territory, where the bicycles are and where he will be in a good position to secure more new sales and get the servicing of the bicycles that he does sell."[65] This was not about selling bicycles to adults. Rather, it focused on the issue of safety and the fact that many of the children who had bicycles were living in the suburbs. Those children's middle-class parents were likely to own cars and be of a white-collar status. This demographic was attractive because it was economically stable, a crucial trait for bicycle boosters. Jefferis said so himself, admitting that he moved his shop to the Highlands area of Louisville, which was only a few miles from downtown, in part, because it was known as a "wealthy section, where there are fine boulevards for fast traveling autos, and a lot of quite streets, a big park, etc."[66] It was not just Jefferis, however, that was making this move to accommodate his business to the changing times and conditions. Other bicycles merchants, such as R. L. Davis, Kline Motorcycle Company, and Indian Motorcycle Sales and Service Company, had also recently "pulled up stakes" and gotten out of the congested downtown area.[67] Jefferis was clear when it came to the impact of the automobile on bicycle business saying, "Dealers have long been too mealy-mouthed in refusing to publicly or otherwise discuss the fact that the automobile has driven the bicycle from the downtown streets. The only people riding bicycles on downtown streets are a few messenger boys."[68] Those messenger boys would have been closer to adulthood, using the bicycle for income and were often merely renting bicycles from their employer.[69] And, as he said, they were few in numbers, less common than suburban children.

In making claims that youth had exhausted the thrill of automobiles, members of the bicycle trade suggested that the automobile was just a fad that would soon fall out of fashion, just as the bicycle had in 1898.[70] It is important to note that this was written in 1925, a year in which "automobile manufacturing slowed its prodigious rate of growth."[71] In 1926 even a General Motors spokesman was somewhat pessimistic, stating publicly, "It seems altogether unlikely that tremendous annual increases will continue."[72] The collective memory of the bicycle industry was also at play. Its experiences with adult consumers in the 1890s inspired pessimism about the prospect of sustaining sales to adults for more than a few years at a time, regardless of the product. This was coupled with a belief that if children were growing bored with the car in 1925, adults would soon follow. The implication was that even adults would come back to the bicycle after their affair with the automobile. Still, the bicycle industry hedged their bets by putting their focus on the juvenile market instead of gearing up for a potential increase in sales as adults came back to the bicycle. The belief that American children would reject the automobile was, no doubt, wishful thinking on the part of bicycle industry officials. Whether they rejected cars or not, the fact that statutory law prohibited children from driving cars certainly worked in the bicycle industry's favor. Even so, manufacturers decided to mimic many design characteristics of motorized vehicles. This suggests that, at least in their opinion, children were indeed fascinated by cars.

The growth of automobile consumption in the 1920s had the bicycle industry on its heels. As cars crowded the streets and roads, adults found the prospect of using a bicycle for commuting or utilitarian purposes decidedly more complicated and possibly dangerous. By 1925 the bicycle industry was clearly preoccupying itself by trying to figure out why adults were no longer riding bikes and what, if anything could be done to solve the problem. Aside from the limited and apparently ineffective efforts to encourage government officials and city planners to take proactive steps that would make cycling safer, the industry seemed in a state of confusion. Merchants and industry elites were at odds over the future direction of bicycle marketing. It was the elites' idea to concentrate on safety and children that would win out. The onset of suburbanization fed into pre-existing opinions that the best course of action was to target children. As a setting that offered safer cycling on sidewalks and streets with a lower volume of traffic and slower speeds, suburbs offered an important opportunity to sell bicycles to white middle-class children. A larger amount of open space, between houses and child-friendly destinations, was well-suited for bicycles as they became an important instrument of juvenile mobility. Regardless of the bicycle industry's reactions to cultural changes, real or perceived, the 1920s represent an era in which bicycle marketing was changing but had yet to find the kind of success that had been sought since the golden age of cycling. Juvenile marketing offered a bandage to declining sales in the 1910s and 1920s but it would appear to be a tonic in the following decades.

7

Surviving the Great Depression

BEFORE THE GREAT DEPRESSION, the bicycle industry already had its fill of lean years. Standard accounts of business and consumerism would lead one to assume things would only get worse after 1929, but that was not the case. Even though the entire economy was on a downward spiral with consumers buying significantly less—hiding money under mattresses and in the back of cupboards—bicycle sales showed no significant decline. This was true even in 1932, when nearly twelve million workers were unemployed.[1] As figure 10 shows, sales were decidedly worse during the 1921 recession—when around five million workers were unemployed—than any time during the Depression.[2] After 1932, bicycle sales began a steady climb. In fact, they would skyrocket during the Depression and hold steady after World War II. Historian Lizabeth Cohen writes that it was the U.S. government's decision to become an "arsenal of democracy" in order to "restaff factories and restuf[f] wallets for the first time in years. Those favorable conditions in turn produced others: booming demand for consumer products, record-breaking retail sales, and the creation of even more jobs to manufacture and to sell long coveted goods. Production of refrigerators increased 164 percent in the first six months of 1941 over the average for 1935–1939; automobiles were up 55 percent and other consumer durables followed suit."[3] Yet bicycle sales reached record levels in 1936 with 1,233,000 units sold.

The secret to success was marketing the bicycle to juveniles. At the same time, marketing to juveniles was a hindrance for the bicycle's

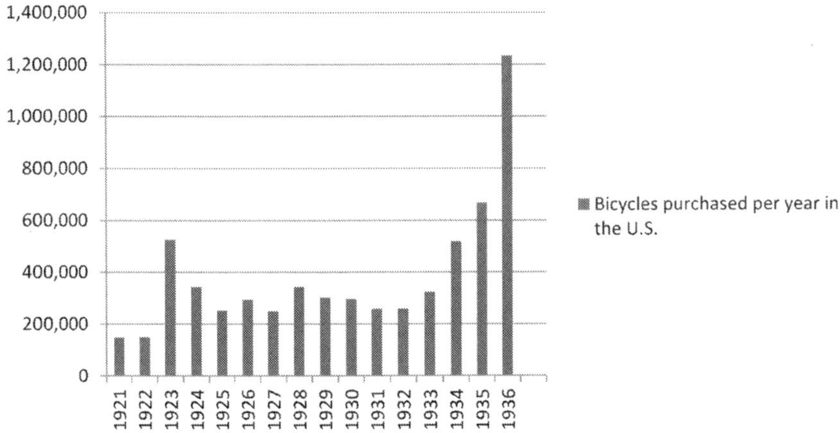

10. Annual bicycle purchases in the United States, 1921–33. Schwinn Bicycle Company, "U.S. Bicycle Market Statistics—1895 to 1979," *Schwinn Reporter*, March 1980.

marketability among adults, but this was a price the industry seemed willing to pay. If the experiences of the past had taught bicycle and parts manufacturers anything, it was that adults were not the key to stabilizing their market. Again in 1936 they would see that increased adult participation in cycling certainly added a nice boost to sales, but it did not provide the kind of numbers that could be depended on or accurately predicted. While the industry's marketing and production designs seriously altered the way Americans would think about the bicycle—not necessarily in a positive way—they also induced the type of record sales that other industries would not experience until after World War II.

Bicycle historian David Herlihy points out that the cycle industry "mounted an impressive comeback in the 1930s." He attributes it to increased participation in recreation, economically devastated adults coming back to the bike for cheap transportation, and the success of the balloon tire for children's models.[4] Recreational interests and balloon tires (as well as other alterations in design) were clearly important but the idea that adults bought bicycles as a cheap alternative form of transportation is less convincing. The 1920s and 1930s were pivotal decades for the American bicycle industry that led to a sea change in our conception of mobility and consumerism; however, these years have received comparatively little attention from bicycle historians.[5]

The 1920s had been decidedly bleak for the bicycle industry but the 1930s would offer some promise. By 1934 the industry was beginning to experience an upturn, one that was forecasted as early as 1930. An advertisement for the New Departure coaster brake exclaimed, "Happy Days Are Here Again! Glorious days for the kiddies—profitable days for cycle dealers. Cycle Trades advertising in the *Post*, *American Boy*, and in comics is pepping up the industry to greater sales efforts and we confidently look for bigger business this year."[6] The exclamation "Happy Days are here again" was no doubt a comment on the state of the bicycle industry, and possibly a sign of optimism regarding the entire economy. The uptick in sales four years later would indeed coincide with a decline in unemployment. Bicycle consumption rose from 323,000 in 1933 to 518,000 in 1934 whereas unemployment fell from 25 percent in 1933 to 22 percent in 1934.[7] The connections between trends in unemployment and bicycle sales were not all that synchronous, however, when looking at the depression as a whole. As table 6 shows, bicycle sales could thrive despite unemployment levels. In fact, bicycles were doing so well that *Motorcycle and Bicycle Illustrated* underwent a significant alteration by changing its name to *American Bicyclist and Motorcyclist*. The bicycle's newfound importance was signified by a change in the order of the title of the magazine, as well as the font—making bicycles the dominant subject. The content of the magazine also became substantially more devoted to the bicycle, while motorcycling content became significantly less common.

Individuals within the bicycle industry were encouraged by the upswing in business, even if they were confused, or divided, on what exactly caused the revival. The number of bicycles sold versus the number of passenger cars registered during the first few years of the Great Depression shows that rebounding bicycle sales were not simply a function of fewer cars being sold. In fact, the trends in bicycles sold and cars registered show similarities. While the numbers are quite a bit different, when bicycle sales experienced the biggest gains so too did

TABLE 6: Unemployment, Bicycles Sold, Cars Registered, 1929–37

Year	1929	1930	1931	1932	1933	1934	1935	1936	1937
Unemployment	3.2%	8.9%	16.3%	23.6%	24.9%	21.7%	20.1%	16.9%	14.3%
Bikes sold (x 1,000)	300	296	258	259	323	518	668	1.233	1.143
Cars registered (per 1,000)	189	187	180	167	164	170	177	188	197

Sources: William H. Young and Nancy K. Young, *The 1930s* (Westport, CT: Greenwood Press, 2002), xvii; Schwinn Bicycle Company, "U.S. Bicycle Market Statistics—1895 to 1979," *Schwinn Reporter*, March 1980; US Department of Commerce, Bureau of the Census, *Historical Statistics of the United States* (2001), no. HS 34, 64.

the number of cars registered. The number of bicycles sold, however, was less affected by drastic increases in unemployment than cars registered. Still, the upswing that the bicycle industry began experiencing in 1933 was shared by the automotive industry one year later. Census data show that many items among "personal consumption expenditures" were bouncing back by 1934, including food, tobacco, clothing, and recreation.[8] The bicycle, however, was doing more than bouncing back; it was surpassing pre-Depression sales figures.

There are a few explanations for the significant uptick in sales. Margaret Guroff and James Longhurst argue that it was due in part to celebrities' interest in the bicycle.[9] Guroff explains that it was at the 1932 Olympics in Los Angeles that they could view bicycle races in person. They were so excited by the spectacle that a number of Hollywood stars began cycling for exercise. An issue of *Toy World and Bicycle World* showed an image of Raquel Torres in a bathing suit astride her bicycle on the beach. The caption read, "Like many of the motion picture stars, Raquel Torres is fond of cycling."[10] With the likes of leading ladies such as Katherine Hepburn and Joan Crawford mounting a bicycle, Hans Ohrt, who sold bicycles to celebrities in Hollywood, believed the fashion would make its way east.[11]

The CTA, at its annual meeting in 1933, also attributed the growth, at least in part, to a rise in the fashionability of cycling. There was no mention of celebrities in particular but cycling as fashion was certainly a point of interest. CTA president W. B. Stephenson said, "We can credit women with the fact that bicycle sales for the first three weeks of August were 295 percent of those in the entire month of August last year."[12] More specifically, the *Chicago Daily Tribune* attributed the revival of the tandem bicycle "to the recent fashion of bicycling established among women."[13] This line of reasoning was similar to the logic in the 1910s. At that time, members of the cycling industry proposed that if the interest of society women was awoken and maintained, cycling would grow in popularity. Such appeals, if successful, would confirm what historian Alan Brinkley argues "was the increasing appeal, even the vice grip, of conformity in many areas of society" during the Great Depression.[14] Connecting bicycle marketing to fashion, however, was shortsighted since fashions, by their very nature, are not permanent. Regardless of the CTA's understanding or clear articulation of the forces that were positively affecting bicycle sales, they would continue to rise until World War II. Sales would have continued to rise in the 1930s without adults, because of the effectiveness of the children's marketing campaign. However, that brief fad of adult cycling, which the industry encouraged but did not create, really sent marketing and manufacturing into high gear.

The steady rise of bicycle sales beginning in 1933, along with the persistent advocacy of groups, organizations, and individuals who put pressure on governmental officials and city planners to think more seriously about cyclists—even when it was done with the sole intent of getting them out of the way—was cause for celebration.[15] The total US market "apparent consumption" (purchases) of bicycles rose from 323,967 in 1933 to over 1.1 million in 1936 and 1937.[16] This was the first time since 1900 that the industry had been able to meet the one million mark. Throughout the 1920s, the industry was only able to break the 400,000 mark in 1923. Its ability to sell over one million bicycles in 1936 and 1937 bolstered opinions in New York that "the marked rise in enthusiasm and growing interest in bicycling on the part of the general public within the city limits" required park executives to study cycling needs and plan facilities.[17]

By 1938 even Robert Moses—"the world's most vocal, effective, and prestigious apologist for the automobile"—responded to the revival by creating safe spaces for bicycles in New York City.[18] In his proposal for bicycle paths, he told Mayor Fiorello La Guardia:

> When on July 9th as one of those participating in the ceremonies in connection with the opening of a two and one half mile section of the outmoded Motor Parkway in Queens, into an experimental bicycle path from which data to satisfy the demands of bicycle traffic will be obtained, I said—"The way to make progress, sometimes, is to go backward," and that the Park Department was planning more than fifty miles of additional paths exclusively for bicyclists throughout the five boroughs, which would turn the calendar back forty years.[19]

In writing, "The way to make progress, sometimes, is to go backward," progress meant unrestrained automobility and cyclists taking up part of the street represented regress, an obstacle to progress that needed a remedy. Mayor La Guardia was of a similar opinion when it came to alternatives to cars. He believed "the automobile represented the best of modern civilization while the trolley was simply an old-fashioned obstacle to progress."[20]

Robert Moses made it clear that the number of children on bicycles had become significant enough to cause city planners to consider young cyclists. In fact, a primary purpose of the proposal was to help get kids off the public streets. But his purpose was twofold, partially so that children could avoid injury, but also to remove a "hazard to motorists." He contradicted T. J. Sullivan's arguments that children were safer on bicycles writing, "Every motorist is aware of the hazard created by children of the adolescent age exploring the whole width of the roadway, and particularly by delivery boys who weave in and out of traffic or steal a tow on the rear of fast-moving vehicles and trolley cars."[21] He continued by suggesting that relegating cyclists to sidewalks was not a viable solution since, in that instance, they would pose just as much of a threat to pedestrians. Clearly Sullivan and Moses were in conflict about the problem but agreement about the solution. Moses's description of the problem, however, was one that could attract more support from motorists and the automotive industry, which was important considering the number of motorists on the roads as opposed to the number of cyclists.

The *New York Times* confirmed Moses's points about the resurgence of the bicycle. Described as a "bicycle army," Marshall Sprague informed readers, "In the past two years, domestic bicycle production has quadrupled. . . . The country's cycle population is said to have reached 6,000,000, far more than existed in the Gay Nineties."[22] The article included five separate photos of men and women—not children—and their bicycles. Two of the pictures were throwbacks to the old days—one showed a woman getting started on a boneshaker; the other pictured a man standing next to his ordinary. Sprague contended, "As a cycling nation, we are creeping up on England, France and Germany."[23] He offered the fact there were "110 youth hostels, rustic inns placed at convenient intervals along popular cycling and hiking trails, where cyclists can get food and lodging . . ." as proof.[24] Sprague pointed out that the bicycle was even popular in "motor-minded" cities like Detroit and Chicago. The rest of the article focused on New York City and the initiative to build more cycling paths spearheaded by Robert Moses and the Department of Parks. In the city, he pointed to the popularity of amateur racing and the growing clarity in which cycling clubs articulated their demands—"bombard[ing] Commissioner Robert Moses and his Park Department with appeals and suggestions for cycling facilities."[25]

Aside from record sales, the bicycle industry had another factor in its favor. The proposed cycling facilities were a part of the Works Progress Administration's (WPA) sponsorship of recreation and attempt at economic recovery. The improvements were to be constructed with "relief labor"; all paths were to "be surfaced with permanent materials so as to require as little maintenance as possible when practical."[26] While a primary goal of the proposed project was to ensure the safety of cyclists and remove hazards from the road for motorists, there was also considerable effort in designing paths that would not be monotonous for cyclists. Moses wanted the project to provide an opportunity for "mental relaxation and physical exercise."[27] Because the overwhelming majority of the mileage created would exist within city parks, the plans were not intent on providing a means for travel throughout the city. Instead of focusing on making cyclists' commute safer or more efficient, they sought to improve the psyche and physical health of New York City residents. For years, the bicycle industry promoted the bicycle as a means of rejuvenating the spirit and improving the health of participants. During the Great Depression, the WPA saw the importance of creating facilities for leisure activities and thereby advocating, in part, on cycling's behalf. Just as governmental support and subsidies would prove crucial for the automotive industry over the next few decades, the bicycle industry also flourished when supported by congressional funding via federal agency.[28]

Believing leisure to be just "as pivotal to the social and political recovery of the nation" as getting people back to work, the New Deal government had an unprecedented level of interest in Americans' leisure activities.[29] Susan Currell's study of leisure during the Great Depression argues, "Although the function of the New Deal government was to get America working again, many of the social programs that took place throughout the decade focused intently on providing the 'right' leisure and correcting the 'wrong' leisure that had emerged."[30] In particular, newer forms of leisure that required passive participation were viewed with the most contempt. "In 1931, Harold Rugg, author of *An Introduction to Problems of American Culture*, listed as 'problematic' those recreations of modern American culture that entailed alterations in traditional customs: automobile driving, movie going, radio listening, jazz dancing, and spectacle sports."[31] Currell argues that the New Deal government looked to European models for inspiration, including Italy, Germany, the Soviet Union, and Great Britain. While she suggests that the United States wanted to correct and therefore control Americans' leisure activities, she sets the United States apart by showing how it ensured there was still an element of choice. Therefore, WPA projects "attempted to diffuse accusations of government interference in community leisure and to create a 'grassroots' approach to the national problem."[32] New Deal efforts to correct its citizens' use of free time, which was much more significant during the Depression than it had been previously, purposefully avoided a heavy-handed approach. Historian Foster Rhea Dulles argues that "Despite the demands made for a great measure of control over popular amusements, the American people continued in the 1930s to maintain the laissez-faire attitude which was felt to be the essence of democracy. . . . Opportunity, not compulsion symbolized the American way."[33] There was a belief that if people were given opportunity for appropriate forms of leisure they would take advantage, as long as there was also an effort to limit access to "undesirable diversions."[34]

With the help of two hundred and fifty thousand New York City residents on the WPA's payroll, the New York Department of Parks' plan called for over fifty miles of bicycle paths in twenty-one different locations across the five boroughs, most notably with more than five miles planned for Central Park—a constant venue for cycling activities from the 1890s to the present era.[35] Outside of New York City, the WPA also helped construct other cycling infrastructure, such as a velodrome for amateur racing in Chicago and a bicycle track at the Butler Fieldhouse in Indianapolis.[36] These facilities for bicycle racing, as well as the races themselves, gave the bicycle industry a lot of good publicity. At county fairs, cycling events were included to draw locals' interest. One newspaper headline proclaimed, "Approximately Twenty Thousand Expected to Throng Grounds on Opening Day Listed and Include Four-Day Speed Program," which was four days of bicycle racing for state championship titles.[37]

Working in tandem with the success of juvenile marketing, renewed interest in amateur racing and sociability afforded by cycling clubs was an important factor in the industry's ability to attain that mark of one million bicycles sold. Even before the WPA created officially designated areas for races, cyclists participated in "'boot-leg' races . . . during the early hours of the morning" on public streets and boulevards.[38] Six-day racing also regained popularity. It was very popular in the first half of the 1920s, grossing as much as $250,000 a week at Madison Square Garden.[39] Even through the 1930s, attendance at the

Garden remained around one hundred thousand paying spectators per week and attracted celebrities like Al Capone and his entourage.[40] The CTA used these competitive events for publicity announcing, "Amateur bicycle road races are popular throughout the spring, summer and fall months—open to all boys and offering opportunity to win valuable prizes."[41] The resurging popularity of amateur races provided an opportunity to fortify those links between health and cycling, which the industry had been working to imprint on American consumers over the past four decades.

The CTA connected the masculinizing effects of cycling as sport to success as an adult, no matter what career was chosen. It argued, "You will be surprised how much a bicycle will help a fellow to make something of himself when he grows up. There is hardly a big star in athletics, in sports, even a big gun in business or profession, who did not build his health and strength by riding a bicycle during his kid days."[42] Included were examples such as Shirley Mason and Dick Barthelmess; athletes like Babe Ruth, Charlie Paddock, Jack Dempsey, and Helen Willis; as well as the Prince of Wales and Charles Lindbergh. Those who were successful in "business or profession" presumably did not have time for the bicycle once they were adults, "but most athletes, aviators, racing drivers, track stars, boxers and all others whose success depends upon rugged health and strength . . ." continued to use the bicycle after adulthood "as a big part of their training."[43] Some effort was made to include girls as beneficiaries of cycling, albeit in a limited context. The CTA added, "All that we have said of bicycle riding for pleasure and health applies equally to the girls. Bicycles are now extensively used by girls of all ages everywhere—at boarding schools, colleges and at the famous and smart winter resorts."[44] Again, girls were treated as something of a catchall and for them, the bicycle was a means for health and pleasure, not strength, independence, or other attributes commonly associated with masculinity. The majority of the points made specifically addressed boys, comments such as "the bike is every boy's birthright" and "every dad wants his boy to have all the wholesome fun he can find."[45]

Competitive cyclists were not the only ones lending legitimacy to cycling; there was also a growing club movement in which some of the riders were more interested in getting out for casual exercise. Rather than seeing how fast they could go, they challenged themselves by traveling greater distances—riding centuries.[46] Still, some were content to simply get out for a ten-mile "stroll." There were around thirty thousand organized cyclists and a number of independent riders in New York, and some eighty thousand citizens who rode bicycles "for the fun of it" in Detroit.[47]

Cycling news was abundant in the *New York Times* during the 1890s but had become an outright rarity in the 1920s and 30s. Hoping for a return to those times, cycle clubs had slogans to "Bring Back the Happy Days of the 1890s" and people like Marshall Sprague were of the opinion that those "happy days" had already returned.[48] In attempt to bring those days back, organizers planned a bicycle parade and carnival to take place in Central Park. "A section of the parade would re-create the cycling craze of the Nineties, when riding a bike was a prime requisite for those who searched to move in higher social circles."[49] To recreate this atmosphere, the participants planned to "wear the costumes of the period, the woman in high-laced shoes, full skirts and shirtwaists, the men in short knickers and roll-necked sweaters. Some of the women would appear in sailor hats with short feathers, too, and even bloomers, as a sign of special daring."[50] Even if the riders were merely dressed up and playing a part, this exercise, and the parade in particular, expressed a deep sense of nostalgia for the "happy days of the 1890s"—not coincidentally, an era that featured a both an economic depression and recovery. Along with many other forms of leisure and recreation, in 1938 cycling served as a popular form of escapism.[51] In her study of leisure during the New Deal, Susan Currell writes, "there . . . emerged a new psychological approach to national welfare that argued for recreation that would help mend the Depression-battered psyche and aid adjustment to the new social and leisured order. . . . National and economic breakdown was paralleled with personal breakdown under the strain of modern living and economic insecurity—leisure provided the most effective and nondivisive path out of this personal and national trauma."[52] Dressing up in 1890s-era costumes and parading about on bicycles provided such a path.

While the American bicycle industry was certainly poised and willing to take advantage of the marketing opportunities afforded by the growth of leisure and competitive cycling, it was otherwise unwilling to redirect a large portion of advertising toward adults or racing models. Frank Schwinn was a notable exception, producing a costly lightweight racing model called the Paramount in 1938. Production of the Paramount, however, proved too expensive to be profitable. It retailed for around $75, the most expensive model in the Schwinn line, and experienced little success outside of the professional track-racing circuit.[53] Aside from Schwinn, bicycle manufacturers stuck to their heavier streamlined models with balloon tires because they seemed to offer stable sales.

There were some industry insiders who were highly critical of this failure to offer lightweight adult models. While admitting that French bicycle consumers were somewhat different from their American counterparts, ex-racer Hans Ohrt believed the progress of the French bicycle industry provided an important lesson. He pointed out that most of the participants of a road race from New York to Philadelphia rode bicycles that were produced in foreign countries.[54] He also called attention to the considerable amount of advertising and promotion for the makes and models of bicycles used to ride to victory in French races. While American bicycles were focusing on bulkier designs that appeared to be sturdier, he contended, "France has increased its volume by concentrating on three models, namely, tourist, Tour de France and ladies. Double-bars, truss frames, stands, weighty saddles and oversize tires have long been excluded in any and all equipment as manufactured by the factories of Continental Europe."[55] In short, the production of heavy bicycles in the United States and lack of attention to lightweight adult models was an "untold handicap for the exportation of American bicycles."[56]

As a whole, the industry viewed leisure and juvenile riders as the more cost-effective share of the market. Both could be sold bicycles made of cheaper materials and they did not require any effort in overcoming changing perceptions about bicycles as a means of fun and diversion. By remaining content to sell heavy inefficient models, the industry did more than simply sit back while the image of the bicycle transformed—it actually encouraged it.

Children's models were significantly heavier because of manufacturer's attempts to imitate automotive and motorcycle designs. The top tube was modified to look like a gas tank, and many bicycles were beginning to include speedometers. While they were not designed to actually go fast, at least they would look like they could, and better yet, boys could pretend they were flying along on a motorcycle, car, or even in a plane. An advertisement for the Elgin Blackhawk bicycle boasted the inclusion of a "Streamline twin bar motorcycle type frame and tank, Rubber cushioned frame, Electric disc style horn, Allstate balloon tires with new treaded sidewall, Chromium plated headlight, rims, handlebars, truss rods and sprockets, Stainless steel mudguards, [and] Motorcycle style streamline luggage carrier."[57] No doubt, hearing a bicycle described much like a motorcycle, or even their fathers' new Ford, made bicycles more desirable for boys who were anxious to achieve manhood.

Balloon tires became a standard on all leisure bicycles. In addition to having a fun-loving, kid-friendly name, the tires were designed to be extremely sturdy and to provide more cushion (fig. 11).[58] At the same time, these tires were heavier and added increased rolling resistance due to their width, tread, and lower pressure. This attention to sturdier bicycle designs for kids allowed them to get more use out of their bikes as they were able to take them off-road, through yards and gravel lots, but they were not suited for fast or efficient travel. First introduced by Schwinn in 1933, the balloon tire was an "undeniable asset for the child's model" and a reason why children's bikes became more popular in the 1930s, argues David Herlihy.[59] There are others who give even more credit to Schwinn calling the uptick in sales a "Schwinn-sparked bike boom" that profited the entire industry.[60] The Arnold, Schwinn & Company incorporated in 1895. It was led by an experienced and driven bicycle expert, Ignaz Schwinn, and a relatively passive partner, Adolph Arnold. Arnold was heavily involved in financing the venture but ended up selling his shares to Ignaz in 1908. The company's name would not change to Schwinn until the late 1960s.[61] It was an important

11. *Ride 'Em Rough Fellows, They Thrive on It!* United States Rubber Company advertisement, *Boys' Life*, June 1935, 27.

member of the industry soon after incorporation, representing about 14 percent of market sales up until the 1930s, at which point it became even more successful growing to control approximately 25 percent of the market by 1940.[62] The effect of the balloon tire on bicycle sales is worth considering since its introduction coincided with the upward trend in sales beginning in 1933. The balloon tire alone, however, was not responsible for the industry's recovery. Census data show that various consumer goods bounced back by 1934 and it was not until 1936 that bicycle sales experienced the exponential growth in sales that went significantly beyond output numbers leading up to 1933.

Bicycles quickly became a boy's primary means for adventure and exploration in the 1930s. They were capable of assisting boys in their pursuit of knowledge about their surrounding neighborhood. A model made by Elgin included a "Loud 'Wildcat' siren."[63] The siren, while a potential safety feature, was more important and functional for kids in its ability to better allow them to imagine themselves as cops as they chased "robbers"—their friends—around the neighborhood. While children may have found their bicycles liberating, parents undoubtedly took comfort in the heavy, inefficient designs, and burdensome gear ratios that served to limit how far their kids could comfortably get from home. Children's bicycles became representative of a lesser form of independence in which bicycle riders were tethered relatively close to home. Ohrt agreed, highlighting the fact that there were seventeen-pound bicycles produced in 1895, yet by 1925 "the school boy is the important user and regardless of wishes or demand he, of about 80 lbs. in weight, is expected to cycle with pleasure on a high geared bicycle of nearly half his weight."[64] In spite of the weight, children took to bicycles with enthusiasm and their numbers continued to grow.

T. J. Sullivan explained the growth of the children's market as a response to the growth of the automotive industry. He wrote, "As soon as automobiles became too thick on the highways, these wise dealers saw that co-operation with parents to keep children off the streets and onto the sidewalks was a good selling point. . . . Dealers sell sidewalk safety vehicles first, then, as children approach the ages where they desire to increase their play range, they sell them bicycles which will convey them to the parks and public playgrounds where they can play in safety."[65] Even though older children's bicycles could convey them greater distances, they were still designed in a manner that made them rather inefficient. Manufacturers focused on comfort, safety, and style. As a result, the bicycles they produced were cumbersome and difficult to ride at high speeds for extended periods. These were bicycles for the neighborhood, not the city. They were great for a kid who just needed to get to a park or a friend's house but they also taught children to think about bicycles in a limited capacity. An unintentional repercussion was that these children would grow up to believe that using the bicycle for transportation around the city, rather than around the neighborhood, was impractical.

Manufacturers who focused on children, often specifically on boys, attempted to make the bicycle more marketable precisely by making their product bulkier and, by design, less efficient. Companies also began recreating and renaming their juvenile models. Bicycle parts were renamed to correspond in description to motorized vehicles. An advertisement for Montgomery Ward & Company advertised, "Here it is Boys! The new 1928 Flyer Motobike, just equipped with New Model C improved multiple disk type New Departure Coaster Brake."[66] The incorporation of automotive industry-type jargon appealed to boys' desire to have the most advanced models, with descriptions that sounded very similar to adult's commodities.

Elgin bicycles also tried to capitalize on notions of "progress." One of their ads featured a picture of a couple riding a tandem from the 1880s next to a picture of their newest model. The ad proclaimed, "Wheels of Progress. 50 YEARS AGO, the contraption at the left was a luxury—TODAY, at Sears prices, beautiful, streamlined, balloon—tired bicycles are within the reach of everyone."[67] The bike included all the finest accoutrements such as a dashboard—with speedometer inlayed—a kickstand, luggage rack, and a new saddle. The front of the frame was even designed to appear to have a headlight, as well as a "hood ornament" attached to the front mudguard. In imitating automobiles, bicycle manufacturers demonstrated that in their own opinion, the best way to improve a bicycle and make it more marketable was to model it after automobiles. A 1940 advertisement for Huffman bicycles told boys, "There's motor-car flash in this streamlined hood and chrome grille, which houses the horn and dual headlites [*sic*]. The slip-stream design of this new chain guard makes it the keenest thing that ever concealed a sprocket. Smooth? You'll say so when you see this streamlined chrome frame luggage carrier with its built-in taillite [*sic*]. This slip-stream rear fender adds the final touch of motor-car styling."[68] Columbia bicycles had similar ads, one of which described a model as having "that rarin'-to-go motor-cycle look. See how that tank is streamlined into the racy-built frame. Look at those deeper, wider fenders, those shining white sidewall tires. And talk about colors—the flashing tones and stripings just knock your eye out!"[69] Advertisements for children's bicycles told young consumers that they not only wanted a bicycle that was fun to ride, nor one that simply had all the latest embellishments, they wanted one that would give them the "thrill" of hearing the "gang" proclaim, "it's a beauty!" They needed a bicycle they would "be proud to parade . . . before [their] friends."[70]

Manufacturers continued to design juvenile bicycles in this ornate style, including increasingly sophisticated components. By 1941 bicycles included such amenities as a "Duo-Beam" stoplight/taillight. The advertisement for the light said, "Scree-ee-eech and traffic pulls up sharp behind you . . . when you slam on your brake and flash this brilliant Stop Light. . . . Brake operates stop light by means of an automatic switch—just like the stop light on dad's automobile. Tail light glows steadily—operates by separate hand switch. Entire unit built into luggage carrier, offered for the first time by Sears!"[71] The advertisement pictured a boy and girl leaning on their bicycles, looking at each other, the boy smiling and the girl with a hand on her cheek, practically swooning over the boy with a bicycle that was nearly as sophisticated as a car.

The girls' model featured many of the same components as the boys' models—as far as safety and design—except there were two noticeable differences—one being the dropped top tube and the other being a dress guard over the back wheel. Both were designed to allow girls more convenience and the ability to ride a bicycle while wearing a dress. This marked difference in frame design was an important distinguishing factor for boys. Whereas girls would sometimes hop on their brother's, or another boy's bike, boys were much less inclined to ride a girl's bicycle. A trade magazine article called this fact to the attention of salesmen, reminding them, "Many girls ride and even prefer a boy's wheel, but no boy will be caught riding a girl's bicycle."[72]

Advertisements and other articles about the virtues of the boy market implied that as soon as boys were old enough to drive, they were unlikely to ride a bicycle at all. They reminded readers, "your dad rode one when he was a boy . . ." attempting to stir a sense of nostalgia in fathers who remembered the fun they had while emphasizing that the bicycle was part of the childhood experience.[73] Because of this, manufacturers and, in turn, merchants did not invest as much of their advertising money on the adult market. Not only were they relatively ignoring those over sixteen, but they were also encouraging those under sixteen to long for the day they were old enough to drive a real car, or motorcycle. The bicycle industry would find it increasingly difficult to foster a market for adults when it was responsible for adding to American consumers' love of cars by imprinting onto children notions that the most desirable bicycles were the ones that were best in blurring the lines between bicycles and automobiles. The only thing that was missing for many of these bicycles was a motor. In their response to consumer desires, bicycle manufactures stirred a fascination with automobiles in a decidedly young and relatively new consumer group that the automotive industry had yet to fully appreciate.[74]

The bicycle, now occupying the status of a child's toy, had become one of the first commodities in Americans' lives that they were led to believe they *had* to have. Once children were conditioned to be consumers, they could be taught to be conspicuous about it. Bicycle advertisements directed at children had already used envy to appeal to kids for a number of years. By the late 1920s, rather than simply selling kids any bicycle, advertisements pushed the bicycles that looked the most advanced and therefore the most expensive models. Boys in advertisements told their friends, "Gee! Dad Went the Limit and Got Me the Best There Is." The ad told boys they could get the regular model "without extra equipment" for $45 or for $50 they could get the "super" model "completely equipped with the latest and best of everything."[75] Advertisements offering bicycles as prizes to entice boys to sell magazine subscriptions said, "Oh Boy! Take a look at this flashy 1935 deluxe model motorbike. It can soon be Yours! Comes fully equipped with electric headlight, chime siren, platform carrier, rear wheel stand, coaster brake, and other outstanding features."[76] By 1940 companies were comfortable being more direct in their ads, "It's just too bad if the other kids are green with envy as you climb on this Deluxe Dayton Mainliner, and lead the bicycle parade by a mile. But, come on—let's go to town in motor car style on the bike that's proud and poised—and packed full of life, looks and eye-catching features. Yeah Man!—make way for the Dayton Mainliner."[77] Newspaper articles demonstrated that boys and bicycles had become so intertwined that it would be a mistake for parents to deny them while simultaneously demonstrating the racial and class divide that existed among bicycle consumers. One such article told of a young boy (presumed African American because of the language and source) who had unsuccessfully attempted to steal a bicycle on more than ten separate occasions—each time his efforts were thwarted by local police. The article rejoiced at the fact that after the police had appealed to the public to buy the young boy a bicycle—so they could stop being bothered by him—an "anonymous life-term convict, a white woman, and a minister . . . forked up the money."[78]

While bicycle manufacturers altered designs and their advertisements homed in on notions of conspicuous consumption and conformity, bicycle shops also altered their tactics. Merely adding children's models to their stock allegedly "enable[d] the small dealer who relies on his repair shop mainly for a livelihood to graduate into the merchant class."[79] T. J. Sullivan argued that offering children's models could "double and treble" the volume of sales because "since the wheeled goods business depends on the patronage of women, the repair shop man who has hitherto exhibited a bicycle or two in a window or on the repair shop floor, promptly realizes that women will not patronize such an establishment. Therefore, he proceeds to separate the repair shop from the sales room and making this so attractive that women are as likely to enter it for shopping as to enter any other store in town."[80] Industry leaders had encouraged merchants to make their shops clean and inviting since the 1910s but this was a much more overt statement about the gendered implications of refashioning bike shops to make products more marketable. It is also unique in its attention to the patronage of women. A majority of the advertisements from this particular era targeted fathers, or told children to get their father to buy them a bike. This direct appeal to women and mothers, however, would become more commonplace, particularly after World War II.

Success for the US bicycle industry began in 1934, when "apparent consumption" reached the five hundred thousand mark, a number it would consistently exceed—excluding 1943 and 1944—into the present.[81] This upturn, however, was something of a mystery for merchants and industry officials, who were divided on the cause of slumping sales and what course of action should be taken to remedy the problem. Treating the resurgence of cycling among adults in the 1930s as only natural, outside of advocating for bicycle paths, little was done in the way of marketing to ensure that the number of adults riding bicycles would grow or even continue. It was apparent that the brevity of the bicycle boom of the 1890s predicated on adult participation in cycling and the long struggle over the 1900s and 1910s to bring adults back to the bike had deeply affected the industry. The move to juvenile marketing was an outward expression of the bicycle industry's distrust of adult consumers. There was little faith that adults were the best demographic for stable sales and little confidence in even being able to attract those consumers after the automobile supplanted the bicycle in some respects. The economic downturn in the 1930s played a bigger role than the industry seemed willing to admit because it showed that the industry's alteration of bicycle marketing and design, which began as early as 1913, had paid off. It demonstrated the stability that juvenile consumers provided, even in the face of an economic downturn. The industry would not know for sure, however, until a decade or two later, once prolonged sales of over one million proved a reality.

Coupled with the Great Depression was a short-lived yet important increase in governmental support of cycling. In their goal of stimulating "desirable" forms of leisure and recreation, the WPA aided in the creation of velodromes and cycling paths, both of which gave adult cyclists venues for cycling safely, away from increasingly crowded streets.[82] These adults rode bicycles because they had considerably more free time and they used recreation as a means to escape and rejuvenate, not for transportation. The velodromes and paths created would have done little to help them navigate the city since one was a track strictly for competition and the paths were too disjointed to piece together routes for commuting. After World War II, governmental support of cycling would take a backseat while subsidies for oil companies and automobile manufacturers would become more prevalent.

For industry elites, heightened sales were predicated on the success of advertising to the juvenile market. Suburbanization provided a convenient and somewhat safe environment for juveniles to ride while greatly complicating utilitarian use of the bicycle among adult suburbanites. The second half of the 1930s, however, showed that there was still some hope, that the bicycle could overcome the automobile in the hearts and minds of American adults. But if increased adult participation came without much of a contribution from bicycle marketing, boosters wondered why they should bother spending their advertising dollars on adults. Manufacturers did not let the influx of adult consumers influence their decisions either.

The fact that some athletes continued riding bicycles after adulthood was used to publicize bicycles, as was the spectacle of amateur and professional bicycle racing. Still, American manufacturers failed to even try to take the next step—to rejuvenate production of racing models for adults or to offer and promote juvenile bicycles that were actually capable of going fast. They expressed excitement about the sight of adults on bicycles en masse, but nothing about marketing or design really seemed to change. The few who did see an opportunity and tried to take advantage of it, like Frank W. Schwinn's Paramount lightweight, were not taken seriously. Frank Schwinn got the sense that he was often swimming against the current, dubbing himself "the heretic."[83]

Even in the case of Schwinn, who was trying to market a top-of-the-line lightweight racing machine, the targeted consumer was the serious competitor, not the leisure rider, which undoubtedly existed in greater quantities than racers. Still, increased involvement in competitive cycling could have netted increased sales of leisure models.[84] It is difficult to judge whether manufacturers could have prolonged adult interest in bicycles beyond 1938 if they had paid attention to the needs of utilitarian and commuting cyclists, but at least it would have made a statement that another option still existed—bicycles were not just for play.

Ultimately the move to marketing and designing bicycles for children would prove a stroke of genius that would pay dividends in the long run. Not only did youthful consumerism keep the industry steady through the Great Depression, it got sales figures back to where they were during cycling's golden age and kept them there.[85] It was not merely a successful marketing strategy, it was a revolution. The bicycle industry would prove to many other American industries that the child consumer was indeed a powerful ally. Even though many began targeting children as early as 1920, the bicycle's success was a major testament that would fortify the entrepreneurial gold rush toward young consumers in the decades to follow.

Success, however, came at a significant price. In focusing their attention on the juvenile market, the industry took a step toward transforming the bicycle from a legitimate form of locomotion and exercise for American adults into a child's toy. While bicycles certainly represented a means of practicing masculine activities, it was not until they graduated to real automobiles—not toy replicas—that boys could truly become men. For a majority of Americans, bicycle-marketing schemes essentially destroyed the bicycle's masculine credibility among adults. New bicycle designs led to the transformation in which the bike became a vehicle for boys to understand their role in the world as would-be masculine figures. As a boy, a bicycle allowed individuals to reconnoiter their neighborhoods, but that was only training for the day that they could pilot a *real* automobile across a much broader landscape. Certainly, for those old enough to drive, automobiles were significantly more desirable than bicycles and the bicycle industry helped insure adults would choose cars over bikes by reshaping the bicycles' image as a second-class consumer object, one that merely tried to impersonate another. By altering bicycles to serve as a stepping stone to motorized vehicles, the bicycle became stigmatized as a lesser means of mobility.

8

Bicycles in the Age of Affluence

THE BICYCLE INDUSTRY had made such great progress by the end of the 1930s that advertisements for a wide array of children's goods incorporated bicycles into their own marketing. They were confident the image of the bicycle, or even just the word, would grab children's attention. An advertisement for Cocomalt, a chocolate milk "protective food drink" showed a boy and girl riding bicycles side by side. The copy proclaimed, "You need Pep to be Popular and here's how to get it!" It continued, "every glass of cocomalt with milk gives you one hour of energy for bicycling." This energy would be vital to children who wanted to be good at sports "a leader at parties . . . , [and] to do all the things that make a boy or girl stand out in the crowd."[1] This ad was reminiscent of advertisements for dietary supplements that claimed to help men reclaim their manhood, which ran alongside bicycle advertisements in the 1890s. Other companies such as Lifebuoy soap and Keds tennis shoes waged similar campaigns, targeting juveniles' desires to be popular among their peers. The tactic of using peer society to influence consumer practices among the juvenile audience had become ubiquitous in children's mass media since the 1920s.[2] What is noteworthy about the Cocomalt advertisement is that the company tied an unrelated consumer item to its own to grab children's attention and encourage them to consume Cocomalt. To be popular, you needed a bike and you needed Cocomalt to give you the energy to use that bicycle to attain fitness. Just as the bicycle was symbolic of class and gender ideals for adults at the end of the nineteenth century, it now symbolized the youth and vigor of white middle-class children.

The fact that advertisements, and entertainment targeting America's youth frequently incorporated the image of the bicycle proved that it had become symbolic of childhood. Youth culture of the 1950s shows that the industry's proclamation that the bicycle was the birthright of every American boy—made in the 1920s—had become widely accepted. This "age of affluence" would prove to be a time for mass consumption of a vast array of luxury and leisure items. It was a period marked by a booming economy.[3] Record levels of consumption were not predicated on adults alone. Lisa Jacobson shows that childhood consumerism, which was accelerating in the postwar era, was under way by 1910.[4] Associating the genesis of children's consumerism with the 1950s is a misconception. The postwar era was, however, a time in which the power of the children's demographic became irrefutable—as it captivated the attention of countless entrepreneurs and manufacturers.

It was in the post–World War II era that the bicycle made its final step in the evolution from a commodity for adults to one for children. The bicycle industry continued attempts to expand its young demographic but the manner in which World War II and its aftermath shaped culture and policy worked for and against bicycle consumption in the United States. The industry, in turn, continued to react to and use those alterations to boost sales. This included a small amount of marketing to adults but only as a means to relive their childhood and demonstrate agelessness, to maintain beauty, or to gradually restore gendered ideals damaged and depleted by traumatic events such as World War II. While automotive sales continued to outpace bicycle sales, the bicycle industry reaped the benefits of a growing culture of consumption among children and teenagers, thereby experiencing a steady growth in sales (see table 7).

After World War II, manufacturers continued to reshape the bicycle to make it more esthetically appealing for young consumers. The Arnold, Schwinn & Company (Schwinn) went so far as to create a whole new department, comprised of men who had previously

TABLE 7: Bicycle and Automobile Consumption, 1947–55

Year	Cars consumed	Bicycles consumed
1947	3.3 million	2.8 million
1949	5 million	1.4 million
1950	6.6 million	2 million
1955	7.8 million	3 million

Sources: Schwinn Bicycle Company, "U.S. Bicycle Market Statistics—1895 to 1979," *Schwinn Reporter*, March 1980; US International Trade Commission, *The U.S. Auto Industry: U.S. Factory Sales, Retail Sales, Imports, Exports, Apparent Consumption, Suggested Retail Prices, and Trade Balances with Selected Countries for Motor Vehicles, 1964–81* (Washington, DC: US International Trade Commission, 1982), 2.

engineered and developed motorcycles. Their mission was to modernize and improve bicycles' appearance and quality.[5] Such departments led the way in redesigning 1930s bicycles to look more sophisticated and bulky. After 1945, manufacturers and bicycle designers would go even further toward remaking the bicycle into an apparatus of child's play. It was at this point that they began creating bicycles that were literally toys, equipping them with holsters for cap guns, and donning them with the insignia of child television stars and comic book heroes, or even cartoon characters such as Donald Duck. Even though bicycle marketing and design was aimed at a decidedly younger audience by the 1950s, the industry reacted to shifts in culture to ensure that the bicycle still served as a gateway to manhood. This was particularly true with juvenile models for boys who had outgrown cartoons, those who had moved on to westerns, comic books, and mysteries. The bicycle's ability to provide masculine training grew in importance as World War II and the Cold War shaped the way Americans thought about manhood. There was a renewed focus on vigor. Suzanne Clark argues, "Manliness itself, and the old warrior ethic it invoked, was on trial. The return from World War II plunged American men into a confusion about identities that literature as well as mass culture struggled to address."[6] This struggle over the way Americans would define manhood also manifested itself in the mass culture and consumer objects directed at boys—the future of American manhood.

In his study of automotive culture in the United States, Cotton Seiler ties gendered ideals of the postwar period to the concept of mobility. He writes, "Promising a return to the mythologized past and heralding a limitless, abundant future, automobility seemed to offer the symbolic means to restore the American character—a character figured as masculine. . . . [D]riving 'masculinized' as the automobile began to colonize the cultural, economic, and political landscape of the United States."[7] The Interstate Highway System, enacted under President Eisenhower, spurred the "radical expansion of automobility" in the 1950s and 1960s onward.[8] That system and the relatively unabated (except by war) rise of automobile consumption continued to shape bicycle marketing. The connections Seiler draws between mobility, masculinity, and Frederick Jackson Turner's frontier thesis were also evident in the bicycle. Similar to Turner's thesis that settling the frontier was pivotal for American strength and individualism, Seiler writes that automobility was "sanctioned as a vehicle for individual and national renascence—a means to resuscitate republican selfhood and reopen the frontier."[9] As opposed to the car, the circumscribed mobility embodied by the bicycle could only serve to either introduce, or repair, the concepts and tenets of white adult masculinity.

World War II—while temporarily hindering bicycle sales—reenergized nationalistic ideals that the bicycle industry could then employ in its own favor. A growing hosteling movement and an emphasis on a child's independence, as well as encouragement for parents to prepare their children for a business career at an early age, were endeavors for which the bicycle was well suited. To a degree, the politics of the postwar era were also beneficial for bicycle and parts manufactures in the United States. President Eisenhower and Chicago mayor Richard J. Daley endorsed the bicycle and enacted policies, or created the infrastructure (in Daley's case) that would encourage cycling. In other ways, however, political policy stifled bicycle use. This was especially true among adults because domestic policy helped make automobiles more pervasive by ensuring that oil companies, gas stations, roadside businesses, the trucking industry, and highway departments would all receive a more than generous amount of monetary support from the federal government in the 1950s.[10]

After temporarily regaining popularity among American adults in 1936–38, the bicycle would not captivate the attention of adults again until the 1970s. To be sure, the Depression and postwar era showed that the bicycle industry had found a source of stability and even growth in the children's market, but its product was often affected by the whims of consumer culture, as well as the decisions of political leaders. American culture, the continued expansion of suburbs, and political decisions regarding infrastructure ensured the proliferation of automobile consumption and intensified changes in bicycle consumption. Simultaneously, the bicycle industry exacerbated the divide between childhood and adulthood as a line that was defined by one's form of mobility.

To argue that the bicycle industry continued tactics used in the 1920s and 1930s and that the transformation of the bicycle was complete by the 1950s does not mean that the bicycle or American culture was stagnant. Certainly the bicycle industry would continue to react and respond to ever-changing consumer culture, and at the same time be affected by governmental and diplomatic decisions. World War II, for instance, brought about governmental decisions and shaped cultural ideals in ways that had an important impact on the bicycle industry. Bicycle sales slumped to less than 200,000 in 1943 and 1944, down from over one million in 1941, but they surpassed all previously recorded sales estimates in 1947—with a total US market consumption of over 2.8 million units. Sales would not dip below one million ever again, and other than a few exceptions, sales continued on an upward trend through the 1960s.[11] The war and its aftermath, however, presented both opportunities and obstacles for the industry.

The most apparent obstacle for bicycle sales during the war was the War Production Board's (WPB) decision to ration bicycle production and sales beginning in March 1942. Manufacturers were first limited to producing only "two types of lightweight models" (one for adult men and one for women). Shortly thereafter, they were banned from selling, shipping, delivering, or transferring bicycles all together, until further notice.[12] The lightweight models were dubbed "Victory" models and the Office of Price Administration (OPA) ordered prices set "between $30 and $40."[13] A WPB official explained, "The order was issued because of the terrific rate at which bicycles have been going to people who don't need them, with too few going to people like defense workers who have to have them or soon will need them."[14] This was a blow to the bicycle industry, which was "expected to come into its own as a result of conversion of the auto industry to war production and the severe rationing of tires."[15]

The WPB's announcement of the coming curtailment of bicycle sales actually worked in the bicycle industry's favor momentarily as it instigated a run on bicycles. In Illinois, bicycle sales in January 1942 were double that of January 1941. The state finance director expected sales figures for February to show even bigger gains due to "anticipation of this week's [March 15] order of the War Production board cutting the bicycle industry's 1942 output to 42 per cent of the 1941 volume."[16] This boom in sales—resulting from anticipation of governmental restrictions—was common among many other consumer goods.[17] Even the temporary sales increase in anticipation of the curb on production, however, was not enough to bankroll the months of forcibly curtailed sales that lay ahead for the bicycle industry.

The restriction on production of adult bicycles was problematic, but not nearly as detrimental for bicycle sales as the ordered cease of production of junior models. During the previous year, 85 percent of the 1.8 million bicycles produced were for juveniles.[18] Even though wartime restrictions on production would reduce sales to a tenth of what they were before the United States entered the war, this was more of a temporary pause in the growth of the industry rather than an event whose effects were insurmountable. Although bicycle and bicycle parts manufacturers were forced to reduce their output, their facilities were not closed. Like automobile, sewing machine, and other manufacturers during the era, bicycle producers, such as Schwinn, retooled to aid the war effort.

By 1944 Schwinn had manufactured and delivered "217 different items to various Army, Navy and Air Corps Departments."[19] This was not the first time bicycle manufacturers retooled for a war effort. Schwinn had "served its country" during World War I, producing training plane motors, bomber plane parts, and many other accessories.[20] Schwinn used this detail, as well as the fact that the company earned the US Navy "E" Award, for self-promotion as a valuable and patriotic contributor to the American way of life. This was no doubt an important point for the company to make since it was founded by a German immigrant. Schwinn's publication, *Fifty Years of Schwinn Built Bicycles: The Story of the Bicycle and Its Contributions to Our Way of Life*, an advertisement that masqueraded as a history of the bicycle, told readers about its service to the country. While congratulating itself for its contribution to the war effort, Schwinn also took a moment to note that, in spite of its production of munitions and other military goods, the busy schedule had not prevented the company from spending "every spare moment and many an evening into the night" planning a "gigantic postwar program." Schwinn planned to produce the largest amount of "new and modern equipment . . . in its history" once the war was over.[21] It would take a few years, but Schwinn was confident that it would get back on track. It promised bigger and better things in the postwar era. The war curbed, but did not put an end to, bicycle usage and sales. Even in 1944 Yosemite National Park recorded over one hundred thousand hours of bicycle rentals.[22] Once the war was over, the industry would succeed at picking things up where they left off.

Getting back to prewar production levels did, however, take some time. Arnold, Schwinn & Company made excuses in their advertisements, thanking bicycle retailers for their patience and assuring them they were working hard to return their factories to prewar status. In one advertisement for the Christmas season to run in *American Bicyclist and Motorcyclist*, Frank Schwinn noted that the copy would read, "With the Season's Greetings, we extend our sincere thanks to our many loyal customers for their patience with our reconversion problems. Already our production has reached impressive proportions and we will soon ship Schwinn Built Bicycles in satisfactory quantities.

And all of them will go to our loyal, pre-war accounts."[23] Though Schwinn and other members of the bicycle and parts-manufacturing industry were unable to return immediately to prewar production and sales levels, which were around the one million mark, 1945 was significantly better than 1944—with an output of 544,721, up from 148,799 in 1944. By 1946 sales were back to prewar levels, 1,664,327, and breaking records in 1947.[24]

Manufacturers worked to satisfy demands for bicycles they were unable to meet during the war and bicycle consumption rose steadily until 1949, when numbers dropped from 2.7 million to 1.4 million. After 1949, sales came back to the two million mark and rose steadily each year from then on.[25] A similar trend occurred among various industries and 1948 saw the highest amount of private investment for the years 1946–49, while 1949 saw somewhat of a recession.[26] As bicycle sales got back on track—meeting and ultimately exceeding prewar levels—many of the marketing tactics and design trends remained the same. The focus on juveniles was maintained and even escalated as bicycles and childhood in America became as inextricably linked as automobile ownership was to achieving ideals of adult masculinity.

The bicycle industry continued to market children's bicycles to parents, running advertisements in *Life* and *Popular Mechanics* that focused heavily on the Christmas season. An advertisement in *Life* read, "See their faces light up when it's a real, honest-to-goodness Schwinn-Built waiting beside their Christmas tree."[27] Schwinn offered parents a "*safe* bike" that could "bring young hearts the zest of motion, while the wind stings their cheeks rose-red and their young legs grow more sturdy with every pedal-turn."[28] Schwinn was a dominant force in the bicycle industry by the 1950s, especially among manufacturers.[29]

Growing legs to become "more sturdy" shows how Schwinn continued the practice of promoting bicycles as a means to prepare boys for manhood. At the same time, the fact that the bicycle was seen as a means to gradually ease one into manhood is also apparent in attempts to create a market for bicycles among soldiers returning from war. For war veterans, the bicycle was a mode of reaffirming and rehabilitating their masculinity, particularly in the case of those returning injured. Under the headline "The Bicycle's Aid to Rehabilitation of Our Wounded Veterans," readers were informed of the bicycle's role, and that of the public, in aiding wounded soldiers' recovery. It proclaimed, "The readjustment and happiness of wounded soldiers and sailors with physical disabilities or nervous manifestations will depend in large measure on the way their families and friends and the public at large behave toward them."[30] The article read more like a public service announcement on the problems wounded veterans could possibly encounter when returning to life in the United States. Using information from the Office of War Information, it told readers that a "formerly able-bodied" man who returned home injured was "almost certain to be emotionally disturbed . . . , [i]n his disturbed state the man has his own idea of what a cripple is—an idea which all too often approaches a popular conception arising from ignorance. A soldier who finds himself without legs, for example, may well think of himself in the situation of the legless beggar . . . and he may think that is how others think of him, too."[31] The physical and mental experiences of war could damage, even destroy, one's masculinity if the veteran and his community did not work to overcome bodily sacrifices and the war's psychological impact.[32]

Two pictures accompanied the article—one featured able-bodied soldiers who had returned home enjoying a leisurely group ride on their bikes along with a few healthy young women. The other pictured a solemn-looking man straddling a bicycle that had been converted to remain stationary, while another man tinkered with the design. The caption reads, "In Algiers, Yankee ingenuity fashioned this bicycle trainer. . . . It is used for rehabilitation as a leg and shoulder conditioner."[33] This was part of the work done by nurses and physicians to restore self-confidence as well as physical health, both of which were requisites of masculinity. This shows a negotiation of ideals promoted by the cult of athleticism, which held that war-related traumas could be conquered through exercise, a degree of forgetfulness, and a modern, psychological-based understanding of male identity, which acknowledged war's mental strain and the benefits of being attuned to those side effects.[34] Just as the bicycle was an initiating device that could aid the transformation from juvenile male into adult male, it could also rehabilitate and restore manhood for wounded veterans insecure about their masculinity. In both instances, the bicycle operated as a step toward, rather than a means to achieve, manhood.

This innovative marketing opportunity was not enough to overcome the curtailment of production, but World War II ultimately turned out to be more of a speed bump for the bicycle industry than a devastating setback. The strict limitations on production put in place by the War Production Board dampened spirits, but many manufacturers such as Schwinn and Bendix were able to push through the war years with their factories in full force, manufacturing parts and accessories for military use. Economic historian Harold Vatter argues that American business in general emerged from the war with "large accumulated reserves of liquid assets, elaborate postwar plans, and a relatively reduced burden of debt charges."[35] This was certainly true for members of the bicycle industry. The pause provided a moment of reflection and breathing room for planning, marketing, and production strategies after the war. Bicycle production increased drastically immediately after World War II but still there was panic that American companies would not be able to produce enough bicycles to meet demand and might, therefore, open up room for imports. The biggest fear was that they would not be able to compete or meet foreign producers' prices due to disparities in workers' wages in European countries and the United States.

In spite of those fears, the postwar period would prove to be very good for the American bicycle industry. That success came through a continued focused on boys. Cultural trends, such as the growth in suburbanization, home-building, and consumption of automobiles, televisions, children's clothing, and toys would all continue to increase dramatically throughout the 1950s and early 1960s.[36] In the process, design trends developed across various industries. For instance, the sophisticated but functionless embellishments incorporated into bicycle design were also apparent among several other consumer items. James Patterson writes, "Automotive design—at its most flamboyant from 1955 to the early 1960s—expressed the dynamic and materialistic mood of the era. The designs deliberately recalled lines of jet planes and generated a streamlined, futurist feeling—one that was emulated in many other products, from toasters to garden furniture to new kitchens that featured all manner of sleekly crafted electrical conveniences."[37] Automobile sales soared during the postwar economic boom. Around 49.3 million cars were registered at the beginning of the 1940s and 73.8 million were registered by the decade's end.[38] "By 1960 nearly 80 percent of American families had at least one car, and 15 percent had two or more."[39] This helped keep the tactic of promoting the bicycle as an item that prepared children for adulthood (driving in particular) firmly intact. In his history of children at play, Howard Chudacoff argues that "in the minds of experts, play was not the opposite of work; rather, it should be a productive activity through which a child rehearsed for modern adulthood by following the guidance of wise, rational adults."[40] This attitude was apparent in bicycle promotional materials, including safety films for children produced by private production companies.

One such film, *Drive Your Bicycle*, suggested that if children thought about and drove their bicycle like a car, they would be safer and better prepared to drive an actual car when they reached the appropriate age. A boy in the film tells a parent that he and his friends have been learning bicycle safety at school. Regarding the weekly class, he says, "We call it learning to drive our bikes. Coach says we have to follow all the same traffic regulations as the cars, so that if we learn all the regulations by driving our bikes we'll be ready to drive a car when we're old enough."[41] Such materials showed that boys could ride and truly enjoy their bicycle while simultaneously daydreaming about being old enough to drive a car. They also showed how pervasive the idea that bicycles were merely preparation for cars had become.

Advertisements and calls for adults to provide bicycles for children also became ubiquitous, coming from individuals and organizations that were seemingly unconnected to the bicycle industry. An article, "Hank Wants a Bicycle for Paper Route," made appeals through attempts to capitalize on the charitable spirit of readers. It alerted them about a young boy in need who had recently learned to ride a borrowed bicycle and desperately wanted one of his own so that he could start a paper route. The article assured readers, "It is good to foster self-reliance in a youngster, and we hope that a bicycle may be located for Hank in order that he might partake of riding fun with other kids and experience his initial business venture, which looms so large on his boyish horizon."[42] This article was not only about charity and benevolent paternalism—it was also an encouragement for adults to train children to be good capitalists and to provide opportunities for socialization with their peers—free from parental supervision. Paul Ringel's study of childhood consumerism argues that time spent among peer groups benefitted businesses by fueling consumer demands.[43]

Another article, "Give Teen-Age Child a Little Independence," explained that the bicycle was a natural means of initiating boys into manhood. It claimed, "This reaching out for new fields to conquer is natural and normal, and we should help our boys to satisfy reasonable desires."[44] Still, being careful not to totally alienate females the article continued, "Boys, and girls, too, need freedom to be on their own, to do things for themselves. The sense of liberty and responsibility for one's own actions that goes with it are valuable experiences."[45] Notions of liberty were stressed—not by coincidence—in the years around World War II, as America developed a heightened spirit of patriotism and an even greater desire to grant others that same freedom and liberty that they experienced themselves.

Heavy bicycle designs of the 1930s would also continue after World War II but manufacturers took juvenile marketing a step further with designs that could incorporate into play for younger/smaller children more easily. The 1950 toy fair included exhibits from dozens of bicycle-manufacturing companies. There were bicycles for "every age group . . . both adult and juvenile, balloon tired and tank models."[46] One exhibit by the D. P. Harris Hardware and Manufacturing Company featured their new 'Hopalong Cassidy' bicycle, which included "shootin' irons, genuine leather holster and fringe, jewels, studs and many other authentic 'Hoppy' features."[47] The 1930s–50s saw the rapid expansion of childhood consumerism and juvenile mass media. By 1950 the bicycle industry, television, radio, and children's magazines all worked in tandem to encourage a mutually beneficial ideal of juvenile masculinity. The *Hopalong Cassidy* series and similarly themed bicycle romanticized and glorified the cowboy of the American West. It was never too early for young boys to begin dreaming about taming the wild and getting back to the rugged individualism of their forefathers. Other juvenile models included a cowboy motif as well. Along with cap guns and holsters, the Gene Autry model by Monark included a "rodeo brown" finish, rhinestones, and a plastic horse's head affixed to the head tube. The 1953 Juvenile Ranger, produced by the Mead Cycle Company (fig. 12), also included cap guns, as well as a saddle blanket, saddlebags, and embellishments to make the seat look more like a cowboy's saddle. The bicycle was just as necessary to aspiring masculine archetypes as a slingshot or air rifle. Used together, boys were more than prepared to settle their suburban landscape.

Bicycle shops continued to alter their tactics as well. Carl Hutchinson of the Hawthorne Cycle Company wrote, "In the 15 years in the bicycle and juvenile wheel goods business . . . we have found that our best bet is the boy. The average boy is more careful of his obligations than are the majority of adults, and we treat him with the same consideration."[48] Hutchinson claimed that nearly 50 percent of his sales were made to boys who used their bicycles for transportation to and from school and often to carry newspapers. Tactically, he admitted, "as the holiday season approaches we give more space to our toys and juvenile wheel goods, a larger corner window being devoted to same. Only at the Christmas season are dolls carried, as we wish to keep the stock predominantly masculine."[49] Store owners such as Hutchinson did not want to confuse the masculinity of boys' bicycles by selling them next to dolls and girls' toys. Similarly, designs made sure to keep a firm line drawn between girls' and boys' models. An article in the *Dry Goods Economist* argued that segregating boys and girls as soon as possible would lead to more profits.[50] Some studies, such as the one by the Cleveland Welding Company, also found that "there was a 'class' appeal in the new models that broadened the spread between the deluxe and competitive lines."[51] Their study focused on rider psychology, especially that of juveniles. It found that the illusion of mass without weight

12. 1953 Mead "Juvenile Ranger." Photo courtesy of the Bicycle Museum of America.

and "complete contrast" between male and female models—attained through the use of dark colors for men's bikes and light feminine colors for the ladies—were two important aspects of rider psychology.[52]

As popular forms of entertainment for children and juveniles proliferated, American adults became increasingly concerned with what their children were thinking and doing. Adults believed certain forms of entertainment were responsible for instilling vices, rather than virtues, in their children. Of particular concern was juvenile delinquency. Social scientists, intellectuals, religious officials, government officials, and law enforcement officials all testified before the Subcommittee on Juvenile Delinquency claiming, "Mass media stood between parent and child. Consequently, parents could no longer impress their value systems on children who were influenced as much by a new peer culture spread by comic books, radio, movies, and television, as by their elders."[53] Senator Robert C. Hendrickson, the subcommittee's chairman, claimed there was a "30 percent increase" in juvenile delinquency from 1948 to 1953.[54] Psychiatrist Fredric Wertham's controversial best-seller, *Seduction of the Innocent*, which blamed juvenile delinquency and antisocial behavior on comic books, heightened alarm.[55] While the concern with juvenile delinquency was certainly more palpable in the postwar period than it had been in the years leading up to the war, James Gilbert argues adults' fears about juveniles were not new—it was merely the source of influence that had changed. In his study of fears of juvenile delinquency, Gilbert contends that such concerns were episodic—using the fear of the 1920's "flaming youth" as an example. Still, he argues the concerns with the 1950's mass culture were "protracted and perhaps more universal and intense than at earlier periods."[56] Mass culture was not unique to juveniles, as televisions, radios, and a rising mail-order industry along with a growing number of chain stores, affected the choices, sensibilities, and mannerisms of adults as well. While American adults readily consumed television and radio, they were simultaneously critical of the media. They believed these new mass-culture forms "deprived adolescents of their innocence, their childhood, and their independence."[57] Much like the bicycle industry, which had taken a more heavy-handed approach at marketing its products to children during the Depression, many other industries were now doing the same.[58]

The effort to stem the tide of comic books waged by Senator Hendrickson and others was somewhat late in coming, and it is questionable whether it had any effect at all. As early as 1947, there was evidence that the comic book industry was over-reaching and the popularity of their product was beginning to fizzle—even without public outcry over juvenile delinquency. Frank Schwinn brought this to the attention of his advertising department, citing a *Wall Street Journal* article that reported comic book sales were slumping and the price of production rising.[59] Schwinn, addressing his employees over forty years before the publication of James Burkhart Gilbert's argument, also recognized that the controversy surrounding comics was not new. Regardless of a belief that comic's popularity would be short-lived, Schwinn advocated using them for what they were worth. He wrote, "Many things such as the comic book are ephemeral. Witness the dime novel of a generation or two ago. I believe that because of the marked similarity between the dime novel and the comic book, it is reasonable to assume that their popularity cycles will be similar but must be adjusted for."[60] After all,

Schwinn was a leader in an industry that had firsthand experience with the instability of consumer fads. He saw the opportunity and limitations they offered.

The bicycle industry made a continual effort to react to, anticipate, or even encourage, social and cultural alterations that would benefit sales. The rise of comic books and children's programs on the radio and television provided a convenient and effective means of promoting bicycles to juveniles; they also created a perceived problem that bicycles could solve. In effect, these cultural shifts, the rise in marketing to children that helped expand childhood consumerism, and the fears that consumption of these new goods led to juvenile delinquency affected the way the bicycle industry would think about and market their product. This put the bicycle industry in the curious position of promoting their product in the very same sources of media that supposedly led to juvenile delinquency, something a bicycle could allegedly curb. That is not to say that the industry opposed comic books or children's programming—to do so would have made them an opponent of the very things juveniles enjoyed. A certain line had to be toed in which bicycles could be promoted to parents as an alternative to comic book reading for their children but simultaneously to children as something that could help them live out their fantasies of being the crime-fighting heroes of the very same comics their parents did not want them reading. Essentially, the industry needed to promote bicycles as a means of independence for children and supervision for adults. Numerous companies catering to child consumers addressed these competing interests. Lisa Jacobson argues that radio clubs like Ovaltine's Little Orphan Annie's Secret Circle and Post Toastie's Inspector Post Junior Detective Corps. were popular because they successfully "straddled two distinct consumer constituencies—parents and children—ultimately hoping to win over children without sacrificing parental goodwill."[61]

One way to negotiate those demands was through encouraging the creation of clubs and group activities. Frank Schwinn saw the rising fears of juvenile delinquency and the resulting growth of clubs as an opportunity to sell more bikes. He told a Schwinn executive, "There is a lot stirring in the way of boys' clubs and activities to help overcome the juvenile delinquency going on in our locality. . . . I think it would be fair to contribute to this movement in light of the possible publicity and business opportunity involved."[62] Schwinn was most likely talking specifically about programs led by the Bicycle Institute of America, which was one of the more vocal groups leading the charge in promoting bicycles as a curative of juvenile delinquency. He saw this as an opportunity to satisfy perceived desires of both child and parent. A bicycle club could give a child the feeling of independence while also ensuring there would be a responsible party to supervise.

Much like earlier trade groups such as the Directorate and Cycle Trades of America, the Bicycle Institute of America (BIA) consisted of retailers, manufacturers, and distributors of bicycles and parts in the United States. In the interest of promoting bicycle riding, the BIA not only bought advertising in children's magazines, it also published books and materials to create an interest in organizing and perpetuating bicycle clubs for kids. It promoted clubs in a manner that stressed the benefits of bicycling for juveniles arguing bicycle clubs could, add "vigor, vitality, and happiness" to communities by "providing an outlet for fraternization, social contacts and stimulating activities that result in lasting friends and boost the morale of its members."[63] The BIA believed the fraternal bonds forged via bicycle were extremely important to the bicycle's future success. In its opinion, the bicycle would continue to grow in popularity because cyclists represented "sports enthusiasts who have achieved a common source of happiness. They have found bicycling an inexpensive form of transportation recreation—a valuable way to enjoy their spare time—a means of improving their physical condition [and] a carefree, happy way of getting closer to nature."[64] This was a continuance of bicycle promotions that predated World War II, the Great Depression, and even the move to juvenile consumers. Cyclists of the 1950s apparently also needed a practical and inexpensive means of escaping the "inevitable pressures of everyday life."[65] Instead of simply providing health and enjoyment for individuals, however, the bicycle of 1950 also allegedly strengthened communities.

In other ways, the BIA was also reactive to the cultural milieu of the postwar era. It continued old appeals, ones it believed worked in the past and were successful among various demographics, yet it also refined some of the language used, particularly in appeals made to parents. It was quick to offer bicycles as the remedy for a culture that adults feared may be spinning out of control. Childhood, with its comic books and television programming, seemed far different for their children than what they experienced growing up. The bicycle, however, offered a means to hold onto traditions. Parents that had had bicycles during their childhood could ensure that their children had the same experiences. For those who grew up too poor for their parents to afford a bicycle, buying one for their own child signified social mobility just as important as owning their own car. By the 1950s, the bicycle was an undeniably fundamental part of the American child's life experience, but the BIA promoted it as even more.

With the memory of war still fresh in Americans' minds, the bicycle industry continued to link bicycles and childhood with nationalistic ideals. In club promotional materials, the BIA reminded readers, specifically those interested in starting cycling clubs, that clubs were indeed important not only to ensure well-behaved children but also national health and it was a duty of responsible citizens to promote such groups. "In our nation today," it implored, "it is not sufficient for any organization to confine itself to its own interests and activities. The responsibility to the community, particularly to its younger members, is an unfailing mark of responsible citizenship and leadership."[66] Attempting to promote the bicycle as a deterrent to the prospect of misled youth, the BIA continued, "The good health and fun derived from bike riding is a perfect antidote to crime and juvenile delinquency. It is a real contribution to the achievement of the American ideal—better, healthier and happier young people who make tomorrow's citizens and help to build a greater country for all to live in."[67] The bicycle, then, guaranteed individual and national health. In the hands of "young people," it was a symbol of America.

By the late 1950s, the BIA published booklets stating, "Many communities across the country have recognized the need for supervised teen-age activity and have formed clubs for this age group."[68] This was somewhat contradictory to other appeals aimed at parents encouraging them to give their child a little independence by buying them a bicycle. With the creation of bicycle clubs, however, parents could be more confident that their child would go on outings via bicycle without worrying that they would get into trouble or be in danger. The clubs would promote bike hikes, community picnics, and bicycle-safety campaigns. With the creation of clubs, there was still a guise of teenagers' full independence. The BIA cautioned adults interested in creating bicycle clubs that "Interest in Youth Fitness and bicycling, sparked from within the ranks of the youngsters themselves, can better build teen-age support than many other projects instigated and controlled by adults."[69] The BIA recognized that a club founded by and run by adults *for* teenagers would prove less appealing than an "authentic" club organized by teens.

This notion of supervision at a distance was the product of negotiations between desires to grant children independence and teaching them responsibility while at the same time addressing real concerns about the preoccupations of juveniles and fears of delinquency. A letter from Frank Schwinn to one of his executives laid out ideas for such a program as early as 1947. Regarding a meeting with the BIA and other manufacturers in January 1948 on the subject of "The Bicycle is an Implement for Fighting Juvenile Delinquency, providing Helpful Recreation and Amusement for Growing Children," Frank Schwinn inquired about what kind of data could be gathered to support the claim.[70] He explained to a Schwinn executive that the BIA would enlist a group of men to "work with . . . the Youth Hostel, boy and girl scout groups, YMCA and . . . other national organizations working for the good of America Youth, to demonstrate that the bicycle is the ideal instrument for the furtherance of healthful and educational group activities for children. It is hoped by the concerted effort . . . we can eventually institute suitable programs in our public grammar and high schools."[71] Naturally, if those hopes came to fruition it would be of considerable benefit to certain members of the bicycle industry.

Bicycle programs in public grammar and high schools would almost guarantee an increase in bicycle sales and excitement about bikes.

The encouragement of parents to grant their teens a little more independence and for teens to seek adventure and health outdoors was well-illustrated by the growth of the hostel movement. *Scholastic* magazine published an article on the virtues of hosteling as early as May 1938.[72] Hostels were imported to the United States by Isabel and Monroe Smith, who studied "peace movements" at Columbia University. After traveling abroad and learning about the hostel movement in England and Germany, the Smiths helped establish the first American Youth Hostel in Northfield, Massachusetts, in 1934. They ascribed to the ideals of the German schoolteacher and creator of the hostel, Richard Schirrmann, that "wandering is school in the open," and that hostels could foster "health, a return to nature, education, joy and friendliness, and the furtherance of peace and understanding among people of different classes, religious and political beliefs, races, and nations."[73] By 1935 there were 35 hostels in America and 1,750 passholders/members. That number grew to 209 hostels and 11,146 passholders by 1939. During peacetime, there were nearly 5,000 hostels in 20 countries.[74] The trips could last up to ten weeks and were gaining notoriety among educators who believed hosteling was "an excellent supplement to a school curriculum."[75] The American Youth Hostel trips were perceived as beneficial to American teens and those in their early twenties because it brought them together with those of different backgrounds. Accommodated in barns, cabins, and private homes, hosteling also allowed children from larger cities and most likely a middle-class background—because of the expenses and resources needed to go on such a trip—to see how other parts of the country lived.

Members of the bicycle industry had been excited about the prospects of the hostel movement among the youth and the implications it would have for their product from the onset. Hostelers could make their excursions on foot or via bicycle but one participant observed that the number using bicycles was nearly double that of those walking.[76] In 1938 the League of American Wheelmen spoke of the growth of the movement and tied it to a call for more cycling paths in the United States.[77] Others pointed out the growing popularity of hostels as well, citing the fact that there were 110 located along popular cycling and hiking routes as further proof of the symbiotic relationship that bicycles and hostels could enjoy.[78] Taking long trips hiking or via bicycle and staying at hostels was encouraged as an activity for American youth because it helped instill many of the ideals that American adults hoped youth would embrace. Not only could the experience help them learn to get along with others from different backgrounds, it also provided the physical activity and adventure that could help them mature physically and mentally. These multi-week trips with their peers encouraged the kind of independence and resourcefulness that were idealistic characteristics of the nation.

Calls for parents' support of the trips often incorporated a play on ideals of masculinity that were twofold. An article in the *Chicago Daily* calling on parents—but aimed specifically at fathers—to grant teens independence provided a narrative that recounted a young boy asking his parents for permission to go on a bicycle adventure for a few weeks. He would undoubtedly stay at hostels during that time. When he asked his parents, "His mother's heart missed a beat or two but she waited. She knew her husband always could handle such things far better than she ever could, because he thinks before he answers, and she usually speaks too soon."[79] Here the goal was to directly appeal to patriarchy. In that pursuit, it is understandable that advertisers would target fathers and reaffirm masculine ideals of men as logical, level-headed patrons and women as overly emotional. Bicycle clubs and the hostel movement were yet another way that the bicycle could transport a juvenile to adulthood. Even better, it could do so in a manner that negotiated the wants of both children and parents.

While promoting bicycles as a curative of the ills of mass culture, the bicycle industry also used mass culture as a venue for its advertisements. Even though Frank Schwinn expressed doubts about the continued popularity of comics, he advocated their use. He claimed they were "the quickest and cheapest way to reach our customer."[80] By 1948 the company created its own comic, *The Schwinn Bicycle Comic*

Book. Advertisements for their comic book appeared in general comics, with emphasis on the "Stories of death defying bicycle racing and stunting, history of the bicycle, how to ride, care for and adjust your bicycle" that could be found in the Schwinn comic.[81] One of the first issues released in 1949 offered just that. On the cover was a drawing commemorating Alfred Letourneur's promotional exploit of riding a modified Schwinn Paramount at 108.92 miles per hour (fig. 13). The smoke in the background, along with the leather cap and aviator goggles, made Letourneur look like a jet pilot, or even a superhero. Instead of flying in the sky, he flew along the ground on a Schwinn-built bicycle.[82] Actual photos from the event show Letourneur without any kind of eye protection and the helmet he wore looked much more like a bicycle helmet, decidedly less sleek than a leather aviator's cap.

By 1957 even the comic books about well-known superheroes incorporated bicycles into their pages. As the bicycle was such an important part of the American juvenile experience, it is little wonder that the writers of *Batman* created a parallel character named Batman Jones. Jones was a juvenile who dressed up like his hero, Batman, and answered the bat signal just as quickly, on his bicycle rather than in the Batmobile. Batman tried to discourage the juvenile imposter but was surprised to find that Batman Jones could fight crime even though he was, in Batman's opinion, "too young" for such a thing. Eventually Batman Jones gives up on crime fighting on his own when he develops an interest in collecting stamps—a comment on the fickleness of juvenile consumers that contradicted opinions among bicycle boosters that they were reliable.[83] The fact that bicycles were so pervasive in the lives of young Americans established a certain level of symbiosis between bicycles and comic books. Batman Jones allowed young readers to envision themselves helping superheroes fight crime and the fact that he did so on a bicycle would arouse a desire for their own bicycle, or possibly a newer model. There were also outright advertisements by bicycle and parts manufactures included in the pages of comics and westerns, popular among juveniles. The American Octanator Corporation told merchants that its advertisements would reach twenty million people with spots in *Captain Marvel*, *Captain Marvel Jr.*, *Whiz Comics*,

13. *108.92 Miles per Hour on a Bicycle*. Arnold, Schwinn & Company, *Schwinn Bicycle Book*, 1949.

Western Hero, *Monte Hale Western*, *Rocky Lane Western*, *Tom Mix Western*, *Hopalong Cassidy*, *Nyoka*, *Bill Boyd Western*, and *Lash LaRue Western*, to name a few.[84]

The bicycle industry would also use television and radio programs to promote their product, particularly to children, but some members expressed concerns about whether radio commercials would benefit their business in any way. In correspondence with Schwinn executive Mr. Bond, Frank Schwinn ordered that he be publicly pessimistic about radio advertising. Regarding a correspondence between the Schwinn Company and Campbell-Ewald—the advertising firm that represented the BIA and CTA—Frank Schwinn wanted Bond to be tight-lipped. He ordered, "With respect to their inquiry re our opinion of the value of mentioning of our product on radio programs, you will inform them that we too have no way of gauging this, do not believe we are getting our money's worth, but are going along 'in a small way' in the hope that we will eventually be able to determine its value. Our present opinion is that we derive little, if any, benefit from it."[85] Other bicycle companies were curious about radio advertisements' effectiveness and this is a primary reason why Schwinn downplayed results.

Advertising agencies reported similar attempts to keep the effectiveness of radio advertising hushed across various industries. A J. Walter Thompson executive claimed radio was so effective in 1930 that "We have had several cases of where our clients were asked to go before meetings for example, to tell about the results of radio advertising and they have refused to do so because they did not want their competitors to know just how good it was. . . . Most everybody on the air does his best to keep the facts from getting to anybody in tangible form."[86] Frank Schwinn believed Campbell-Ewald, since it represented the BIA and was closely associated with many bicycle and parts manufacturers that Schwinn saw as competition, was "sympathetic with eastern manufacturers" and, therefore, not to be trusted. These eastern manufacturers were New Departure, Morrow, Westfield Manufacturing, US Rubber Company, Diamond Chain Company, and others, which Frank Schwinn believed to be very powerful and controlling of the bicycle industry. Even in spite of the growth of his own company and western manufacturers, he wrote, "[their] control is still strong and its strength bases upon the fact that the industry could not operate; in fact, would be brought to a standstill if Diamond Chain and New Departure were suddenly eliminated."[87]

The use of radio and, subsequently, television, for bicycle marketing was apparently effective. Soon the bicycle industry would not simply use television and radio as a venue; it also employed the help of real television stars, not just comic books and puppets like Howdy Doody. Schwinn ran advertisements telling potential customers to write in for a free copy of their cyclorama catalog, which included "full-color pictures of Hollywood stars and latest Schwinn-Built models."[88] Frank Schwinn believed the incorporation of movie stars into bicycle advertisements was effective because a "movie star's picture and name will stop the reader whereas just a bicycle ad would not. . . . Once that attention was had some of it could be diverted to the bicycle."[89] Schwinn also ran advertisements in trade journals telling dealers about their cyclorama campaign as proof that Schwinn was working hard to market their brand and "provid[ing] the best in consumer advertising to bring the customers to [dealers'] store[s]."[90] Frank Schwinn instructed that the copy should read, "Already 350,000 (or whatever figure may be at that time) American boys have written to us for a copy of the famous Schwinn cyclorama and we know that before the year is out, well over half a million boys and girls will have."[91]

The returns on their campaign were substantial. One of Schwinn's executives reported shipping over 384,000 cycloramas between June and August 1946 alone.[92] Similar advertisements were placed in girls' magazines, such as *American Girl*, and on television and radio programs directed at girls. Still, the marketing directed at girls is less apparent and often couched in terms of good health, rather than independence, fun, or adventure. There are countless publicity shots of movie stars on bicycles from the 1930s to the 1950s in part because many of the larger Hollywood lots kept "fleets of Schwinns, Shelbys, Raleighs, and Rollfasts so its actors, writers and crew could get from one giant soundstage to another."[93] A wide array of movies incorporated bicycles into their storylines, often in ways that connected the bicycle to youthfulness, young love, eccentricity, or comedic antics. In *The Quiet Man*, John Wayne and Maureen O'Hara jump on a tandem bicycle to escape the confines of supervised courtship, making their way to the countryside where they share their first kiss.[94] It is also important to note that *The Quiet Man* was set in Ireland and in the film the bicycle represented a kind of foreign quaintness as well as young love. With movies such as

Woman of the River, *Athena*, and *Today We Live*, as well as popular movie stars ranging from Gary Cooper to Lauren Bacall employing bicycles while still exuding beauty, exuberance, and coolness, Hollywood undoubtedly shaped views of the bicycle—particularly among those who emulated celebrities.[95] Of course, the bicycle made appearances in countless television programs as well. Instructing others in how to promote the bicycle on television, the Bicycle Institute of America told potential bicycle boosters, "Women's shows will be interested in bike fashions and the advantages of cycling for health and figure control."[96] Some companies, Schwinn for instance, compensated celebrities with a bicycle in exchange for their photo. Frank Schwinn preferred to use the image of celebrities to simply grab consumer's attention, but there was also the potential to sell bicycles out of consumer desire to imitate the stars they idolized. This harkens back to the marketing ideas at the turn of the century, which argued that if the industry could merely get society women (i.e., stylish women and upper-class women), to ride bicycles, all other women would follow.

Along with its emphasis on boys, the bicycle industry continued the trend of producing heavier bicycles with large balloon tires in the postwar era. The bicycles were bulky in part because manufacturers believed children needed something sturdy that could take their abuse but also because they were cheaper to produce than were bicycles consisting of lightweight materials. Lightweights required more sophisticated—and therefore costly—methods of engineering and welding. By the 1950s, however, it was evident that some consumers desired, or even preferred, a lighter-style bicycle with narrower tires, many of which also included multiple gears. These bicycles were considerably more efficient and could go "fast" over varying gradients more easily than a bicycle with only one gear. In an answer to lagging sales of ladies' and girls' models, Frank Schwinn suggested a lady's model with 1.75-inch-wide tires to associates. He believed it might be popular since "small tires at higher inflation pressures will provide less rolling resistance, which would be a factor in increasing popularity in ladies models."[97] His suggestion reveals a belief that women were not cycling because it was perceived as too strenuous. It was also a step toward correcting the American trend of producing heavy and inefficient machines.

American consumers began referring to such bicycles with skinnier tires and multiple gears as "English Style" models, a description American bicycle manufacturers would also use in catalogs in the late 1950s. Others, such as Columbia, called them "American Lightweights" once they began actually producing and selling that particular model.[98] Schwinn also expanded their production and sales of lightweights during the first part of the 1950s as well. A six-month sales comparison with the industry showed that Schwinn lost around 65 percent of lightweight sales, which was an improvement from the loss of 71 percent in 1952 and 82 percent in 1951.[99] The large super-balloon tires first introduced by Schwinn in the 1930s had dominated the industry but now, in the face of competition from European companies, American manufacturers and tire producers were forced to accept that many American consumers preferred a smaller, harder tire because of its efficiency. To refuse to cede to consumer demand would mean losing as many as 85,000 sales out of a total of around one million in the span of six months. For Schwinn, which accounted for 194,904 of those sales, the piece of the pie that lightweights represented was too much to leave on the table.[100]

Not only did American bicycle companies initially ignore this particular segment of the market—a segment that had been highlighted as early as the 1920s as a direction in which the industry needed to devote more attention—it also sought political help to make bicycles imported from Europe more expensive.[101] Most notably, the Bicycle Manufacturers Association of America called on the US Trade Commission in October 1951. Its request for an "escape clause" from lowered tariffs was initially denied but reconsidered in 1955 after imports rose drastically. At that point, the US Trade Commission recommended President Eisenhower raise the tariff on bicycles to 22.5 percent.[102] Eisenhower would ultimately prove to be a valuable advocate for the bicycle industry, but it was not without some prodding. In this particular instance, he enacted a 50 percent increase in tariffs on imported bicycles, thus raising the duty from 11.25 percent to the US Trade

Commission's recommendation of 22.5 percent. It was raised specifically to "protect American producers from 'serious injury . . . resulting in part from tariff concessions.'"[103] Most of the bicycles imported came from Great Britain, West Germany, Austria, France, Belgium, Netherlands, and Luxembourg. The number of bikes imported reportedly "mushroomed from fewer than 20,000 units a year from 1947–49 to 963,000 [in 1954]" and they were estimated to be as high as 1,250,000 in 1955.[104] This was due largely to the fact that the imported bicycles were cheaper. In a memo to his associates, Frank Schwinn lamented:

> About 12 months ago, people began to awaken to the large difference in price between foreign and domestic cycles and began to buy them. Like a snowball rolling down hill, the trend grew as the lightweight type of foreign cycle increased in popularity with the youngsters. These cycles are now acceptable. We, in the business, are prone to delude ourselves with isolated reports and instances such as—Foreign cycles don't stand up, dealers won't repair, dealers overcharge for repair, dealers do not like them because of cut-rate competition, etc., etc. The phenomenal increase in the sales of imports attests to the fallacy of these delusions, and—The good makes of imports stand up as well as domestic cycles.[105]

The cause for the expansion of the US market was pinned on the growing consumption of "large wheel light-weight bicycles" and the fact that "the domestic industry manufacture[d] almost no bicycles of [that] type."[106] The British bicycle industry in particular was "dismayed" by the announcement of the increased tariff because of the damage it would do to their businesses. H. M. Palin, director of the British Cycle and Motorcycle Manufacturers Union, believed the potential impact very harmful for both economies. He commented, "The increased tariff is all the more regrettable because it will hinder the cycle industry's efforts to earn dollars and so help to maintain the balance of payments between this country and the United States."[107] This was a sticky issue for President Eisenhower since he maintained, "this nation's firmly rooted policy of seeking ever expanding levels of international trade and investment is in no respect altered by this decision."[108]

In 1954 Frank Schwinn complained about the effects of the policy of fair trade on the previous year's sales. He qualified figures saying, "If we had not adopted fair trade, we also would have shown a gain this year, or at least no loss."[109] Schwinn was extremely concerned with how his company could continue to compete against both domestic and foreign competition.

On the subject of sales, Schwinn told marketing supervisor Ray Burch, "I'm not anxious to make any changes now, nor until we know whether Washington will give us a reprieve. If you have occasion to write the President, use the old Roman gladiator's salute—'Caesar, those about to die salute you.'"[110] Just seven months later, Schwinn would have his reprieve. Eisenhower's increased tariff on imports, however, may not have been as big as American bicycle manufactures had hoped. The president took a middle-of-the-road approach that was simultaneously not enough in American manufacturers' opinion, yet too much in the opinion of foreign manufacturers. Eisenhower saw the increase in tariffs, but his decision to scale back the amount of the increase suggested by the Tariff Commission as a compromise, one that would "assure foreign manufactures of 'an excellent competitive chance to share handsomely in our large and growing market for bicycles.'"[111] While it may not have been as much of an increase as certain members of the bicycle industry and Tariff Commission wanted, it undoubtedly helped to protect manufacturers from bankrupting themselves trying to compete with foreign manufactures.

Taking action to increase bike tariffs on imported bicycles was not the only time that Eisenhower would make headlines in a move that benefitted the American bicycle industry. The president also offered their marketing campaign a little more credibility when he echoed endorsements for cycling found in trade magazines and general advertisements for the public. In particular, he advocated the bicycle as a means of improving health, especially among America's youth, a matter of concern that in 1954 prompted him to call a conference on the physical fitness of the nation. American youth had recently tested poorly—50 percent actually failed the "standard minimum muscular fitness tests which had been conducted among" the youth in the United States and abroad.[112] In an interview, Eisenhower argued that the reason statistics on the strength and health of American children looked "very depressing" in contrast with those of other countries was not because of "any deliberate desire to be affluent and soft." Instead, he explained, "American children ride buses to schools farther away than four to eight blocks, whereas European children walk or ride bicycles. [A phenomenon which] he attributed . . . to parental fear of 'so much traffic on the roads.'"[113] Cycling to school was, no doubt, affected by parents' fear of traffic more significantly than walking. Because a block is an urban unit of measurement, the settings that the president described were necessarily urban and therefore likely to have sidewalks to keep pedestrians safe from traffic. Those riding bicycles, on the other hand, were expected to share the street with automotive traffic.

The bicycle industry's campaign to promote cycling as a safe activity for children, which had been ongoing since the 1930s, had yet to convince the public that it was indeed safe, but it had made some inroads. In areas where there were no bicycle paths, members of the President's Council on Youth Fitness such as Dr. Shane MacCarthy, suggested that city streets that were lightly used on weekends could be blocked off to automotive traffic and designated as bike recreation areas. MacCarthy also proposed that "secondary roads, left practically untraveled because of new highway building programs, could be easily converted into protected trails for the exclusive use of cycle enthusiasts."[114] Even though the genesis and construction of Eisenhower's interstate highway system is explained as arising out of desires to transport military items across the United States, interstates also reduced the traffic burdens for smaller highways and thoroughfares. Inadvertently, the interstate system had the potential to increase cycling's safety and, therefore, popularity. Still, this development was not as beneficial as it would have been for the president to put more effort into creating bicycle paths separate from automobiles. Even Robert Moses, who had successfully created bicycle paths in New York before World War II, took steps to ensure that the automobile would be king. To the detriment of even public transportation, Moses ordered bridges on New York City parkways be built so low that busses could not travel beneath them, effectively barring everyone without their own car from getting into the city quickly or efficiently.[115]

Still, there were some that pushed for bicycle infrastructure. Eisenhower's enthusiasm for cycling, at least in part, was attributable to Dr. Paul Dudley White, a cardiologist who treated the president after a heart attack. As well as advocating bicycles for children, White wanted to see more adults riding bikes. He told audiences, "A bike ride a day keeps the heart doctor away."[116] Dr. White admitted that for everyone to ride a bike to work every day might be a tall order, especially for those in cities like New York. Consequently, he petitioned leaders of Baltimore, Chicago, Boston, Richmond, and San Francisco to make bicycle paths in parks and along roadways a priority.[117] Dr. White appeared to get other politicians on board with his promotion of cycling. A picture included in the BIA's booklet, *Bike Fitness*, showed Dr. White and Mayor Richard J. Daley riding a tandem bicycle together—White in front, concentrating and smiling while Mayor Daley looked carefree on the back. The photo was taken as part of the publicity at the opening of Chicago's bicycle paths.[118]

The BIA was ecstatic over endorsements from President Eisenhower and his doctor. It included a newspaper clipping inside the cover of *Bike Fitness* proclaiming, "Hey Kids! Ike's Hep about Bicycles."[119] It also reported that when President Eisenhower obtained a report by the Citizen's Advisory Committee on Youth Fitness from Vice President Nixon, "he stated that he would like to see more young Americans riding bicycles. He pointed out that in his travels through Europe he had noted the continuing popularity of this sport which probably accounted for the high physical fitness ratio of European youths."[120] Concerns about youth fitness were beneficial to the bicycle industry as a whole. The BIA played on ideas of nationalism saying, "Youth Fitness is National Fitness." Their booklet pictured a bald eagle in flight against the backdrop of red, white, and blue.[121]

Others were optimistic about the effects of Eisenhower's support of cycling as well. The *New York Times* reported, "Trade sources expect bicycle sales soon to start pedaling at a very fast clip as a result of President Eisenhower's interest in the sport."[122] Even though the president had only endorsed cycling relatively recently, Steve Masters, president of Masters, Inc., claimed that his store had already experienced a 20 percent increase in sales over a two-week period by January 13, 1957.[123] Robert W. Kerr, vice president of the American Machine and Foundry (AMF), believed that sales were likely to rise. Referencing Dr. White's endorsement of cycling the previous year, Kerr said, "Our experience in the past has been that praise of cycling from White House circles has been followed by an upsurge in demand for wheel goods."[124] Even though manufacturers and members of the industry gave a lot of credit to the White House, sales were continuing a general upward trend, increasing each year after 1949—going from 1,451,685 to 2,625,554 in 1957.[125] Aside from the political support, bicycle manufactures believed sales were increasing because of "the introduction by domestic producers of new, streamlined 'middleweight' bikes similar to the popular foreign ones. They added that the continuing trend to the suburbs and the opening of more and more facilities for safe cycling in cities and towns throughout the country had also spurred volume."[126] The middleweight bicycle, which was introduced in 1955, reportedly accounted for 65 percent of "all domestic manufacturers' sales" in 1956.[127]

While the president's promotion of cycling was good for the American bicycle industry, it also had the effect of improving diplomatic relations with foreign countries, which had been strained by his decision to increase the tariff on imported bicycles. The Dutch were enthusiastic about Eisenhower's support of cycling and reportedly saw "promise of better relations with the U.S." as a result. Figures on bicycle ownership estimated there were approximately 500 bicycles for every 1,000 people and 25 cars per 1,000 in the Netherlands.[128] Conversely, in 1957, there were 15.41 bicycles per 1,000 people in the United States and 326 cars per 1,000.[129] As a country that consumed bicycles with great zeal, the Dutch agreed wholeheartedly when Eisenhower spoke of the health benefits and could point to the fact that the life expectancy in the Netherlands exceeded the United States as proof.[130] Of course, there is a lot more that factors into a country's life expectancy than whether they ride bicycles or not. Still, Eisenhower pointed out an important way in which American culture was different from that of European countries. It is important to note, however, that Eisenhower promoted cycling as exercise, not necessarily as a practical form of transportation. To do so would be a possible cause for concern among the automotive industry. While the White House's promotion of the bicycle was important and undoubtedly beneficial for the industry, it was not the sort of sea change regarding the image of the bicycle that was needed to get adults back on bikes. The president was not saying *ride your bike and leave your car at home or buy a bike, not a car*. He was saying *ride a bike for health*, which maintained the youthful image of the bicycle as an implement best suited for leisure and/or strenuous work.

The expectation that Americans would give up their car for a bike was far too much to ask, and Eisenhower's suggestion that the Netherlands was somewhat superior in terms of health because of their cycling culture was merely political maneuvering. Still, bicycles and parts manufacturers had come a long way. Bicycle production and consumption would reach unprecedented heights shortly after World War II. The war and its aftermath was beneficial for any consumer item that could be promoted as a curative to all the insecurities that war brought, particularly in terms of gendered ideals like vigor and independence. Bicycle marketing easily stepped into that role. After all, bicycles had been promoted as a way to maintain vigor and experience freedom of movement for over fifty years. Even in advertisements for children's models, members of the bicycle industry linked their product to a heightened sense of nationalism and patriotism by incorporating gendered ideals. The bicycle could prepare boys for manhood and girls for a version of womanhood that men found attractive. Older children, boys in particular, could use their bicycles to become more independent and self-sufficient by going on multi-day excursions, staying at hostels, aiding in the war effort, or to create their own revenue stream. In this manner, the bicycle not only led to independence but also instilled a spirit of capitalistic individualism that would mold him into an ideal American man. As the BIA would point out, the bicycle promoted vigor, vitality, fraternization, and happiness. While making young boys stronger, it also kept them out of trouble—protecting them from the scourge of juvenile delinquency.

The bicycle was not only a tool for instilling masculine ideals—it also had the ability to restore masculinity. For injured World War II veterans, it was the perfect means of reintroducing one to their masculine, prewar state because of its ability to ease them back into manhood. The bicycle could be a tool for vigorous exercise or leisurely enjoyment; it was up to the rider to decide. To that end, promotional ads using the images of Hollywood celebrities and beautiful women encouraged women and young girls to take up the bicycle to keep their figure. All of this did much to secure the place of the bicycle in American society. As a symbol of American youth and exuberance, bicycle consumption not only stabilized, it saw dramatic gains in the hands of a booming population that was arguably more prosperous than it had ever been.[131] Economic prosperity among Americans in the 1950s was not only a boon to the bicycle industry—many other household and consumer goods were thriving. The automobile became even more emblematic of American-ness as car consumption grew exponentially after the war's end. As a result, the bicycle industry seemed content to let their product remain an adolescent form of mobility. Its advertisements were largely unconcerned with the automotive industry. Aside from dispelling fears of cyclists' safety in light of increased automotive traffic or describing bicycles in terms similar to automobiles, there was no sense that by the 1950s the bicycle industry even saw the automotive industry as a competitor.[132] While they had once competed for the same business, bicycles and cars had become two completely different objects used for entirely different ends.

The trials and tribulations facing men during World War II and the Cold War played a role in the way Americans idealized childhood. The bicycle—the most desired of all children's commodities after World War II—was marketed in a manner that took advantage of concerns about American manhood, while at the same time heightening parent's concern about their children's choice of recreation.[133] The bicycle was a quintessential part of the American experience postwar, but one that was most closely associated with developmental stages of life, and marketing suggested it was more important for boys than girls. As a tool that allowed boys to rehearse for manhood, bicycles were means of training individuals for business, driving, and an introduction to independence. Bicycles had become the birthright of nearly every American boy, but that relationship was soon severed as the boy reached maturity. While riding a bicycle and then graduating to the automobile was a fundamental step in becoming a man, the bicycle could only prepare one for manhood, not confer it. Bicycle designs and the industry's marketing strategies did little to overcome the stigma that bicycles were children's toys. In fact, it fed into those ideals and helped affirm conceptions of mobility that have remained an important aspect of American identity.

9

High-Risers and Multi-Geared Redeemers

ALTHOUGH THE BICYCLE INDUSTRY seemed to be on solid ground by the 1950s, some key members recognized the need to temper appeals to juveniles. In some cases, it seemed there was a need to uncouple images of the bicycle and childhood all together. The Bicycle Institute of America (BIA), for instance, was aware that the image of the bicycle as a consumer item was so closely associated with childhood that even older teenagers were likely to turn away. It believed the best way to repair the bicycle's status as a child's toy was for adults, particularly parents, to take the bicycle more seriously. Because the BIA believed children were influenced most heavily by their parents, it suggested that parents take the whole family out for cycling excursions. The BIA argued, "If parents think of the bicycle as a toy, only to be used by kiddies, a similar opinion will grow in the mind of the child. Some teenagers think of the bike as 'kid stuff,' and refuse to ride, while it is their age group which needs the exercise most. If parents participate in family bike hikes, their example will convince the youngsters that cycling is an adult means of exercise and transportation."[1] Simultaneously, while telling parents to take the bike a little more seriously and show their children that it was an adult means of exercise, the BIA and the bicycle industry as a whole remained relatively focused on marketing bicycles to children.

Booklets with titles like *Bike Fun* were stuffed full of pictures, guides, and rules for games to play with bicycles. The industry was still counting on the juvenile market to bring continued success and growth in sales for the 1960s. When asked if sales would "really soar" during that decade, several leaders of bicycle manufacturing and component companies responded optimistically citing a growth in population and subsequently more children in need of a wheel. C. Williams of Williams Rims said, "As more children reach the bicycle riding age, our dreams of selling four million bicycles a year becomes a realizable goal." Similarly, A. Todry of Otto Todry & Son shared his company's view that "With more youngsters than ever crowding schools, the constant move of the population to the suburbs, the bicycle is an important part in every child's life. These style conscious boys and girls want a new model bicycle just like Mom and Dad want that new car every year."[2] Even though members of the bicycle industry were growing cognizant of the drawbacks of marketing strategies that focused on children, they provided little evidence in their own materials that the bicycle had any adult characteristics. They believed they would be able to continue to rely on children to increase sales as the baby boom generation aged into adolescence.[3]

Consequently, over a decade after first recognizing the seeming inseparability of bicycles and childhood as a potential problem, efforts to disassociate the two had yet to begin in earnest. An article written in 1964 and appearing in *Today's Health* echoed the sentiments of those within the industry that wanted to decouple the bicycle and children in the 1950s. It was accompanied by a stock photo from Arnold, Schwinn & Company and quotes from the bicycle's leading health advocate, Dr. Paul Dudley White. He argued, "The bicycle should not be thought of simply as a small child's toy, but rather as an instrument for daily use, not only by teen-agers but by adults of all ages. Some teen-agers think they are too old to ride a bike. This is ridiculous."[4]

Early efforts to change the bicycle's image did not target adults so much as they attempted to alter the notion that bicycles were merely toys. To that end, as early as 1945 Arnold, Schwinn & Company ran a comic-strip advertisement in the pages of various comics such as *Wonder Woman*, *Mutt & Jeff*, and *Green Lantern*. In the comic, a boy who is asked by a friend if his dad was going to buy him a bike replies, "Nope! Gee! You'd think I was asking for a toy instead o' somethin' useful like a bike." The boy then goes to prove to his father just how useful a bicycle can be when he is able to use a friend's bike to bring his dad the briefcase he forgot at home just before his train leaves the station.[5] This comic strip–styled advertisement was not trying to distance bicycles from youthfulness or contest the idea that bicycles were for kids. Rather, it was merely suggesting that kids could use their bicycles to help their parents. This was an old tactic that had been around since the 1910s as companies promoted bicycles as a means for children to run errands for parents and useful for pharmacies, grocery stores, and even Western Union in allowing young workers to deliver goods more quickly and efficiently.[6] In the same vein, bicycle advertisements that appealed to social and cultural ideals of boyhood incorporated the same themes as advertisements that appealed to manhood at the end of the nineteenth century.

Even though bicycle marketing and the way in which leaders spoke of the industry's future did not seem to change from the 1920s through the 1950s, by 1960 bicycle designs did indeed begin to offer a little more diversity. It was in that year that Schwinn, tired of losing a significant number of sales to imported multi-geared bicycles, introduced the Varsity model with an eight-speed derailleur. Derailleurs were developed first in England but significantly improved in France. They proved extremely popular among French bicycle-touring enthusiasts in the 1930s and soon caught on in England as well but it would take more than twenty years for American companies to start producing derailleur-equipped bicycles.[7] The name of Schwinn's Varsity model made it apparent that there was a conscious effort to keep teens on bikes well into their high school years. The addition of eight speeds and narrower tires made the Varsity capable of going faster and farther with less work than previous streamlined one-speed bikes and three-speed English models. By 1965 Schwinn offered five different models of derailleur-equipped bikes and other manufacturers followed suit. Sales steadily increased from 3.6 million in 1961 to 7.4 million in 1968 (see table 8).[8]

The steady growth in sales during the first half of the 1960s was specifically credited to a renewed interest in cycling among adults.

TABLE 8: **US Bicycle Sales, 1961–69 (x 1,000)**

Year	1961	1962	1963	1964	1965	1966	1967	1968	1969
Total sales	3,664	4,216	4,410	5,088	5,654	5,747	6,292	7,494	7,053
Twenty-inch wheels	500	550	650	650	2,058	2,900	4,157	5,655	4,292
Middleweights	2,170	2,499	2,465	2,528	2,324	1,794	1,241	810	1,330
Lightweights	994	1,295	1,295	1,210	1,274	1,053	894	969	863

Source: Frank Berto, "The Great American Bicycle Boom," in *Cycle History 10: Proceedings of the 10th International Cycling History Conference*, ed. Frank Berto (San Francisco: Van der Plas Publications, 2000), 135.

In an article titled "Return of the Cycle," James Hayes of the BIA reported, "Grownups have come back to the bicycle. . . . They're the fastest growing part of the market."[9] Even so, according to the same article, adults only represented 25 percent of sales, which may sound unimpressive but that was significant growth compared to the 15 percent adults represented in 1941.[10] The figure was included to show the degree to which adult participation had indeed grown. Focusing on commuters in urban areas such as New York City and Washington, DC, it argued that cycling was rising in popularity among adults who were using it for leisure and exercise, noting that a big reason was "to escape from the automobile." An image accompanying the article pictured a young woman on a bicycle with the caption "Exercising: Away from the Fumes."[11] Writing for *Today's Health*, James Godfrey Harmount made the analogous point that cycling was a popular means for "getting close to nature, for physical fitness but most of all just plain fun."[12] Adult cyclists in the 1890s often took to the bicycle for similar reasons. Instead of escaping from the fumes of automobiles, they were escaping industrialized cities' polluted air. A subsequent article in the same magazine proclaimed, "Incredible as it may seem, history is repeating. The bicycle has come into its own again."[13] Both the 1890s and 1960s saw the bicycle promoted as a vehicle to health. In the 1960s, however, the bicycle was not necessarily demonstrative of masculinity but it was a potential curative during a time of increasing fears among the medical community that Americans were too sedentary. Previously named *Hygeia*, *Today's Health* was an American Medical Association publication that was often found in doctor's offices and schools. In *Today's Health*, Harmount summed up the concerns with health in the 1960s describing it as "a period of our national history when we must provide greater outlets for physical fitness."[14] These concerns worked to boost the sales of adult models; however, they would soon be eclipsed, once again, by juvenile models.

All sales remained somewhat stable during the first half of the 1960s. Most experienced gradual increases, but things were clearly changing by 1965, the year in which sales of twenty-inch wheels—the size often found on children's bicycles—exploded. Consequently, sales of both middleweights and lightweights fell but the middleweight's decline was more substantial. Bicycle historian Frank Berto points out that this swing in sales was due to the birth of the high-rise bicycle. He argues that at first, kids made their own high-rise models with spare parts.[15] However, when pointing out the success of the high-rise bicycle in 1966, the executive secretary of the National Bicycle Dealers Association (NBDA) attributed the genesis of the high-rise to enterprising dealers in San Diego, not kids. He explained that there was as an abundance of cheap banana seats, so cheap they were bought in spite of the fact that they were not selling, and "at the same time motorcycle-type bike handlebars were being offered in the same area. Dealers who were then rebuilding used bikes used these cheap items in the process, and the fad was begun. Service men home on leave picked up the items and started riding them along with their children. Monkey see, monkey do, and in a few short years the Monkey-bike has spread throughout the world."[16]

The bikes looked like the chopper version of a motorcycle with banana seats and high handlebars atop twenty-inch wheels (see fig. 14). The industry soon took notice, especially with agencies like the NBDA pointing out, "By far, the greatest volume seller in '66 was the high rise banana bike. Not only was this the highest volume in domestic production, but it was also the leader in imports."[17] Numerous manufacturers had set to work creating their own high-rise models, one of the most

14. 1968 Schwinn "Orange Krate" high-rise model. Photo courtesy of the Bicycle Museum of America.

popular versions being Schwinn's "Sting-Ray." The high-rise fad soon peaked, however, in 1968 and began to decline by 1969. Still, sales were significantly high. The total sales of bicycles would also drop in 1969 and 1970 but surpass previous totals in 1971 and increase more than 60 percent from 1971 to 1972 in what has been dubbed the "Great American Bicycle Boom" because European markets did not experience this explosion in sales.[18]

Unlike increasing sales from 1965 to 1968, the explosion in growth from 8.8 million in 1971 to 13.8 million in 1972 cannot be attributed to high-rise twenty-inch-wheeled models. Twenty-inch sales continued

TABLE 9: **US Bicycle Sales, 1970–77 (x 1,000)**

Year	1970	1971	1972	1973	1974	1975	1976	1977
Total sales	6,891	8,849	13,897	15,210	14,106	7,294	7,804	9,413
Twenty-inch wheels	4,048	4,054	3,594	3,821	3,083	2,584	3,377	3,640
Middleweights	1,290	640	580	620	550	363	781	1,119
Lightweights	1,152	3,763	9,385	10,563	10,354	4,374	3,646	4,654

Source: Frank J. Berto, "The Great American Bicycle Boom," in *Cycle History 10: Proceedings of the 10th International Cycling History Conference* (San Francisco: Van der Plas Publications, 2000), 135–37.

their slow drop from 4.2 million in 1969 to 3 million by 1974. Lightweights, on the other hand, experienced phenomenal growth in sales from 860,000 to 10.3 million during the same period. By 1974 lightweights represented approximately 73 percent of total sales. Even though they seemed to peak one year earlier with 10.5 million sales in 1973, their precipitous drop to 4.3 million in 1975 and 3.6 million in 1976 was still more than 3 million more models than were ever sold in a single year throughout the 1960s (see table 9).[19]

A number of popular magazines published articles in 1971 about the bike boom with such titles as "Look Ma, No Engine," "Bicycle Madness," "Bike Boom: A Way out for Commuters?," "Bike Comes Back," "Riding a Bike for Health, Economy, and Ecology," and "Bicycle Boom Still in High Gear."[20] An article in *Popular Science* took notice of the lightweight's growing popularity announcing, "Big Boom in the Hot New Bikes." The article started off by immediately addressing the image of the bicycle as a child's toy writing, "If you think bikes are for kids, you've never tried a 10-speed lightweight. It's the sports car of bicycles. It makes that three-speed 'English racer' you're familiar with feel like an old truck. Hills you'd walk up with the three-speed are ones you can take sitting down on the lightweight."[21] It argued that the weight of around twenty-two pounds, the stiff and responsive frame materials, and all the gears were the secret to the lightweight's success. *Time* also took notice of the phenomenon and reported on retailers' fears that they would run out of stock before Christmas. It explained that the potential shortage resulted from "the bicycle's biggest wave of popularity in its 154-year history."[22]

Several articles describing the growth of the bicycle's popularity in 1971 attributed it to adults' increased participation in cycling because of environmental and/or ecological reasons. This was not entirely novel. In 1967 New York City Parks commissioner Thomas P. F. Hoving "unoficially made Sundays bicycle day in New York City." He explained, "There is a sad phenomenon going on in this country today. . . . It seems the car has become more important than people, whose servant it is supposed to be. Facilities for cars, from gigantic parking lots to super highways, are eating up the land by millions of acres a year." His solution was "more bikes, less cars."[23] By 1971, *Time* explained, "Environmentalists are turning to the bike as a pollution solution," but it added that there were also "physical fitness fans" and commuters trying to find a faster alternative to the clogged city streets.[24] In all three explanations there is an underlying concern or reaction to growth of urban areas and sedentary lifestyles. A writer for the *Atlantic Monthly* described himself, like so many others, as being "afflicted with contemporary megalopolis-itis," and fallen prey to a "sedentary life."[25] Echoing concerns about neursthenia at the end of the nineteenth century, Americans once again seemed convinced that increasing technology could have a physcial and psychological toll.

Concerns with the potential disadvantages of civilization were also apparent in the growth of jogging and aerobics as popular forms of exercise. The introduction for a 1968 aerobics manual proclaimed, "In this age of mechanization and automation, we know that our normal work activities do not provide the exercise our bodies, our muscles, and our hearts and lungs require."[26] In her study of the rise of fitness culture in America, Shelly McKenzie argues that the catalyst was rising attention to the "cardiac crisis" that began in the 1950s. By the 1970s, however, it seemed Americans were jogging for a variety of reasons. It was at this point that "A second, younger group, motivated by environmental and spiritual concerns, adopted jogging . . . for its own, often political and pyschological, purposes."[27] Running was even promoted during the oil crisis as a solution to gas shortages. *Runner's World* told readers, "This oil shortage could be the impetus we've needed to get people to use that long neglected source of energy—the human body. The time is approaching when runners will be considered as prophets who long ago began preparing for the oil shortage."[28] Cyclists also seemed poised to take their place as "prophets" of the coming revolution in energy consumption but while the United States stood at the precipice of that revolution, it managed to keep from falling over the edge—at least temporarily. The promotion of bicycles as a solution to high gas prices would be repeated in the following decades—such was the case with a 1990 bicycle advocacy article titled "Beating Saddam."[29]

The 1973 energy crisis undoubtedly compounded the public's awareness of an over-reliance on petroleum-powered transportation. In November of that year, President Nixon announced plans for "Project Independence." He told reporters that the "United States of America as the greatest industrial power of the world with 7 percent of the world's people and using 30 percent of the world's energy shouldn't have to depend on any other country for energy that provides . . . jobs . . . transportations . . . light and . . . heat. We can become self-sufficient."[30] The oil shortage, however, does not deserve all the credit for the 1970s bicycle boom. As bicycle historian David Herlihy argues, the crisis probably did add an "unexpected boost," but as Frank Berto points out, the shortage did not hit the United States until late 1973, at which point bicycle sales had already experienced their precipitous rise, and 1974 would see a slight decline.[31] If anything, the oil shortage may have extended a high rate of bicycles sales and resulted in a less severe drop in sales for 1974 than it would have been otherwise. The oil crisis did not seem to actually have any long-lasting impact on energy usage in the United States. As historian Natasha Zaretsky has argued, the two problems that the crisis shed the most light on—American dependence on foreign oil and energy consumption—in fact worsened after 1974.[32] By 1975 bicycle sales were back down to around seven million. Still, the 1975 slump experienced sales that were only slightly less than the peak of the 1960s and it was a level at which sales could apparently be maintained. Sales would fall below that number only one time after 1976.

The 1960s and 1970s were crucial for the redemption of the bicycle's image. As James Longhurst argues, it is difficult to identify one single factor leading to adult's decision to come back to the bike. Rather, it was a combination of improved bike technology, growing environmentalism, and a physical fitness fad.[33] Adult models' sales would remain more in line with juvenile models, if not surpassing them, well into the twenty-first century. David Herlihy explains, "The second boom helped reestablish cycing as a healthy and rewarding adult activity. Americans would no longer consider the bicycle a mere child's toy, and would gladly spend several hundred dollars or more on a well-made machine."[34] At the close of the 1970s, Samuel Wilkens, executive vice president of the Chain Bike Corporation, believed that the bicycle industry would continue to grow in the 1980s and 1990s. He supported his faith in the industry's future on predictions of a growth in population from 220 million in 1979 to 264 million by the year 2000, "a significant rise of approximately 20%."[35] This would not merely mean there would be a growth in potential for sales of children's models. Wilkens explained, "The industry has witnessed a burgeoining market for 10-speed bicycles over the past several years. By charting and analyzing changing patterns within the various age groups, there is considerable evidence of an increasing adult population and a corresponding potential demand for 26-inch and 27-inch bicycles."[36] Even still, Wilkens argued that the sales growth between 1946 and 1970 was largely based on the growth of a "new class of riders, those in the 13–35 age-category." He believed that group had been "largely satsified" and so charged the industry with three objectives: "Keep the present number of riders on bicycles. Interest more people of all ages in riding bicycles. Create interest among the very young to strart riding and owning their first bicycle."[37] In an effort to attain these goals, his own company, the Ross Bicycle Organization, sought to keep bicycles in the "public eye" by making "appreences on TV shows that stress many important bicycle themes" and by "stay[ing] in close contact with various legislators, helping them create programs favorable to cyclists and bicycling" such as creating bicycle lanes and other such infrastructure in urban areas.[38]

Sales from 1980 through 1982 suggested Wilkens's predictions might be wrong. They slipped from 10.8 million in 1979 to 6.7 million by 1982. That would be as far as they would fall, however, jumping back to 9 million in 1983 and staying at or above 10 million thereafter. Two emerging forms of competitve cycling were important to the recovery and stability of sales in the 1980s and 1990s—bicycle motocross (BMX) and mountain biking. Both inspired new styles and designs. The BMX bike was most often built around twenty-inch wheels, while mountain bikes would settle on twenty-six-inch wheels.

As early as 1979, some members of the bicycle industry believed that BMX bikes were the wave of the future. Bicycle merchants were told of shop owners like James Fonder of New Jersey, who proclaimed BMX to be the "fastest growing sport in the country" and attributed BMX to increased profits—after Fonder became actively involved in the sport in late 1977. Merchants were encouraged to learn all they could about the sport and to sponsor their own team.[39] BMX sales were important, but they did more to keep sales of twenty-inch bicycles steady with a slight increase from 3.6 million sold in 1977 to a peak of 5.2 million in 1987. The focus on BMX design and production was also a tactic employed by the industry to combat the growing competition from imported bicycles—since American companies believed they were better able to stay on top of the latest trends in design. At approximately 42 percent of the market share by 1985, imports became a real threat to bicycles manufactured in the United States. Much of that competition came from Asian manufacturers that priced bicycles 10–15 percent below domestic brands.[40] As a result, American companies like Murray Ohio Manufacturing Company and Huffy stepped up attempts to improve their brand's image. Murray sponsored professional and amateur riders to increase brand recognition and in hopes of cashing in on BMX's growing popularity. Along with spending an estimated $750,000 to supply bicycles to sponsored riders like Olympic gold medalist in track cycling, Mark Gorski, Murray also chose to "concentrate its marketing clout on the 6 to 15-year-old market—the age group, it believe[d] that ha[d] the biggest appetite for new trends and distinctive bike styles." To that end, Murray "made licensing deals to use such trade names as Rainbow Brite, Barbie and Masters of the Universe to help boost bike sales." The company also used focus groups of kids to "help fashion its TV commercials and . . . decals."[41] The BMX style became iconic of youth and adventure by the mid-1980s, playing a supporting role in several movies for younger audiences including *E.T.*, *The Goonies*, and *The Karate Kid*. While the hero's bike in *E.T.* was an imported brand, Murray made sure the characters in *Goonies* would employ Murray-branded bicycles in their pursuit of hidden treasure.[42] Movie producers jumped on the bandwagon wholeheartedly with the 1986 movie *Rad*, in which a teenager chooses to skip college-entrance exams in order to attend a BMX race called Helltrack because winning could potentially lead to his sponsorship and a BMX career.[43] BMX would continue to have supporters in the 1990s but by the end of the decade, it was associated more with ESPN's X Games and/or counterculture. By this time, mountain bikes had overtaken BMX bikes in sales.

Initially, bicycle manufacturers had little reason for hope when it came to the mountain bike's marketability. Like the high-rise bike, mountain bikes were created by enterprising bicycle enthusiasts, rather than industry leaders. Thrill seekers like Gary Fisher, Charlie Kelley, and Tom Ritchey were part of a growing sport that involved riding modified antique bicycles, particularly the balloon-tire models of the 1930s–1950s, and racing down the fire roads of Mount Tamalpais in Marin County, California.[44] As the participants tinkered and modified their bikes to suit the needs of such a riding style, they concentrated on stronger designs that gave more stability, greater stopping power, and multiple gears for riding up and down the mountain. The balloon-tire models they were on were so ill-suited for the amount of braking needed for an off-road race downhill that they had to reapply grease to the bearings of their coaster-brake-equipped hubs after each trip down the mountain. Thus these events were often referred to as a "Repack."[45] Four years after the industry embraced the new designs and began mass-producing their own versions of mountain bikes, sales were still "underwhelming."[46] They would, however, prove to be much more popular over time.

TABLE 10: **US Bicycle Sales, 1979–92 (x 1,000,000)**

Year	**1979**	**1980**	**1981**	**1982**	**1984**	**1986**	**1988**	**1990**	**1992**
Total sales	10.8	9.0	8.9	6.7	9.0	12.3	9.9	10.8	11.6
Twenty-inch wheels	4.5	3.7	3.7	3.2	4.4	4.7	3.5	3.5	4.1
Lightweights	6.0	4.9	4.6	3.2	4.9	6.1	4.3	1.9	.8
All others	.3	.4	.6	.3	.8	1.5	2.1	5.4	6.7

Sources: "The '88 Market in Review," *American Bicyclist and Motorcyclist*, April 1989, 55; "The 1992 Bicycle Market in Review," *American Bicyclist and Motorcyclist*, April 1993, 8.

The Bicycle Manufacturers Association did not initially keep track of how many mountain bikes were sold. Instead, they were categorized with "all others" in manufacturing reports. The production of that category was nominal in 1979 but it came to represent more than half of total production by 1992. Producing only 300,000 bicycles considered "others" not lightweight and not twenty-inch in 1979, the number grew to 6.7 million by 1992 (see table 10).[47] The growth of mountain-bike sales is attributable to mountain biking, but certainly not all mountain bikes sold would be used off-road at all. They were sold as a more versatile and comfortable option. The handlebars and geometry allowed for a more upright position and the thicker tires could handle city streets, sidewalks, gravel, or dirt. Mountain bikes also came with multiple gears, usually with smaller gearing than the typical ten-speed so they would seem easier to pedal up steep hills, something a commuter or utilitarian cyclist was sure to appreciate.

Mountain bikes had grown so popular by 1990 that *Bicycling* asked, "are road bikes dead?" In an article that began as a mock obituary, the author cited production figures and conversations with "people on the front line of bicycle sales" to point out that mountain bikes had already captured "65–80% of the market."[48] Tracing the "demise" of the road bike, the article argued that since the 1970s, "most Americans have ridden a knockoff of the classic European road racer. If the bike was good and the rider was reasonably fit, it became a match made in heaven. Usually, though, the relationship ended in a quick divorce. The grounds: irreconciable differences caused by a skimpy saddle, interminable top tube, and a nagging drop bar. Many road bikes became garage bikes."[49] The mountain bike provided an answer to all those problems. On a mountain bike the rider enjoyed a more relaxed and comfortable position. The road bike, a direct descendant of racing bikes, seemed to demand more from the rider. With a road bike, there was a perceived pressure to ride fast and to look fit while doing so. This was referred to as the "psych-out factor" of road bikes.[50] David Campbell, product manager for the US bicycle manufacturerer Cannondale, claimed that entry-level road-bike models were suffering declining sales because mountain bikes had become "the introductory bike of choice."[51] Mountain bikes were also more forgiving for newer riders. Their increased stability, puncture-resistant tires, and upright position made mountain bikes less intimidating for the novice.

The production and sales of road bikes were certainly high in the 1970s, with a short but dramatic peak in 1974. Bill Wilkinson, executive director of the BIA, suggested that maybe that was actually a hindrance for bicycle usage. An underlying point of both Wilkinson's comments and the article "Are Road Bikes Dead?" was that the heightened sales of the 1970s belied actual usage. As the article suggests, many of those bikes may have been ridden a few times and then hung in the garage to collect dust. Wilkinson said that the mountain bike should have been the bike that Americans were able to buy in 1972–74. "Unfortunately," he explained, "they were lured by European flash and sold the European-style racing bike. The ten speed became as synonymous with bicycling as Kleenex is with tissue. It was the wrong thing in the first place . . . [and] it probably did more to frustrate the growth of cycling through the '70s than anything else."[52] With the growth of ten-speed bikes in the 1970s came a rise in the marketing of cycling apparel. *American Bicyclist and Motorcyclist* made sure bicycle retailers were aware of this new sales opportunity. Under the headline "Bike Boom Inspires Bike Fashions," it told readers, "It's happened, and it's happened big, the Bicycle Boom has brought forth the first bicycle-inspired sportswear line." More of an advertisment than an article, the one fashion line that was mentioned specifically was Catalina's Cycle-Mates, which adapted "authentic European racing styles."[53] The 1970s embrace of European-designed ten-speed racing bikes, complete with form-fitting racing-styled clothing, was undoubtedly beneficial to the mountain bike's appeal by the 1980s.

Just like the 1984 Bruce Springsteen album, mountain bikes were "born in the USA." Partipants in "Repacks" (mountain-bike races) often raced down the mountain in jeans, flannel shirts, and boots.[54] This was a far cry from the ten-speed cyclist's form-fitting shorts and special cycling shoes. Mountain bikes liberated consumers from the pressure to dress a certain way. Some were also attracted to mountain bikes and off-road riding because it allowed riders "to get pig filthy and act rude."[55] Neal Murdoch, a moutain bike race organizer, denounced ten-speed bicycles as "a scam on the American public . . . [because] Americans in the Fifties began seeing TV shows of European road races and demanded those kinds of bikes."[56] The first mountain-bike enthusiasts were therefore described as "rabid revisionists of cycling, the John Birch Society of sport. Hard-line American-firsters" who believed "European racer's dropped handlebars and narrow tires" resulted in a "high-strung, overbred machine." Describing the opposing characteristics of mountain bikes, Murdoch explained, "Mountain bikers ride upright to take in the American scenery. They like to ease on down the road, which in this country is likely to be a rural dirt lane or a cratered urban street. . . . What we finally have in the fat-tire bike is an American piece of transportation for American conditions."[57] Murdoch and others were seemingly denouncing what they saw as the elitism of the ten-speed bicycle.

Similarly, the transition from the 1970s to 1980s, argues Gillian Frank, also experienced a backlash against the percieved elitism and gayness of disco music. He shows how "the discourse surrounding disco was highly sexualized and framed by homo-heterosexual definitions."[58] Bicycles did not have the same sexualized associations but ten-speeds were apparently viewed as foreign/un-American, even if they were produced domestically. A 1980 Oscar-winning film, *Breaking Away*, touched on this particular aspect. The main character, Dave, provokes his father's ire when he becomes obsessed with bicycle racing and Italian cyclists in particular. He begins to study Italian independently and even begins speaking with a fake Italian accent. His father, a former quarry worker turned used-car salesman, calls it "I-dee talk." When he attempts to confront his son about how "weird" he has become, he inadvertanly walks in on him shaving his legs. His anger is soon replaced by shock and fear of what his small-town boy has become.[59] Dave eventually makes his father proud, although reluctantly, when he uses his bicyle-racing prowess to defeat collegiate cyclists at Indiana University—students who are portrayed as outsiders and wealthy elitists throughout the movie.

Mountain bikers such as Murdoch certainly did not see themselves as strange or elitist. Charlie Kelly, an important figure in the growth of mountain biking, expressed this perspective when explaining the motivation for the creation of a long-distance mountain-bike ride that traversed the Pearl Pass from Crested Butte, Colorado, to Aspen. Aspen, a scenic destination for the "international rich and famous," was the subject of a great deal of scorn from many Crested Butte residents. They viewed the whole culture of Aspen as elitist. After a group of Aspenites crossed the Pearl Pass into Crested Butte on motorcycles, the mountain bikers of Crested Butte decided to one-up them and complete the same trek on their bicycles. Charlie Kelly explained, guys showed up to ride in the morning hungover and ill-equipped for the cold temperatures on the pass but they managed the ride because "they were not about to let those Aspen faggots go up on motorcycles and not get themselves up, too."[60] David Leverenz argues, "The word 'faggot' has nothing to do with homosexual experience or even with fears of homosexuals. Instead, it is "a label of ultimate contempt for anyone who seems sissy, untough, uncool."[61] Charlie Kelly was likely associating the Aspenite version of masculinity with homosexuality as a rejection of its percieved elitism or self-righteousness. Competitive road cyclists were often seen as belonging to the same elitist ilk. A female mountain biker described her abandonment of road biking and embrace of the mountain bike as a reaction to the "sanctimounessness in the road-biking community."[62] Clearly, some saw mountain biking as an answer to the eltitism and otherness of road biking but a number of Americans who chose a new mountain bike over a road bike may not have even associated ten-speeds with European culture or elitism. What they saw was the style of bike more and more people were riding and they were simultaneously encouraged to buy a mountain bike by retaliers who told them it was more practical than a road bike because of its versatility.

Road cycling did receive more attention by the mid-1980s as the first American team competed in the Tour de France and American Greg LeMond became the first person outside of Europe to win the Tour in 1986. He won again in 1989 and 1990. American networks such as CBS and ABC's *Wide World of Sports* brought European bicycle racing into American homes. This did not have a sustaining impact on the sales of lightweight (ten-speed) sales, however. Sales did climb some after early television covereage, going from 4.2 million in 1983 to 6.1 million in 1986, the year LeMond won his first Tour de France, but they fell to 1.9 million by 1990. The level of excitement for cycling that American success abroad may have stirred is hard to gauge, but it appeared brief at best. By 1992 lightweight sales had fallen to around eight hundred thousand.[63] The road bike's decline was written about as potentially tragic but explanations for why it was happening suggested that mountain bikes were not only eclipsing road bikes in sales, they also represented a model that was used regularly—as opposed to the road bike, which was allegedly purchased and soon forgotten. The price tag and cost of producing the two different models were apparently not all that diffent, so the rise of mountain bikes seemed to be a positive development for the bicycle industry as a whole. Heightened sales were one thing, but continued usage meant more profits for components manufacturers and local shops that serviced and repaired bicycles.

The mountain bike was able to maintain its popularity throughout the 1990s and 2000s but it has faced more and more competition from hybrid bikes (including cyclocross). In 2012, the hybrid/cross category represented 24 percent of production, while mountain bikes represented 25 percent and road bikes 20 percent.[64] Even in 2005, at the height of Lance Armstrong's career, road bikes were 16 percent of total sales while mountain bikes were 29 percent, thus making it seem that the "Lance factor," as Trek Bicycles Corporation executives described it, was largely hyperbole.[65] Road-bike production came back to surpass that of mountain bikes in 2010 and 2011 by one percentage point but it slipped back to 20 percent in 2012. Youth models, on the other hand, fell to 12 percent of the market. Research by the National Sporting Goods Association has found that cycling participation has declined somewhat since 1995, the year of peak participation. The National Bicycle Dealers Association attributes much of that to declining youth participation.[66] A study they commissioned found that the number of children riding bicycles fell by 43 percent from 2000 to 2013.[67] Another organization, People for Bikes, found that while the number of children commuting to school on bicycles has certainly dropped since the mid-1970s, overall youth biking has actually remained relatively flat.[68] These findings are more consistent with overall sales of youth models. Aside from the odd spike in 2000, industry production has also been relativly flat, with 5.4 million youth models produced in 2001 and 5.6 million in 2014. The average has been around 5.4 million per year from 2001 to 2014.[69] The number of women who ocassionally rode a bicycle also fell by 13 percent from 2000 to 2013, but the number of women who were considered enthusiasts, riding at least 110 days a year, rose by 8 percent.[70] In spite of proclamations of a loss of interest among some, overall bicycle production in the United States has remained flat. Production was 11.9 million in 2000, and while it dipped to 11.3 million in 2001, it bounced back to 13.6 million in 2002 and stayed above 11.9 million for the rest of the decade. In 2015, total production was 12.5 million.[71] While youth models certainly make up a sizeable portion of the bicycle industry's annual sales, the current state of the industry appears much more diverse and less dependent on any one group than it was from the 1930s to the 1960s. Headlines proclaiming another bike boom seem perennial but the past few decades show steady sales with a shifting demographic—a move away from children back to adults.

After the ten-speed boom of 1972–74, the image of the bicycle became somewhat more complicated than simply a child's toy. Weekend warriors in local parks and commuters in urban areas made significant steps toward reclaiming the bicycle. Even so, cycling is more likely to be associated with environmentalism, poverty, eccentricity, or health. Rarely is the act representative of adult masculinity today and then only to a small group of people, mostly those who participate in the sport or know someone who does. To some, mountain bikes represented Peter Pan masculinity. Commenting on the rising popularity of mountain biking in 1985, *Rolling Stone* writer Trip Gabriel argued, "To breeze down a mountain on an updated paper-boy bike is a fantasy realized. The high-performance fat-tire bike taps into the primitive, preadolescent brain. Mountain bikes are Peter Pan bikes, the closest thing to flying out the bedroom window to whisk about the neighborhood." He preposed a revision to the earlier thoughts on children's motivations for riding bikes, writing, "Old Ignaz [Schwinn] had it backward. Children on bicycles don't want to imitate grown-ups driving cars. Just the opposite. On a high-tech fat-tire bike, you do not have to leave the hermetically sealed terrarium of kiddom. You can remain eleven years old forever."[72] To be sure, some today still take to bicycles in an attempt to chase down their youth, just as those in the 1890s mounted bicycles to reclaim their youthful vigor, but bicycle usage for utilitarian purposes has risen in recent years. Bike-share programs and the number of bike lanes, for example, have grown tremendously.

Tulsa, Oklahoma, launched the first automated bike-share program in 2007 and Washington, DC, quickly followed suit.[73] By 2012, there were over twenty citites with bike-share programs, and five years later there were 119 bike-share systems in the United States.[74] Census data also show that "the number of U.S. workers who traveled to work by bicycle increased from around 488,000 in 2000 to 786,000 in 2008–2012, a larger percentage increase than that of any other commuting mode."[75] The League of American Bicyclists has reported that, in comparison to 2005, bicycle commuting has risen by at least 10 percent in forty states.[76] Cities all across the United States have responded to the growing number of bicycle commuters by adding various types of bicycle lanes. From 2012 to 2014, 113 protected lanes were added to US streets, thereby seperating cyclists from autoists for increased safety. That is even more significant when considering the fact that from 1874 to 2011, only 78 such lanes were created.[77] Margaret Guroff argues, "the growth of bike lanes involves a sort of feedback loop" in which the push for safer routes and subsequent creation of bike lanes helps people feel more comfortable cycling. More riders on city streets leads to a push for even more lanes.[78] Clearly, the way US consumers think about the bicycle is moving away from the narrow view that they are only toys, but such opinions are still in the minority and the use of a car for transportation far supasses any other mode for Americans as a whole. Of work commutes made in the United States from 2008 to 2012, 86.2 percent were made via car, truck, or van—compared to less than 1 percent made by bicycle.[79] A 2008 study of transportation habits showed that Germans were eight times more likely to use the bicycle for transportation than Americans. The Dutch were twenty-six times more likely to do so.[80] While consumption and usage of the bicycle is certainly changing in the United States, it is still hard to forsee a day when bicycle usage will surpass that of automobiles—barring environmental or electrotechnological calamity. The days of the bicycle being seen solely as a child's toy, however, seem to be at an end.

CONCLUSION

Consumers as Derailleurs

BY THE LATE NINETEENTH CENTURY, ideals of nation were increasingly linked to consumption. Rather than defining themselves by what they produced, Americans began to define themselves by what they consumed.[1] As automobile consumption grew, the United States became a nation of autoists. The bicycle's changing status compounded this alteration. It became a means for children to prepare for adulthood with the understanding that once they grew into adults, they had outgrown the bicycle. It had, after all, prepared them to drive cars. Understanding the shifts in bicycle marketing and consumption lends insights into Americans' unique conceptions of gender and mobility. The story of the bicycle's staying power despite all the changes that have occurred since the 1880s demonstrates its mutability as a consumer object.

The severity of both the boom and bust in the 1890s had long-lasting effects on the bicycle industry. Cycling's meteoric rise in popularity was a bonanza for the industry—leading many entrepreneurs to enter the trade and inspiring a false sense of optimism. Americans' fascination with the bicycle, however, quickly diminished with the same intensity as it had previously flourished. Changes in the American middle class's ideals of gender had a significant impact. Men turned to bicycles in the 1880s and 1890s in reaction to a growing belief that the industrialized city and new forms of labor that did not require physical exertion were making them effete and nervous—shells of the men who came before. The "cult of fitness" that came to pass—with its emphasis on living a strenuous life in the fresh open air—was of considerable benefit to the bicycle industry. The increasing ease of riding a bicycle, which came with the invention of the safety bicycle, the inclusion of pneumatic tires, and decreasing prices made cycling more accessible. These developments also blurred the lines of gender and class that the high-wheeler had previously demonstrated. In turn, they led to a middle-class exodus from cycling, but bicycle marketers were reluctant to respond. Throughout the first decade of the twentieth century, the bicycle industry continued to promote middle-class ideals of health. Instead of targeting the lower classes directly, the industry believed that advertisements targeting the middle class would also speak to laborers who sought to emulate their social superiors.[2]

During the first half of the twentieth century, the bicycle industry waxed nostalgic about the prosperity of the golden age with the hope that it could lead the way back to similar sales figures—of over one million units. Many members of the industry learned a lesson from the rise and fall during the 1890s. They led the charge not only to recover sales and production levels, but to do so in a way that would impart a sense of stability. Those attempts, however, were greatly complicated by the rising popularity of automobiles. Still, members of the bicycle industry believed that cars would also experience a loss of appeal—just as bicycles had ten years prior. Though some bicycle and parts manufacturers seemed wary of boosting sales based on consumer fads, there were others who attempted to get middle-class men and society women back on bicycles in the hope that it would lead to a resurgence of cycling's fashionability. The industry was ultimately forced to come to terms with the fact that their target market had moved on.

The automobile proved to be more than just a passing fad and as it continued to maintain the attention of all classes, the bicycle industry targeted a consumer group that would never be able to buy (or drive) cars—children. Cars preoccupied consumers' imaginations and thereby changed the way Americans thought about mobility. The automobile became the standard by which all other forms of mobility were measured and as sales began to outpace those of bicycles, the car became a symbol of the nation. The car became synonymous with freedom and as prices decreased it was held up as a beacon of America's democratic promise. The changing ideals of mobility in which the car became the epitome of masculinity and patriotism reaffirmed the bicycle industry's need to concentrate on children.

In reaction, the industry did not change the nature of its marketing, it simply shifted to a different demographic. Concentrating on children afforded the bicycle industry an opportunity to stimulate sales, but it was also a matter of convenience because it did not require a reworking of the ideals associated with cycling. Alterations in bicycle marketing to focus on children occurred at the dawn of a new era in which childhood consumerism would become too powerful and too pervasive to ignore. The bicycle's history reveals how efforts to train Americans to be good consumers and therefore good citizens began during childhood. Indeed, childhood was changing from a time of frivolity into a period in which one prepared for adulthood. This made the move to children—particularly boys—doubly convenient for the bicycle industry. Traits that were once virtues for adults—such as independence, strength, health, and consumerism—were implanted into ideals of childhood, thereby allowing bicycle boosters to repurpose old marketing strategies. This meant that the industry did not have to re-create the symbolic nature of the bicycle. In some ways, however, it inadvertently did just that—at least for a while.

Bicycle boosters' success in marketing the bicycle as a means of independence, health, and fun for boys led the bicycle to become increasingly associated with boyhood. As bicycles became a means for boys to train for manhood, the bicycle was transformed into a commodity that was primarily for a single stage in life. Once a person moved beyond that stage, they left bicycles behind. Just as the car had grown to become a symbol of American adulthood and success, bicycles were symbolic of childhood. These interconnections between the bicycle and childhood, while successful in selling bicycles to children, had an adverse impact on cycling's appeal to American adults. In its efforts to increase and stabilize sales, the bicycle industry alienated adult consumers and inadvertently stigmatized their product.

To a degree, the bicycle industry's effort to make their product more appealing to children during the first half of the twentieth century was the right thing to do. This was especially true considering the post–World War II population boom. That influx of children, however, would become adults soon enough. In order to reach its fullest potential, the bicycle industry needed to avoid limiting its appeals to children. But how could it reconcile successful efforts to make bicycles the subject of childhood fantasy with the need to promote a side of cycling that was suitable for adults? Manufacturers busied themselves creating bicycles with holsters for cap guns, fake gas tanks, and other embellishments that made it impractical—indeed laughable—for adults. They devoted considerably less time or effort trying to improve adult models. After successfully marketing bicycles to children, either adults would have to be pushed into cycling by outside forces or the industry would have to re-create the image of the bicycle as a commodity for adults *and* children. Adult models would have to look significantly different from children's models.

This came to pass with the introduction and mass production of ten-speed bicycles at the close of the 1960s. It would take until 1972, however, before the sales of lightweight ten-speeds would eclipse twenty-inch models due in large part to the high-rise bicycle craze that began around 1965. The swing in demographics toward adult participation was undoubtedly clear by 1971. The ten-speed boom was relatively short-lived but sales stayed significantly higher than numbers experienced before the boom. It helped adults think about bicycles as something that could be a little more serious than a toy but perhaps it was too serious as the mountain bike soon replaced the ten-speed as the most popular model for adult consumers.

The bicycle has successfully navigated numerous transitions as a consumer item since its creation and that process highlights a unique relationship between consumers and marketers. Rather than the bicycle industry leading the consumer, the bicycle's history shows that the power in the relationship was most often in consumers' hands. The bicycle industry has often found itself reacting to changing trends—some inspired by creative and enterprising consumers. Neither the high-rise or the moutain bike were ideas that came from bicycle manufacturers. Rather, they came from the bottom-up. Once the bicycle industry recognized the marketing potential of both, manufacturers quickly began producing their own versions of the new designs. With the child's bicycle of the 1920s, however, the bicycle industry deserves much more credit in contributing to the growth in popularity. Of course, even then, the industry was aided by changing ideals for childhood and its tactics had harmful side effects. At other times, such as the boom of the 1890s and the great American bicycle boom of the 1970s, the industry was reacting to a demand that already existed, rather than creating it. The industry certainly fostered the demand in those cases and often took steps to increase desires for bicycles but then it was only fanning the flames, not starting the fire.

The growth of road cycling and utilitarian riding in the past few decades are also trends that the bicycle industry did not necessarily inspire, but has cultivated to the best of its ability. More recently, the industry is witnessing a growth of electronic bikes (e-bikes) on public roads and showroom floors. There is considerable speculation that e-bikes will change the future of cycling. The industry has also been moving toward increasingly nuanced specialty bikes instead of all-purpose bikes. In theory, this means enthusiasts will need several different types of bicycles—a road bike, mountain bike, fat bike for winter, gravel bike, and cyclo-cross bike—for instance. Whatever the next major trend may be, it is unlikely that there will be advertisments on television, the radio, or even streaming video services. There will undoubtedly be articles in cycling magazines, however. Advertisements might even appear in the social-media feed of individuals with the appropriate browsing history. It is a brave new world for an old piece of technology that has already weathered significant shifts in culture and consumer desires. If its history tells us anything, the bicycle will endure.

Notes

Bibliography

Index

Notes

Introduction

1. Judith Crown and Glenn Coleman, *No Hands: The Rise and Fall of the Schwinn Bicycle Company an American Institution* (New York: Henry Holt and Company, 1996), 66.

2. Ross Petty, "Peddling Schwinn Bicycles: Marketing Lessons from the Leading Post–WWII US Bicycle Brand," Quinnipiac University CHARM Symposium Papers 2007, 167.

3. Barbara W. Tuchman, *The Proud Tower: A Portrait of the World Before the War, 1890–1914* (New York: Macmillan, 1966), 122–23.

4. Victor Fleming, dir., *The Wizard of Oz* (Burbank, CA: Warner Bros. Pictures, 1939).

5. Judd Apatow, dir. *The 40 Year Old Virgin* (Universal City, CA: Universal Pictures, 2005). Other examples include: Denis Reynolds's comment, "people that aren't retarded usually drive," on *It's Always Sunny in Philadelphia*, season 3, episode 9, "Sweet Dee's Dating a Retarded Person," directed by Rob McElhenney, aired on October 11, 2007, on FX; and Brad Pitt's character in *Burn After Reading*, directed by Joel and Ethan Coen (Universal City, CA: Universal Studios Home Entertainment, 2008). Some of these examples are also used in Zach Furness, *One Less Car: Bicycles and the Politics of Automobility* (Philadelphia: Temple Univ. Press, 2010).

6. Norman L. Dunham, "The Bicycle Era in American History" (PhD diss., Harvard University, 1956), 447; Maurice Green, "A Review of '94," *Recreation*, December 1894, 121; Issac B. Potter, "The Bicycle Outlook," *Century*, September 1896, 789. Dunham says there were 4 million while Potter says there were 2.5 million.

7. Susan B. Carter, *Historical Statistics of the United States: Earliest Times to the Present*, vol. 4 (New York: Cambridge Univ. Press, 2006), 4–640.

8. Luis A. Vivanco, *Reconsidering the Bicycle: An Anthropological Perspective on a New (Old) Thing* (New York: Routledge, 2013), 40.

9. Vivanco, *Reconsidering the Bicycle*, xxi.

10. Jeremy Withers and Daniel P. Shea, *Culture on Two Wheels: The Bicycle in Literature and Film* (Lincoln: Univ. of Nebraska Press, 2016), 3.

11. See Robert Smith, *A Social History of the Bicycle: Its Early Life and Times in America* (New York: American Heritage Press, 1972); Andrew Ritchie, *King of the Road: An Illustrated History of Cycling* (London: Wildwood House, 1975); David Herlihy, *Bicycle: The History* (New Haven, CT: Yale Univ. Press, 2004); Peter Nye, *Hearts of Lions: The History of American Bicycle Racing* (New York: W. W. Norton, 1988).

12. Evan Friss, *The Cycling City: Bicycles and Urban America in the 1890s* (Chicago: Univ. of Chicago Press, 2015), 10.

13. In the process of recounting the story of the bicycle's relegation to the status of child's toy, this book implicitly highlights the increasing divergence of American culture from other cultures—as cycling fell out of favor among adults in the United States but maintained popularity in other countries. In 2008, around 9 percent of trips were via bicycle in Germany, 19 percent in Denmark, and 27 percent in the Netherlands. That same figure for the United States was 1 percent. At the same time, this work does not intend to offer a proper comparative study of the bicycle. It will, however, aid other authors in producing such a work in the future. The aforementioned statistics come from John Pucher and Ralph Buehler, "Cycling for Everyone: Lessons from Europe," *Transportation Research Record* no. 2074 (2008): 3.

14. Thomas Cameron Burr, "Markets as Producers and Consumers: The French and U.S. National Bicycle Markets, 1875–1910" (PhD diss., University of California, Davis, 2005); Glenn Norcliffe, *The Ride to Modernity: The Bicycle in Canada, 1869–1900* (Toronto: Univ. of Toronto Press, 2001). Burr makes this argument about the United States, while Norcliffe suggests a similar development in Canada. This work's contention that the bicycle industry is culpable in the bicycle's loss of status in the United States will go beyond Thomas Burr's 2005 dissertation, which is the most detailed account of the bicycle's declining status from 1875 to 1910. Burr suggests that "bicycles lost social legitimacy in the United States and retained it in France," arguing that this was due in part to the overproduction of bicycles in the United States during the 1890s. This led to a dramatic decrease in price, thereby allowing members of the lower classes the opportunity to participate in cycling. Burr and Glen Norcliffe both argue that as bicycles grew ubiquitous and less expensive their popularity waned, as a bicycle became less of a status symbol and more of a common diversion for the masses. Comparatively speaking, Burr contends that because France was more moderate in terms of bicycle production, it did not suffer the boom and bust cycle that occurred in the United States.

15. Charles E. Pratt, "A Sketch of American Bicycling and Its Founder," *Outing: An Illustrated Monthly Magazine of Recreation*, July 1891, 342–43. Pope produced the Columbia bicycle. It would grow to be one of the most powerful companies during the bicycle's early years. See Bruce D. Epperson, *Peddling Bicycles to America: The Rise of an Industry* (Jefferson, NC: McFarland, 2010).

16. For a history of the bicycle see Robert Smith, *A Social History of the Bicycle*; Ritchie, *King of the Road*; and Herlihy, *Bicycle*.

17. Issac B. Potter, "The Bicycle Outlook," *Century*, September 1896, 789.

18. Vanguard Cycle Company, *Vanguard Cycle Company Catalog* (Indianapolis: Vanguard Cycle Company, 1900); Acme Cycle Company, *Acme Bicycles* (Elkhart, IN: Acme Cycle Company, 1898); Nell Irvin Painter, *Standing at Armageddon: The United States, 1877–1919* (New York: W. W. Norton, 1987) xx; Steven Duboff, "A Method for Estimating the Economic Welfare of American Families of any Composition: 1860–1901," *Historical Methods* 13, no. 3 (Summer 1980): 177. The poverty line had increased from "$506 per year in 1877 to $553 per year in 1900."

1. Cycling's Rise and American Manhood

1. Margaret Guroff, *The Mechanical Horse: How the Bicycle Reshaped American Life* (Austin: Univ. of Texas Press, 2016), 18–19; David V. Herlihy, *Bicycle: The History* (New Haven, CT: Yale Univ. Press, 2004), 103–5.

2. Herlihy, *Bicycle*, 116.

3. Herlihy, 121.

4. Glen Norcliffe and Phillip Gordon Mackintosh, "Men, Women and the Bicycle in the Late Nineteenth Century," in *Critical Geographies of Cycling: History, Political Economy and Culture*, ed. Glen Norcliffe (Farnham, England: Ashgate, 2015), 158. Norcliffe and Mackintosh argue that the number of women who rode the velocipede was actually quite small, in spite of images, mostly from Paris, that show women with velocipedes.

5. Paul Smethurst, *The Bicycle: Towards a Global History* (New York: Palgrave Macmillan, 2015), 24. There has been some debate about who deserves credit for inventing the velocipede. See Herlihy, *Bicycle*, 75–101.

6. Smethurst, *The Bicycle*, 32.

7. Smethurst, 30

8. Guroff, *The Mechanical Horse*, 23.

9. *Leavenworth Times*, February 24, 1869.

10. Herlihy, *Bicycle*, 120.

11. Herlihy, 124–26.

12. Pratt, "A Sketch of American Bicycling and Its Founder," 342–43.

13. Herlihy, *Bicycle*, 188–89.

14. Herlihy, 198.

15. Schwinn Bicycle Company, "U.S. Bicycle Market Statistics—1895 to 1979," *Schwinn Reporter*, March 1980; Carter, *Historical Statistics of the United States*, 4–640. The numbers in table 1 are based on Bruce Epperson's revised estimates. He argues conventional numbers for the peak years overestimated production. Still, the general

trend remains the same. See Bruce Epperson, "How Many Bikes: An Investigation into the Quantification of Bicycling, 1878–1914," in *Cycle History 11: Proceedings of the 11th International Cycling History Conference*, ed. Andrew Ritchie and Rob Van der Plas (San Francisco: Van der Plas Publications, 2001), 49.

16. Herlihy, *Bicycle*, 202.

17. Ellen Gruber Garvey, "Reframing the Bicycle: Advertising-Supported Magazines and Scorching Women," *American Quarterly* 47, no. 1 (March 1995): 72; Clare Simpson, "Capitalising on Curiosity: Women's Professional Cycle Racing in the Late Nineteenth Century," in *Cycling and Society*, ed. Dave Horton, Paul Rosen, and Peter Cox (Abingdon, United Kingdom: Ashgate, 2007), 49–50.

18. Herlihy, *Bicycle*, 201.

19. Peter Zheutlin, *Around the World on Two Wheels: Annie Londonderry's Extraordinary Ride* (New York: Kensington Books, 2013), 29. Annie Londonderry began her legendary trip around the world on bicycle wearing a traditional dress. She soon found it cumbersome and restrictive, switching to bloomers and, ultimately, to a man's riding suit.

20. Dzierziak, *The Evolution of American Bicycle Racing*, 13.

21. Zheutlin, *Around the World on Two Wheels*, 27.

22. Herlihy, *Bicycle*, 250.

23. See Patricia Marks, *Bicycles, Bangs, and Bloomers: The New Woman in the Popular Press* (Lexington: Univ. Press of Kentucky, 1990), 174–203; Garvey, "Reframing the Bicycle: Advertising-Supported Magazines and Scorching Women"; Lisa S. Strange and Robert S. Brown, "The Bicycle, Women's Rights, and Elizabeth Cady Stanton," *Women's Studies* 31 (2002): 609–26; Julia Marie Brock, "The Bicycle As Vehicle to Women's Emancipation As Reflected in Popular Culture, 1888–1900" (master's thesis, University of Houston–Clear Lake, 2004); Evan Friss, *The Cycling City: Bicycles and Urban America in the 1890s* (Chicago: Univ. of Chicago Press, 2015), 160–85; James Longhurst, *Bike Battles: A History of Sharing the American Road* (Seattle: Univ. of Washington Press, 2015), 57–60; and Sarah Hallenbeck, *Claiming the Bicycle: Women, Rhetoric, and Technology in Nineteenth-Century America* (Carbondale: Southern Illinois Univ. Press, 2016), 1–32.

24. Robert Smith, *A Social History of the Bicycle* (New York: American Heritage Press, 1972), 65.

25. John Higham, "The Reorientation of America in the 1890s," in *Writing American History*, ed. John Higham (Bloomington: Indiana Univ. Press, 1970), 79; Michael McGerr, *A Fierce Discontent: The Rise and Fall of the Progressive Movement in America, 1870–1920* (New York: Oxford Univ. Press, 2003), 63.

26. Higham, "The Reorientation of America in the 1890s," 79.

27. Price Collier, "Sport's Place in the Nation's Well-Being," *Outing: An Illustrated Monthly Magazine of Recreation*, July 1898, 383.

28. Collier, "Sport's Place in the Nation's Well-Being," 383.

29. Gail Bederman, *Manliness and Civilization: A Cultural History of Gender and Race in the United States, 1880–1917* (Chicago: Univ. of Chicago Press, 1995), 14.

30. Bederman, *Manliness and Civilization*, 14.

31. Kevin J. Hayes, *The Two-Wheeled World of George B. Thayer* (Lincoln: Univ. of Nebraska Press, 2015), 89, 92, 198.

32. Friss, *The Cycling City*, 130–31. Friss documents how physicians prescribed cycling as a cure for insufficient vigor, neurasthenia, and other ailments.

33. "The Hygiene of Cycling," *Scientific American*, November 27, 1886, 341.

34. "The Hygiene of Cycling," 341.

35. Jeremy Withers and Daniel P. Shea, *Culture on Two Wheels: The Bicycle in Literature and Film* (Lincoln: Univ. of Nebraska Press, 2016), 44; Stephen B. Goddard, *Colonel Albert Pope and His American Dream Machines: The Life and Times of a Bicycle Tycoon Turned Automotive Pioneer* (Jefferson NC: McFarland, 2000), 82.

36. Charles E. Pratt, *The American Bicycler: A Manual for the Observer, the Learner, and the Expert* (Boston: Osgood and Company, 1879), 30.

37. Pratt, *The American Bicycler*, 31.

38. Stefan Szymanski "locates the origin of English sports in eighteenth-century associativity rather than nineteenth-century industrialization." Pratt certainly makes an appeal to the benefits of associativity; however, he is also specifically articulating a notion of manhood that was a response to industrialization. See Stefan Szymanski, "The Theory of the Evolution of Modern Sport," *Journal of Sport History* 35, no. 1 (Spring 2008): 4.

39. "The Ravages of the Bicycle Boom," *Scientific American*, April 20, 1896, 391.

40. Smith, *A Social History of the Bicycle*, 52.

41. Childs, "Training for Cycling Competitions," 347.

42. "Health on Wheels," *Outing: An Illustrated Monthly Magazine of Recreation*, July 1885, 495; This article is quoting W. Gordon Stables, MD, *Health on Wheels* (London: Iliffe & Son, 1885).

43. "Health on Wheels," 495.

44. Pratt, *The American Bicycler*, 32; Bederman, *Manliness and Civilization*, 6–7. As Gail Bederman argues, "Attempting to define manhood as a coherent set of prescriptive ideals, traits, or sex roles obscures the complexities and contradictions of any historical moment. . . . Envisioning manhood as a unified set of traits gives us no way to . . . understand how men themselves negotiated the contradictions [they faced]." It is apparent that the self-reliance, strength, resolve, and courage cycling demanded of its participants as a sport, were in fact, traits that were often associated with manhood.

45. See McGerr, *A Fierce Discontent*. Michael McGerr highlights some of the contradictions of the Progressive movement in the United States, such as the way it glorified the yeoman farmer yet seemed unwilling to embrace the agriculture movement and celebrated new technologies such as cars and airplanes.

46. For an argument that the bicycle represented modernity, see William H. Beezley, *Judas at the Jockey Club and other Episodes of Porfirian Mexico* (Lincoln: Univ. of Nebraska Press, 1987).

47. Richard Harmond, "Progress and Flight: An Interpretation of the American Cycle Craze of the 1890s," *Journal of Social History* 5, no. 2 (Winter 1971–72): 236. As table 1 shows, the craze was not over by 1896 but many bicycle historians agree that by 1898 the "bust" was in sight.

48. Pratt, *The American Bicycler*, 31–32.

49. "The Outing Club," *Outing: An Illustrated Monthly Magazine of Recreation*, April 1885, 103. For S. S. McClure (muckraking journalist and cofounder of *McClure's* magazine) as editor of *Outing* see Robert A. Smith, *A Social History of the Bicycle*, 9.

50. David Herlihy, *The Lost Cyclist: The Epic Tale of an American Adventurer and His Mysterious Disappearance* (Boston: Houghton Mifflin Harcourt, 2010), 59, 285.

51. Roland Marchand, *Advertising the American Dream: Making Way for Modernity, 1920–1940* (Berkeley: Univ. of California Press, 1985), xxi.

52. Pope Manufacturing Company, "Without Car Fare," *Scientific American*, October 8, 1892, 238.

53. Workers of the lower classes whose labor required physical strength did not have quite the same need to demonstrate their vigor.

54. Herlihy, *Bicycle*, 7. Herlihy says the "transition from a rich man's toy to a poor man's carriage" was not complete until the early twentieth century.

55. T. J. Jackson Lears, *No Place of Grace: Antimodernism and the Transformation of American Culture, 1880–1920* (Chicago: Univ. of Chicago Press, 1994), 51.

56. Lears, 108.

57. Harbison and Gathright, "Natures Rule," *Louisville Courier Journal*, July 1, 1896, 6.

58. Friss, *The Cycling City*, 120. Friss, however, does not associate the intensified focus on health with gender.

59. Toledo Medical and Surgical Reporter, "Bicycle Riding," *Scientific American*, February 16, 1895, 105.

60. McGerr, *A Fierce Discontent*, 63.

61. *Puck*, July 1, 1896. Reproduced in David Herlihy, *Bicycle*, 266.

62. London Lancet, "Cycling," *Scientific American*, October 13, 1894, 231.

63. Erie Medical Company, "Men of All Ages," *Louisville Courier Journal*, July 3, 1896, 7.

64. Lears, *No Place of Grace*, 47–58.

65. Erie Medical Company, "Weak Men," *Louisville Courier Journal*, July 12, 1896, 7.

66. Pratt, *The American Bicycler*, 174.

67. For a complete story of Major Taylor's life and career see Major Taylor, *The Fastest Bicycle Rider in the World: The Autobiography of Major Taylor* (Brattleboro, VT: S. Greene Press, 1972); Andrew Ritchie, *Major Taylor: The Extraordinary Career of a Champion Bicycle Racer* (Baltimore: Johns Hopkins Univ. Press, 1988); and Todd Balf, *Major: A Black Athlete, a White Era, and the Fight to be the World's Fastest Human Being* (New York: Crown, 2008). There were individual chapters of the League of American Wheelmen in each state and the ultimate authority over race entry was controlled by the state chapters.

68. Quoted in, Garvey, "Reframing the Bicycle," 72.

69. See Zheutlin, *Around the World on Two Wheels.*

70. Zheutlin, 66. See also Ellen Gruber Garvey, *The Admen in the Parlor: Magazines and the Gendering of Consumer Culture, 1880s to 1910s* (New York: Oxford Univ. Press, 1996), 112–22.

71. E. D. Page, "Women and the Bicycle," *Brooklyn Medical Journal* 11 (1897): 84. Quoted in Garvey, "Reframing the Bicycle," 74.

72. Robert L. Dickinson, "Bicycling for Women from the Standpoint of the Gynecologist," *American Journal of Obstetrics and Diseases of Women and Children* 21 (1895): 24–37; quoted in Hallenbeck, *Claiming the Bicycle*, 53–54.

73. Garvey, "Reframing the Bicycle," 74.

74. Zheutlin, *Around the World on Two Wheels*, 25.

75. William Blackwood and Sons, "Modern Mannish Maidens," *Blackwood's Edinburgh Magazine*, February 1890, 254.

76. Blackwood and Sons, "Modern Mannish Maidens," 255.

77. Kennedy Childs, "Training for Cycle Competitions," *Outing: An Illustrated Monthly Magazine of Recreation*, July 1888, 347.

78. Dunham, "The Bicycle Era in American History," 465.

79. Hallenbeck, *Claiming the Bicycle*, 157.

80. Smith, *A Social History of the Bicycle*, 66.

81. Lisa S. Strange and Robert S. Brown, "The Bicycle, Women's Rights, and Elizabeth Candy Stanton," *Women's Studies* 31 (2002): 615.

82. Frances E. Willard, *A Wheel within a Wheel* (Bedford, MA: Applewood Books, 1997 [1895]), 11–14.

83. Pope Manufacturing Company, "Two by Two," *Scientific American*, May 27, 1893, 336.

84. See Frances E. Willard, *A Wheel within a Wheel*; Brock, "The Bicycle As Vehicle to Women's Emancipation As Reflected in Popular Culture"; Dunham, "The Bicycle Era in American History"; Ross D. Petty, "Women and the Wheel: The Bicycle's Impact on Women," in *Cycle History: Proceedings of the 7th International Cycle History Conference*, ed. Rob van der Plas (San Francisco: Van der Plas Publications, 1997); and Friss, *The Cycling City*, 160–85.

85. Garvey, "Reframing the Bicycle," 66–67; Clare Simpson also talks about advertising directed at the new woman in Horton, Rosen, and Cox, *Cycling and Society*, 60.

86. Garvey, "Reframing the Bicycle," 95.

87. "In These Bicycle Days," *Outing: An Illustrated Monthly Magazine of Recreation*, October 1896, 106.

88. *Puck*, July 7, 1897. Reproduced in Herlihy, *Bicycle*, 268.

89. Pamela Walker Laird, *Advertising Progress: American Business and the Rise of Consumer Marketing* (Baltimore: John Hopkins Univ. Press, 1998), 326.

90. Laird, *Advertising Progress*, 326.

91. Burr, "Markets as Producers and Consumers," 219–20, 234, 240.

92. Burr, 229; *Bicycling World*, May 27, 1898, 21.

93. Garvey, "Reframing the Bicycle," 96.

2. Automobiles and a World at War

1. "Why We Love the Good Old Bicycle," *Motorcycle and Bicycle Illustrated*, January 15, 1917, 19.

2. "Why We Love the Good Old Bicycle," 19.

3. Christopher W. Wells, *Car Country: An Environmental History* (Seattle: Univ. of Washington Press, 2012), 85.

4. *Apparent consumption* is the term used in the *Schwinn Reporter*. See Schwinn Bicycle Company, "U.S. Bicycle Market Statistics." Census statics estimate the physical output of bicycles to be 1.11 million in 1899, 230,000 in 1904, 170,000 in 1909, 300,000 in 1914, and 470,000 in 1919. See Susan B. Carter et al. eds., *Historical Statistics of the United States, Millennial Edition Online* (New York: Cambridge Univ. Press, 2006), 4–641. Tables 2 and 4 use the revised estimates provided in Bruce Epperson's essay on bicycle production from 1878 to 1914. He suggests there were several years in which conventional estimates exaggerate actual output. Still, the larger trends remain the same. See Epperson, "How Many Bikes?" 49.

5. "More Bicycles Than Other Vehicles," *Bicycling World and Motorcycle Review*, October 21, 1911, 205.

6. US Census Bureau, *Statistical Abstracts of the United States: 2003*, "Transportation Indicators for Motor Vehicles and Airlines: 1900 to 2001," no. HS-41, 77.

7. *Automobile*, July 25, 1912, 165; Michael L. Bromley, *William Howard Taft and the First Motoring Presidency* (Jefferson, NC: McFarland, 2003), 387.

8. Model T prices and sales come from Clay McShane, *Down the Asphalt Path: The Automobile and the American City* (New York: Columbia Univ. Press, 1994), 135.

9. "Topics of the Times," *New York Times*, December 10, 1907, 8.

10. Herlihy, *Bicycle*, 377, 380. Herlihy speculates that people were also attending races for gambling opportunities.

11. Tim Cresswell, *On the Move: Mobility in the Modern Western World* (New York: Routledge, 2006), 10. The cancan and Taylorism both emerged in the nineteenth century. The height of Taylorism's popularity occurred in the 1910s.

12. Cresswell, *On the Move*, 159. Tim Cresswell uses Supreme Court cases beginning in 1865 to show how the court has ruled that mobility is a "virtually unconditional aspect of liberty and citizenship despite the lack of formal protection in the Constitution."

13. Wells, *Car Country*, 80.

14. Cotten Seiler, *Republic of Drivers: A Cultural History of Automobility in America* (Chicago: Univ. of Chicago Press, 2008), 54. Like masculine associations with cycling in the 1890s, those of the automobile were certainly soon challenged by women, who used cars to "break down the gender segregation of modern life." Michael McGerr, *A Fierce Discontent: The Rise and Fall of the Progressive Movement in American, 1870–1920* (New York: Free Press, 2003), 231.

15. Seiler, *Republic of Drivers*, 47.

16. Bromley, *William Howard Taft and the First Motoring Presidency*, 387.

17. Quoted in Bromley, *William Howard Taft and the First Motoring Presidency*, 5.

18. Wells, *Car Country*, 80–82; Seiler, *Republic of Drivers*, 64.

19. Peter D. Norton, *Fighting Traffic: The Dawn of the Motor Age in the American City* (Cambridge, MA: MIT Press, 2008), 7.

20. "Week's Doings Portrayed in Pen Drawings," *Motorcycling*, December 14, 1914, 3.

21. "Week's Doings Portrayed in Pen Drawings," 3.

22. "New Haven Asks, What is a Bicycle?" *Motorcycling*, December 14, 1914, 43.

23. "New Haven Asks, What is a Bicycle?," 43

24. "New Jersey's New Bicycle Law," *Bicycling News*, July 1915, 7.

25. Seiler, *Republic of Drivers*, 46.

26. Foster Rhea Dulles, *The United States since 1865* (Ann Arbor: Univ. of Michigan Press, 1969), 203.

27. Quoted in Dulles, *The United States since 1865*, 213.

28. "Some Figures on the Cycle Trade," *Motorcycling*, October 26, 1914, 8. US manufacturers had enjoyed a high protective tariff for a number of years but progressive calls for a lower tariff, in support of farmers, brought about the Payne-Aldrich Tariff under President Taft in 1909 but it was a tariff of compromise that did little other than split the Republican Party. The Underwood-Simmons Tariff of 1913, enacted under President Woodrow Wilson, finally reduced the duties, which is the reason bicycle and motorcycle duties dropped from 45 percent to 25 percent.

29. Harold Underwood Faulkner, *American Economic History* (New York: Harper & Row, 1960), 583.

30. Cover of *Motorcycling*, October 26, 1914.

31. "Record Foreign Trade," *MotorCycling and Bicycling*, August 16, 1915), 1.

32. "Record Foreign Trade," 2.

33. William E. Leuchtenburg, *The Perils of Prosperity, 1914–32* (Chicago: Univ. of Chicago Press, 1958), 16. Leuchtenburg writes, "The outbreak of war in Europe at first produced a serious economic recession in the country, but by the spring of 1915 Allied war orders were stoking American industry and opening up new markets for farm products."

34. Leuchtenburg, *The Perils of Prosperity*, 16.

35. "Good Steady Wages Mean More Sales," *MotorCycling and Bicycling*, August 23, 1915, 12.

36. "Good Steady Wages Mean More Sales," 12.

37. David M. Kennedy, *Over Here: The First World War and American Society* (New York: Oxford Univ. Press, 1980), 55.

38. Herbert Hoover, testimony before Senate Committee on Agriculture, June 19, 1917; quoted in Kennedy, *Over Here*, 118.

39. Kennedy, *Over Here*, 118.

40. Dulles, *The United States since 1865*, 261.

41. L. Stanton Pugh, "Ride a Bicycle and Do Your Bit," *MotorCycling and Bicycling*, July 30, 1917, 37.

42. Pugh, "Ride a Bicycle and Do Your Bit," 37.

43. Pugh, 37.

44. "A Cycle Sign of the Times, Society Women 'Hooverize' by Going Back to the Bicycle," *MotorCycling and Bicycling*, October 22, 1917, 24–25. *Hooverize* (meaning to make sacrifices for the war effort) was a popular expression at the time because of Herbert Hoover's actions as head of the US Food Administration.

45. "A Cycle Sign of the Times," 25.

46. Historian James Longhurst comes to a similar conclusion independently. See Longhurst, *Bike Battles*, 150.

47. "New Departure Expands," *MotorCycling and Bicycling*, August 16, 1915, 2.

48. "New Departure Expands," 2.

49. "Efficiency of the Bicycle Police," *Bicycle News*, October 1915, 27; "Rid Staten Island of Criminal Class," *New York Times*, August 26, 1915, 5.

50. "Efficiency of the Bicycle Police," 27.

51. "Rid Staten Island of Criminal Class," 5.

52. A picture of the Salt Lake City police force and their Pierce bicycles is included in *MotorCycling and Bicycling*, July 23, 1917, 23.

53. "True to His Old Love," *MotorCycling and Bicycling*, July 26, 1915, 49.

54. Frank A. Eagan, "From the Inside Looking Out," *Bicycle News*, October 1915, 25.

55. "Motorcycles on RFD Prove Profitable," *Bicycling World and Motorcycle Review*, October 21, 1911, 199.

56. "Motorcycles on RFD Prove Profitable," 199.

57. Eagan, "From the Inside Looking Out," 25.

58. "Fight for R.F.D. Business," *MotorCycling and Bicycling*, August 2, 1915, 1.

59. "Fight for R.F.D. Business," 2.

60. "Fight for R.F.D. Business," 1.

61. "Fight for R.F.D. Business," 1.

62. A. E. Lonn, "Bicycle Usefulness in Business," *MotorCycling and Bicycling*, December 8, 1917, 28.

63. These ads appear in nearly every issue of *MotorCycling and Bicycling* in 1917.

64. Herlihy, *Bicycle*, 258. Pope donated forty bicycles to the Connecticut National Guard in 1891 to prove their practicality. The First Signal Corps "confirmed that bicycles 'could bring reinforcements into the field quickly and silently' and convey messages when 'signaling or other means of communications are impractical.'"

65. "Pope Gets Contract for 10,000 War Bikes," *MotorCycling and Bicycling*, October 29, 1917, 14.

66. Schwinn Bicycle Company, "U.S. Bicycle Market Statistics." Total sales in 1917 were 606,918.

67. "U.S. to Buy 100,000 Bicycles for War," *MotorCycling and Bicycling*, November 5, 1917, 10.

68. Sears & Roebuck Company, *Catalog no. 134* (Chicago: Sears & Roebuck Company, 1917), 954. The $360 price for a Model T is based on prices listed in McShane, *Down the Asphalt Path*, 135.

69. Gregory J. Downey, *Telegraph Messenger Boys: Labor, Technology, and Geography, 1850–1950* (New York: Routledge, 2002), 106.

70. Downey, *Telegraph Messenger Boys*, 76–77.

3. Cooperation and Confusion

1. "Twixt Nigger and the Devil," *Motorcycling*, October 26, 1914, 8. Black cyclists are a topic that demands more scholarly attention.

2. Leuchtenburg, *The Perils of Prosperity*, 159.

3. "Big Opportunity for the Bicycle Dealers," *MotorCycling and Bicycling*, August 2, 1915, 32.

4. "Big Opportunity for the Bicycle Dealers," 32.

5. "Big Opportunity for the Bicycle Dealers," 32.

6. "Society Women Ride Bicycles and Form a Club," *MotorCycling and Bicycling*, November 15, 1915, 45.

7. "Big Opportunity for the Bicycle Dealers," *MotorCycling and Bicycling*, 32. *Live Dealers* was a term for dealers who actively tried to boost sales, as opposed to those who were "dead," or inactive.

8. Elizabeth Skelding Moore, "Why College Girls Ride Bicycles," *MotorCycling and Bicycling*, November 5, 1917, 33.

9. Moore, "Why College Girls Ride Bicycles," 33.

10. McShane, *Down the Asphalt Path*, 135. The Model T was $850 in 1908 but $260 in 1921. John Bell Rae, *American Automotive Manufacturers: The First Forty Years* (Philadelphia: Chilton Company Publishing, 1959), 108. A Ford touring car was less than $400 in 1916. Meanwhile, a new bicycle was less than $20.

11. "Directors' Report Traces Growth of Big Idea," *Motorcycle and Bicycle Illustrated*, August 9, 1917, 21.

12. "Bicycle Dealers Organize," *MotorCycling and Bicycling*, December 27, 1915, 45.

13. "Remarkable Bicycle Booster Aids," *MotorCycling and Bicycling*, September 27, 1915. 48.

14. "The Power behind New Departure Sales," *Motorcycle Illustrated*, February 10, 1916, 27.

15. "Remarkable Bicycle Booster Aids," 48.

16. "Remarkable Bicycle Booster Aids," 48.

17. New Departure, "The New Departure Coaster Brake Company," *MotorCycling and Bicycling*, September 13, 1915, 39.

18. *Pittsburgh Press*, March 4, 1928, 83; United Cycle Trade Directorate *Report, 1916–17*, 17; "$40,000 for 1913 New Goodyear Slogan," *San Francisco Call*, February 16, 1913, 39.

19. Goodyear Tire and Rubber Company, "1,000,000 Bicycles for 1916, It CAN Be Done," *MotorCycling and Bicycling*, November 15, 1915, 48.

20. Goodyear Tire and Rubber Company, "1,000,000 Bicycles for 1916," 48.

21. Goodyear Tire and Rubber Company, "Free to All Stores That Sell Bicycle Tires," *Motorcycling*, January 11, 1915, 81.

22. Goodyear Tire and Rubber Company, "Free to All Stores That Sell Bicycle Tires," 81.

23. Goodyear Tire and Rubber Company, 81.

24. United Cycle Trade Directorate, *Report, 1916–17*, 23. There were more parts manufacturers listed than bicycle manufacturers, however, and the donations per bicycle manufacture is not listed. It is for parts manufacturers.

25. Frank W. Schwinn to Mr. Bond, November 20, 1948, Interoffice notes to advertising department from Frank W. Schwinn, April 1943–December 1948, Bicycle Museum of American, New Bremen, Ohio. Schwinn told an executive that if New Departure and the Diamond Chain Company were eliminated the entire industry would

be brought to a standstill. Bruce Epperson, a transportation planner and attorney who has written extensively about the bicycle industry, also argues that parts manufacturers had a majority share of control over the industry. Bruce Epperson, conversation with the author, Paris, France, May 27, 2011.

26. Pope Manufacturing Company, *Cleveland Bicycle Catalog*, 1909, 2. Located in the Bicycle Museum of America, New Bremen, Ohio. The catalog stressed the words *made* and *assembled* by printing them in bold.

27. United Cycle Trade Directorate, *Report, 1916–17*.

28. "Goodyear Bicycle Boosting," *MotorCycling and Bicycling*, December 6, 1915, 39.

29. United Cycle Trade Directorate, *Report, 1916–17*, 1.

30. United Cycle Trade Directorate, 25. The dollar amount was $20,162.29 spent on window displays out of a total budget of $36,844.95.

31. United Cycle Trade Directorate, 2.

32. United Cycle Trade Directorate, 19.

33. United Cycle Trade Directorate, 30.

34. "Bicycle Drive Aims to Create New Users," *Printers' Ink*, April 11, 1918, 82.

35. "Bicycle Drive Aims to Create New Users," 81.

36. "Bicycle Drive Aims to Create New Users," 81.

37. Burr, "Markets as Producers and Consumers," 240. Burr documents the steep drop in prices after the bicycle boom occurred. In 1895 the Pope Manufacturing Company lowered the price of their Columbia bicycles from $125, $150, and $160 for the racing model to a base price of $100 for all models. Prices in the Sears catalog fell from $55.95 to $48.90. After the bicycle boom, however, prices fell much more drastically. In 1899 the Pope Manufacturing Company's most expensive model was $75 and Sears offered bicycles for $13.95. The falling prices brought record sales but the bottom soon dropped out.

38. Quoted in Herlihy, *Bicycle*, 377, 347.

39. T. J. Sullivan, "Atlanta Bicycle Business Prosperous," *MotorCycling and Bicycling*, February 19, 1917, 17. The choice of boll weevil was a contemporary comment on noncooperating dealers' destruction to the bicycle business comparing them to the boll weevil's destruction of agricultural profits.

40. Sullivan, "Atlanta Bicycle Business Prosperous," 17.

41. "Getting Ready for the Starter's Pistol Shot," *Bicycle News*, March 1917, 8. According to *Bicycle News*, the article was taken "From the Racing Number of the 'Million Bicycles' Bulletin for February."

42. "Getting Ready for the Starter's Pistol Shot," 8.

43. "Getting Ready for the Starter's Pistol Shot," 8.

44. W. F. Emerson, "Make Every Day in the Year Bicycle Day," *Bicycle News*, March 1917, 9. This was part of the push to sell one million bicycles. W. F. Emerson was president of the Buffalo Metal Goods Company.

45. Emerson, "Make Every Day in the Year Bicycle Day," 9.

46. Burr, "Markets as Producers and Consumers," 408. Burr provides a graph of the number of bicycle shops per one hundred thousand people from 1895 to 1910 in Denver, Providence, Baltimore, and St. Louis. The trend in all cities is a steady rise from 1895 with a peak in either 1897 or 1898 and then a general decline.

47. Emerson, "Make Every Day in the Year Bicycle Day," 9.

48. Charles Fuller Gates, "Merchandising for the Bicycle Dealer," *MotorCycling and Bicycling*, April 23, 1917, 86.

49. Gates, "Merchandising for the Bicycle Dealer," 86.

50. Gates, 86.

51. "Picture of A. W. Nourse in his store at Lansing, Michigan," *MotorCycling and Bicycling*, September 13, 1915, 55. Nourse had reportedly sold about one hundred bicycles that season and was doing so well that he was going to stop selling firearms and focus all of his attention on bicycles.

52. Buffalo Metal Goods Company, "Messages That Sell Bicycles," *MotorCycling and Bicycling*, April 23, 1917, 57.

53. Buffalo Metal Goods Company, "Messages That Sell Bicycles," 57.

54. "Selling No. 5 Shoes for No. 10 Feet," *MotorCycling and Bicycling*, September 17, 1917, 34.

55. "Selling No. 5 Shoes for No. 10 Feet," 34.

56. "Selling No. 5 Shoes for No. 10 Feet," 34. Bicycle gears are measured by number of teeth. The largest chain ring that comes standard on today's bicycles is a fifty-three. Professional riders would not even consider a ninety-six unless they were going to go for a record on a flat surface while being moto-paced, like Alfred Letourneur's record of 108 mph in 1941.

57. W. T. Farwell "Importance of Gearing to the Trade," *MotorCycling and Bicycling*, October 8, 1917, 45.

58. Farwell, "Importance of Gearing to the Trade," 45.

59. Farwell, 45. Farwell was also a contributor to *Scribner's* and *Outing* before joining the Directorate.

60. *Report of the United Cycle Trade Directorate*, August 1917, 13, https://archive.org/stream/annualreport1916cycl/annualreport1916cycl_djvu.txt.

61. Selling No. 5 Shoes for No. 10 Feet," 34.

62. "Getting after the 'Inside Man,'" *MotorCycling and Bicycling*, December 27, 1915, 21.

63. Bicycles, however, consistently outsold motorcycles and did not appear to be as adversely effected by motorcycles as they were by automobiles. Ranging from around $175 to $200, there were 125,000 registered motorcycles in 1910, 175,000 in 1911, and the "high-water mark" of domestic production during the era occurred in 1913 with 71,000 units sold. See Harry V. Sucher, *Inside American Motorcycling and*

the American Motorcycle Association, 1900–1990 (Laguna Niguel, CA: Infosport, 1995), 20–30.

64. Charles Fuller Gates, "Live Wire Ways to Get After Prospects," *MotorCycling and Bicycling*, February 5, 1917, 25.

65. Gates, "Live Wire Ways to Get After Prospects," 25.

66. They reappeared in such volumes that by 1921 T. J. Sullivan would ask, "Shall Germans or Americans Make Our Bicycles?" *MotorCycling and Bicycling*, February 2, 1921, 8.

4. The Child Consumer

1. Arnold, Schwinn & Company, *Fifty Years of Schwinn-Built Bicycles: The Story of the Bicycle and Its Contributions to Our Way of Life, 1895–1945* (Chicago: Arnold, Schwinn & Company, 1945), 55.

2. Richard Wightman Fox and T. J. Jackson Lears, eds., *The Culture of Consumption: Critical Essays in American History, 1880–1980* (New York: Pantheon Books, 1983), x.

3. Steven Mintz, *Huck's Raft: A History of American Childhood* (Cambridge, MA: Belknap Press, 2004), 217.

4. Paul B. Ringel, *Commercializing Childhood: Children's Magazines, Urban Gentility, and the Ideal of the Child Consumer in the United States, 1823–1918* (Amherst: Univ. of Massachusetts Press, 2015), 4; Daniel Thomas Cook, *The Commodification of Childhood: The Children's Clothing Industry and the Rise of the Child Consumer* (Durham, NC: Duke Univ. Press, 2004), 78. Daniel Cook seems to agree, writing, "From about 1915 onward, merchants realized that treating children as individuals with identifiable desires and concerns of their own could increase business."

5. Lisa Jacobson, *Raising Consumers: Children and the American Mass Market in the Early Twentieth Century* (New York: Columbia Univ. Press, 2004), 16–17.

6. Jacobson, *Raising Consumers*, 28.

7. Jacobson, 105.

8. Jacobson, 123.

9. See Benedict Anderson, *Imagined Communities: Reflections on the Origin and Spread of Nationalism* (London: Verso, 1991); E. J. Hobsbawm, *Nations and Nationalism since 1780: Programme, Myth, Reality* (Cambridge: Cambridge Univ. Press, 1990.

10. Charles McGovern, *Sold American: Consumption and Citizenship, 1890–1945* (Chapel Hill: Univ. of North Carolina Press, 2006), 9.

11. Roland Marchand, *Advertising the American Dream: Making Way for Modernity, 1920–1940* (Berkeley: Univ. of California Press, 1985), xxi.

12. T. J. Sullivan, "'Get After the Boy' Says Farrell," *MotorCycling and Bicycling*, September 3, 1917, 35.

13. David M. Kennedy, *Over Here: The First World War and American Society* (New York: Oxford Univ. Press, 1980), 53. Kennedy devotes an entire chapter to "The War

for the American Mind," showing how President Wilson and conservative organizations "mantled their activities in the raiment of patriotism." The war for the American mind even infiltrated the nation's public schools.

14. Ringel, *Commercializing Childhood*, 151.

15. Sullivan, "'Get After the Boy,'" 35. Children's velocipedes are commonly referred to as tricycles today.

16. In 1909 there were just over 300,000 cars registered in the United States; by 1918 that number surpassed 5.5 million. See table 4.

17. Tim Cresswell, *On the Move: Mobility in the Modern Western World* (New York: Routledge, 2006), 196–97. Cotten Seiler argues that the car was somewhat effete at first but "as automobility 'trickled down' to the lower classes . . . it would necessarily be accorded a more masculine character." Cotten Seiler, *Republic of Drivers: A Cultural History of Automobility in America* (Chicago: Univ. of Chicago Press, 2008), 54.

18. Hendee Manufacturing Company, "Are You Ready," *MotorCycling and Bicycling*, November 26, 1917, 30.

19. "Christmas Business for Cycle Dealers," *MotorCycling and Bicycling*, December 6, 1915, 17.

20. New Departure Manufacturing Company, "A Bicycle for Christmas: Can You Beat It?" *MotorCycling and Bicycling*, December 20, 1915, 51.

21. Both the editor and publisher of *MotorCycling and Bicycling* were members of these organizations.

22. "Extensive Bicycle Advertising Campaign," *MotorCycling and Bicycling*, October 1, 1919, 51. The Davis Sewing Machine Company also manufactured bicycles.

23. Hendee Manufacturing Company, *Popular Mechanics*, December 1917, 113.

24. Extensive Bicycle Advertising Campaign," *MotorCycling and Bicycling*, October 1, 1919, 51.

25. United States Tires, *Popular Mechanics*, December 1917, 116.

26. Extensive Bicycle Advertising Campaign," 51.

27. "The Christmas Bicycle Sales Campaign," *MotorCycling and Bicycling*, October 29, 1917, 22.

28. "Christmas Business for Cycle Dealers," 16.

29. "Christmas Business for Cycle Dealers," 17.

30. Tee Bee, "Creating Desire for Bikes in the Young," *MotorCycling and Bicycling*, December 29, 1917, 33.

31. Bee, "Creating Desire for Bikes in the Young," 33.

32. Bee, 33.

33. Ira A. Alexander, "How One Dealer Got Cycle Prospects," *MotorCycling and Bicycling*, December 29, 1917, 17.

34. Jacobson, *Raising Consumers*, 93.

35. "Selling Cycles by Interesting the Boys," *MotorCycling and Bicycling*, September 24, 1917, 29. Dues were a convenient way for clubs to exclude undesirable classes.

36. "Twixt Nigger and the Devil," *Motorcycling*, October 26, 1914, 8.

37. "Selling Cycles by Interesting the Boys," 29.

38. "Selling Cycles by Interesting the Boys," 29.

39. "Selling Cycles by Interesting the Boys," 29.

40. "Work Ahead for Motorcyclists!" *Motorcycling Illustrated*, January 18, 1917, 7. T. J. Sullivan was a member of the Motorcycle and Allied Trades Association, which aligned itself with the Directorate, and then the CTA, a larger umbrella organization intent on selling bicycles.

41. T. J. Sullivan, "How Emerson Gets the Boys and Keeps 'Em," *MotorCycling and Bicycling*, September 3, 1917, 35.

42. Sullivan, "How Emerson Gets the Boys and Keeps 'Em," 35.

43. "Bicycle News: Going after the Bicycle Business," *Motorcycle and Bicycle Illustrated*, February 10, 1921, 35.

44. "Bicycle News," 35.

45. Harley Davidson Motor Company, *Boys' Life*, April 1918, 55.

46. Westfield Manufacturing Company, *Boys' Life*, April 1917, 39.

47. "Christmas Business for Cycle Dealers," 17.

48. Martin A. Delaney, "Boys' Clubs Can Spend Vacation Best on Bicycles," *MotorCycling and Bicycling*, July 16, 1917, 35.

49. Delaney, "Boys' Clubs Can Spend Vacation Best on Bicycles," 35. Crouching over the bars was a reference to racing posture and therefore associated with extreme physical exertion.

50. Blackwood and Sons, "Modern Mannish Maidens," 255. For a discussion of women's position on bicycles see Ellen Gruber Garvey, "Reframing the Bicycle: Advertising-Supported Magazines and Scorching Women," *American Quarterly* 47, no. 1 (March 1995): 75.

51. "A Just-Before-Christmas Letter from Santa Claus," *MotorCycling (Including the Bicycling World)*, December 9, 1925, 39.

52. Haverford Cycle Company, *Black Beauty Bicycles: All that the Name Implies*, Catalog, 1920, 8.

53. New Departure Manufacturing Company, "The Boys behind the Army," *Boys' Life*, April 1918, 49.

54. New Departure, "The Boys behind the Army," 33.

55. J. F. Richter Jr., "Uncle Sam's Endorsement in Advertising Copy," *Printers' Ink*, May 3, 1923, 8–12. Quoted in Charles McGovern, *Sold American: Consumption and Citizenship, 1890–1945* (Chapel Hill: Univ. of North Carolina Press, 2006), 112.

56. McGovern, *Sold American*, 112.

57. U.S. Rubber Company, "One Boy in 1918 Is Worth 3 Boys of 1914," *Boys' Life*, April 1918, 50.

58. B. F. Goodrich Rubber Company, "A Boy's War Book," *Boys' Life*, July 1918, 49.

59. "How the Boy Scouts Help in the War," *Boys' Life*, June 1917, 7.

60. "Getting after the Boy Scout Business," *MotorCycling and Bicycling*, July 9, 1917, 29.

61. "Getting after the Boy Scout Business," 29.

62. Cynthia H. Enloe, "Was It 'The Good War' for Women?" *American Quarterly* 37 no. 4 (Autumn 1985): 629; Phil Goodman, "'Patriotic Femininity': Women's Morals and Men's Morale during the Second World War," *Gender and History* 10 no. 2 (August 1998): 278–79.

63. Bill Brown, *The Material Unconscious: American Amusement, Stephen Crane, and the Economics of Play* (Cambridge, MA: Harvard Univ. Press, 1996), 177.

64. "How the Boy Scouts Help in the War," 7.

65. "Getting after the Boy Scout Business," 29.

66. "Getting after the Boy Scout Business," 30.

67. "Getting after the Boy Scout Business," 30.

68. "Boy Scouts Bikers Prepare for War," *MotorCycling and Bicycling*, December 22, 1917, 45. Of course, there was also the fact that the US government had ordered the production of one hundred thousand bicycles to assist in the war effort.

5. The Postwar Slump

1. Schwinn Bicycle Company, "U.S. Bicycle Market Statistics–1895 to 1979," *Schwinn Reporter*, March 1980.

2. Schwinn Bicycle Company, "U.S. Bicycle Market Statistics."

3. Schwinn Bicycle Company.

4. "Get Business," *Motorcycle & Bicycle Illustrated*, July 16, 1919, 41.

5. "The Cycle Trades under One Big Tent," *Motorcycle & Bicycle Illustrated*, August 13, 1919, 9.

6. "The Cycle Trades under One Big Tent," 9.

7. "The Cycle Trades under One Big Tent," 14.

8. "The Cycle Trades under One Big Tent," 9.

9. "The Cycle Trades under One Big Tent," 9.

10. "The Cycle Trades under One Big Tent," 15.

11. "Bicycles in Industrial Transportation," *MotorCycling and Bicycling* August 6, 1919, 33.

12. "Bicycles in Industrial Transportation," 33.

13. "Bicycles in Industrial Transportation," 33.

14. "Bicycles in Industrial Transportation," 34.

15. "Bicycles in Industrial Transportation," 33. The cars the author is talking about are mostly likely street cars since he or she also talks about cars being crowded.

16. *Printers' Ink*, February 19, 1920, 26. Reproduced in Herlihy, *Bicycle*, 324. *Printers' Ink* was a trade journal for the advertising industry that often included examples of noteworthy or exemplary advertisements.

17. *Printers' Ink*, 26.

18. Pope Manufacturing Company, "Without Car Fare," *Scientific American*, October 8, 1892, 238.

19. Herlihy, *Bicycle*, 325.

20. "How the Boy Market Stacks Up for Size," *Motorcycle and Bicycle Illustrated*, February 17, 1921, 24; E. Evalyn Grumbine McNally, *Reaching Juvenile Markets: How to Advertise, Sell, and Merchandise Through Boys and Girls* (New York: McGraw-Hill, 1938), 116. McNally felt the belief that juvenile consumers could be controlled was rampant among merchants and needed to be corrected.

21. Schwinn Bicycle Company, "U.S. Bicycle Market Statistics."

22. A. B. Coffman, "Why 1921 Will Be a Good Bicycle Year," *MotorCycling and Bicycling*, January 5, 1921, 11.

23. Edward Arnhem, "More Bicycle Sales in 1921 than in 1920," *MotorCycling and Bicycling*, January 5, 1921, 10.

24. Arnhem, "More Bicycle Sales in 1921 than in 1920," 10.

25. Sam Fetter, "Present Conditions the Acid Test of Business," *MotorCycling and Bicycling*, January 5, 1921, 11.

26. Barry W. Poulson, *Economic History of the United States* (New York: Macmillan, 1981), 599–600; W. Elliot Brownlee, *Dynamics of Ascent: A History of the American Economy* (Chicago: Dorsey Press, 1988), 297–98.

27. Faulkner, *American Economic History*, 583–85.

28. Leuchtenburg, *The Perils of Prosperity*, 17. See also Brownlee, *Dynamics of Ascent*, 367–69.

29. Faulkner, *American Economic History*, 583; Leuchtenburg, *The Perils of Prosperity*, 17.

30. Brownlee, *Dynamics of Ascent*, 378; table 5 is based on Faulkner, *American Economic History*, 585.

31. Mead Cycle Company, *Popular Mechanics*, April 1914, 158; Mead Cycle Company, *Popular Mechanics*, April 1917, 193.

32. Sam Fetter, "Present Conditions the Acid Test of Business," *MotorCycling and Bicycling*, January 5, 1921, 11.

33. Hugh H. C. Weed, "The Thing to do Now is Fight," *MotorCycling and Bicycling*, January 5, 1921, 13. The number of automobiles registered in 1919 was 6,679,000, in 1920 it was 8,132,000, and by 1921 it was 9,212,000. It grew each year but the increase from 1920 to 1921 was less than increases from 1919 to 1920 or even 1921 to 1922,

when the number of cars registered reached 10,704,000. US Census Bureau, *Statistical Abstract of the United States: 2003*, 77.

34. Weed, "The Thing to do Now is Fight," 13.

35. Weed, 13.

36. A. H. Bartsch, "1921 Marks the Biggest Battle of Brains Industry Has Ever Known," *MotorCycling and Bicycling*, January 5, 1921, 12.

37. Bartsch, "1921 Marks the Biggest Battle of Brains," 12.

38. Bartsch, 12.

39. Irving Beck, "Plenty of Money Left, Cycle Dealers Can Get Their Share," *MotorCycling and Bicycling*, January 5, 1921, 13.

40. Beck, "Plenty of Money Left," 13.

41. *Historical Statistics of the United States: Colonial Times to 1970* (Washington, DC: US Department of Commerce, Bureau of the Census, 1975), 126.

42. A. E. McGavin, "1921, The Best Season for the R-S," *MotorCycling and Bicycling*, January 5, 1921, 10.

43. Brownlee, *Dynamics of Ascent*, 380.

44. McGavin, "1921, The Best Season for the R-S," 10.

45. McGavin, 10.

46. McGavin, 10.

47. Burr, "Markets as Producers and Consumers," 280–82.

48. Schwinn Bicycle Company, "U.S. Bicycle Market Statistics."

49. W. D. Callender, "Buy it Now," *MotorCycling and Bicycling*, February 2, 1921, 3–7.

50. Callender, "Buy it Now," 3–7.

51. Callender, 3–7.

52. Callender, 3–7.

53. James Longhurst comes to a similar conclusion saying the bicycle industry and Boy Scouts of America worked in "lockstep." He points out that the cyclist merit badge pamphlet was created by two members of the CTA—C. F. Olin and W. T. Farwell. See Longhurst, *Bike Battles*, 115–16.

54. Woody Register, *The Kid of Coney Island: Fred Thompson and the Rise of American Amusements* (New York: Oxford Univ. Press, 2001), 15. Quoted in Jacobson, *Raising Consumers*, 13.

55. Charles E. Pratt, *The American Bicycler: A Manual for the Observer, the Learner, and the Expert* (Boston: Houghton, Osgood and Company, 1879), 30–32. Pratt proclaimed, "As a sport, bicycling is manly, innocent, humane and rational." He defined the bicycle's manly virtues as its ability to develop "the training of eye and ear, the alertness and suppleness of limb and joint and muscle, the quick observation, the prompt decision in emergency, the strength and courage and self-reliance."

56. Cycle Trades of America, *Sixth Annual Year Book 1924–25* (New York: Peter J. Carey and Sons, 1925), 11.

57. "Does Your Boy Have This Opportunity?" *Motorcycle and Bicycle Illustrated*, February 24, 1921, 31.

58. Girl Scouts, http://girlscouts.org/who_we_are/history/timeline/1912_1919.asp.

59. "Does Your Boy Have This Opportunity?" 31.

60. "Bicycle News: Once Again—The Bicycle," *Motorcycle and Bicycle Illustrated*, February 17, 1921, 25.

61. "Bicycle News: Going After the Bicycle Business," 36.

62. "It's the Boy Who Creates the Demand of Bicycles!" *Motorcycle and Bicycle Illustrated*, June 2, 1921, 40.

63. "Doubly Effective," *Printers' Ink*, October 14, 1920, 15.

64. "Doubly Effective," 15.

65. "How the Boy Market Stacks Up for Size," *Motorcycle and Bicycle Illustrated*, 24.

66. "How the Boy Market Stacks Up for Size," 24.

67. The idea that children were passive consumers who were easily convinced by marketing tactics was pervasive among advertisers at the time, but by the 1930s they would prove to be somewhat sophisticated consumers. See McNally, *Reaching Juvenile Markets*, 116. By 1938, McNally was cautioning advertisers "to be mindful of children's consumer savvy." Quoted in Jacobson, *Raising Consumers*, 203. See also 184. She makes a correction to the "conventional histories of children's marketing," which have perpetuated the assumption that children were gullible and obedient consumers who were exploited by advertisers. As she shows, advertisers soon found that children were not as pliant as they hoped.

68. "The Biggest Share of the Pie," *Motorcycle and Bicycle Illustrated*, March 10, 1921, 30.

69. "The Biggest Share of the Pie," 30.

70. *MotorCycling and Bicycling*, January 19, 1921, 31.

71. C. B. T. Hamilton, "Landing the Business," *MotorCycling and Bicycling*, February 9, 1921, 35.

72. Hamilton, "Landing the Business," 35.

73. "First for Sales!" *Motorcycle and Bicycle Illustrated*, April 7, 1921, 68.

74. "First for Sales!" 68.

75. Cycle Trades of America, *Sixth Annual Year Book 1924–25*, 14.

76. Cycle Trades of America, 14.

77. New Departure Manufacturing Company, *Boys' Life*, May 1922, 45.

78. Cycle Trades of America, *Sixth Annual Year Book 1924–25*, 15.

79. Cycle Trades of America, 14.

80. Cycle Trades of America, 12.

81. Mead Cycle Company, *Popular Mechanics*, November 1922, 145.

82. Rex McConnell, "Christmas Trade Booms in Akron," *Motorcycling (Including the Bicycling World)*, December 19, 1928, 26.

83. McConnell, "Christmas Trade Booms in Akron," 26.

84. "A Just-Before-Christmas Letter from Santa Claus," *Motorcycling (Including the Bicycling World)*, December 9, 1925, 39. Dealers were told to try a similar letter on their customers for Christmas trade.

85. Dan Beard, "Hiking and Camping with a Bike," *Boys' Life*, May 1922, 26; W. C. Wessel, "Bike Hiking," *Boys' Life*, May 1922, 27.

86. David Q. Hammond, "The Blue Byke," *St. Nicholas*, July 1921, 712–17.

87. G. G. Livermore, "Snooper Smith, Detective," *Boys' Life*, May 1922, 16.

88. William S. Biscoe, "A Happy Incident," *St. Nicholas*, July 1921, 859.

89. Louise Corcoran, "My Happiest Memory (A True Story)," *St. Nicholas*, May 1920, 666.

90. National Recovery Administration, "Code of Fair Competition for the Bicycle Manufacturing Industry," Approved Code no. 437, Registry no. 1407-1-02, Approved on May 21, 1934, 288.

91. National Recovery Administration, "Code of Fair Competition," 289.

6. The Safety of Cycling

1. Herlihy, *Bicycle*, 325–27.

2. Steven A. Riess, *City Games: The Evolution of American Urban Society and the Rise of Sports* (Urbana: Univ. of Illinois Press, 1989), 65.

3. Riess, *City Games*, 65; Sidney H. Aronson, "The Sociology of the Bicycle," *Social Forces* 30, no. 3 (March 1952): 312. Aronson writes, "Of course, the automobile, for the most part, displaced the bicycle as a means of transportation, but made full use of the institutions which accompanied the two-wheeled vehicle. See also Richard Harmond, "Progress and Flight: An Interpretation of the American Cycle Craze of the 1890s," *Journal of Social History* 5, no. 2 (Winter 1971–72): 251. Harmond argues, "The bicycle, as inventor Hiram P. Maxim pointed out, created a demand which it could no longer satisfy. 'A mechanically propelled vehicle was wanted instead of a foot-propelled one,' he wrote, 'and we now know that the automobile was the answer.' In this, as in so many other respects, the bicycle had prepared the way for the automobile."

4. Norton, *Fighting Traffic*, 22.

5. National Recovery Administration, "Code of Fair Competition for the Bicycle Manufacturing Industry," 288.

6. John Urry, "The System of Automobility," *Theory, Culture & Society* 21, no. 4/5 (2016): 30; Norton, *Fighting Traffic*, 1–18. Norton's introduction does an excellent job explaining this transformation, which he calls the social reconstruction of the city street.

7. Wells, *Car Country*, 9.

8. Herlihy, *Bicycle*, 328.

9. Burr, "Markets As Producers and Consumers," 298.

10. "A Generation Discovers the Bike," *New York Times*, October 18, 1925.

11. "Foresees Revival of Bicycle Vogue," *New York Times*, September 14, 1922.

12. "Bicycle Makers Cut 40% off Retail Price," *New York Times*, September 15, 1922.

13. Burr, "Markets as Producers and Consumers," 315. Burr gives much of the credit to the automobile suggesting that it "led to the development of two very different markets at the end of the decade. The two national elites exited the market, and working-class riders entered the market in large numbers, but the middle classes in each country took very different paths, and since the markets were, at this time, predominantly middle-class, this led to different markets."

14. Burr, 338.

15. Herlihy, *Bicycle*, 325.

16. Hans Ohrt, "Optimism anent American Bicycles: What Remains to Be Done," *Motorcycling (Including the Bicycling World)*, November 11, 1925, 16.

17. Kenneth T. Jackson, *Crabgrass Frontier: The Suburbanization of America* (New York: Oxford Univ. Press, 1985), 163. According to table 9, in 1920 the United States led with one passenger vehicle for every 13 inhabitants, while it was one for every 228 in the United Kingdom and one for every 247 in France. In 1930 there was one car for every 5 inhabitants in the United States, one for every 42 in the United Kingdom, and one for every 37 in France.

18. Ohrt, "Optimism anent American Bicycles," 16.

19. Ohrt, 16.

20. "Bicycles Big Transportation Factor in Germany," *Motorcycling (Including the Bicycling World)*, March 14, 1928, 29.

21. "Bicycles Big Transportation Factor in Germany," 29.

22. "Bicycles Big Transportation Factor in Germany," 29. For much more detail on the struggle for separate paths and wheelways for cyclists see Robert L. McCullough, *Old Wheelways: Traces of Bicycle History on the Land* (Cambridge, MA: MIT Press, 2015).

23. Schwinn Bicycle Company, "U.S. Bicycle Market Statistics—1895 to 1979," *Schwinn Reporter*, March 1980. The only outlier to this trend was 1923, when consumption was estimated at 525,000. This is based on census data for "apparent consumption," which is the number of bicycles produced in the United States per year plus imports minus exports. The 1929 stock market crash had a relatively small effect on sales in the years to follow, during the Great Depression.

24. "Dealers Tell What Ails Bicycle," *Motorcycling (Including the Bicycling World)*, July 22, 1925, 40.

25. "Dealers Tell What Ails Bicycle," 40.

26. "Dealers Tell What Ails Bicycle," 40.

27. "Dealers Tell What Ails Bicycle," 40.

28. "Dealers Tell What Ails Bicycle," 40.

29. W. T. Farwell Jr., "Well, Why Don't They?" *Motorcycling (Including the Bicycling World)*, October 24, 1928, 27.

30. Farwell, "Well, Why Don't They?" 27.

31. See William H. Beezley, *Judas at the Jockey Club and Other Episodes of Porfirian Mexico* (Lincoln: Univ. of Nebraska Press, 1987) 45–49 and 125–29. See also Glen Norcliffe, *The Ride to Modernity: The Bicycle in Canada, 1869–1900* (Toronto: Univ. of Toronto Press, 2001).

32. Cycle Trades of America, *Cycle-Logical Ways to Happier Days* (New York: New Departure Press, 1930), 7.

33. Farwell, "Well, Why Don't They?" 27.

34. Chrysler Motor Corporation, "The Chrysler Six Gives Results Never Before Achieved," *Saturday Evening Post*, April 5, 1924, 43.

35. Robert Smith, *A Social History of the Bicycle* (New York: American Heritage Press, 1972), 247. Smith does not include the number of bicycle accidents and fatalities for previous years. He simply says the number "climbed."

36. "Decline of Cycling Here," *New York Times*, May 8, 1928.

37. "6-Day Race Drew More Than $200,000," *New York Times*, December 9, 1924.

38. L. Viajero, "Stepping Out and Doing Things to Boost Business," *Motorcycling (Including the Bicycling World)*, June 20, 1928, 30.

39. Viajero, "Stepping Out and Doing Things to Boost Business," 30.

40. Viajero, 30.

41. Viajero, 30.

42. T. J. Sullivan, "Bicycle Safety for Children," *Motorcycling (Including the Bicycling World)*, April 29, 1925, 33.

43. Sullivan, "Bicycle Safety for Children," 33.

44. Sullivan, 33.

45. Norton, *Fighting Traffic*, 22, 24.

46. "Bicycles Take Kids off the Streets," *Motorcycling (Including the Bicycling World)*, May 27, 1925, 35.

47. "Bicycles Take Kids off the Streets," 35.

48. T. J. Sullivan, "Save Children by Buying Them Bikes," *Motorcycling (Including the Bicycling World)*, June 10, 1925, 39.

49. Sullivan, "Save Children by Buying Them Bikes," 39.

50. T. J. Sullivan was also most likely the author of the article from the previous month, "Bicycles Take Kids off the Streets," in which an author's name was not provided but Sullivan was an editor and contributor to the magazine.

51. "Bicycles Take Kids off the Streets," 39.

52. Fairfax Downey, "The Adventures of Old Things," *Saturday Evening Post*, April 25, 1925, 80; City of New York Department of Parks, "Program of Proposed Facilities for Bicycling," New York Public Library (1938): 1.

53. Downey, "The Adventures of Old Things," 80.

54. See Phillip P. Mason, "The League of American Wheelmen and the Good-Roads Movement, 1880–1905" (master's thesis, University of Michigan, 1958).

55. "Bicycles Take Kids off the Streets," 35.

56. Lobdell-Emery Manufacturing Company, *Boys' Life*, May 1929, 67.

57. T. J. Sullivan, "Safety Vehicles as a Sales Plea," *Motorcycling (Including the Bicycling World)*, July 8, 1925, 20.

58. Sullivan, "Safety Vehicles as a Sales Plea," 20.

59. New Departure Company, "Who's Up?" *Boys' Life*, May 1928, 52.

60. "A New Generation Discovers the Bike," *New York Times*, October 18, 1925. Apparent consumption was around 150,000 in 1921 and 1922, 525,000 in 1923, and 343,000 in 1924. See Schwinn Bicycle Company, "U.S. Bicycle Market Statistics."

61. "A New Generation Discovers the Bike," *New York Times*, October 18, 1925.

62. "A New Generation Discovers the Bike."

63. "A New Generation Discovers the Bike." DeWitt Page was a member of the Cycle Trades of America as a representative of New Departure, a subsidiary of GM that made coaster brakes and bearings used on bicycles.

64. "Bicycles Take Kids off the Streets," 35.

65. A. W. Williams, "Cycle Dealers Prefer Suburban Locations," *Motorcycling (Including the Bicycling World)*, July 18, 1928, 29.

66. Williams, "Cycle Dealers Prefer Suburban Locations," 29.

67. Williams, 29. At the time, motorcycles and bicycles were often manufactured and sold by the same business.

68. Williams, 29.

69. See Gregory J. Downey, *Telegraph Messenger Boys: Labor, Technology, and Geography, 1850–1950* (Abingdon, United Kingdom: Routledge, 2013).

70. "A New Generation Discovers the Bike."

71. David M. Kennedy, *Freedom from Fear: The American People in Depression and War, 1929–1945* (New York: Oxford Univ. Press, 2005), 34–35.

72. Albert Bradley, "Setting up a Forecasting Program," *Annual Convention Series*, American Management Association, no. 41, March 1926; quoted in Kennedy, *Freedom from Fear*, 22.

7. Surviving the Great Depression

1. Samuel Eliot Morison, *The Oxford History of the American People* (New York: Oxford Univ. Press, 1965), 944.

2. David M. Kennedy, *Freedom from Fear: The American People in Depression and War, 1929–1945* (New York: Oxford Univ. Press, 2005), 48.

3. Lizabeth Cohen, *A Consumers' Republic: The Politics of Mass Consumption in Postwar America* (New York: Knopf, 2003), 63.

4. Herlihy, *Bicycle*, 327.

5. Robert A. Smith, *A Social History of the Bicycle: Its Early Life and Times in America* (New York: American Heritage Press, 1972), 246–47. Smith explains that the "bicycle made little noise" in the 1920s but that there was a "bicycle revival" in the 1930s, which were "grim" years for the automobile. He cites a contemporary newspaper report "that Americans had taken once again to the cycle because it was the most convenient means at hand to express their biological and spiritual dissatisfaction with the machine age" but quickly refutes the reporter's claim. Failing to consider the resurgence in adult cycling, Smith argues the revival "was a phenomenon confined predominantly to youngsters." His proof that it was a phenomenon confined to youngsters is based on the developments during World War II. "The bicycle was immediately seen as a partial solution to the problem of gasoline rationing, and the government encouraged bicycle makers to produce more. But it is significant that the production of all children's machines was halted, and these had accounted for 85 percent of those produced in 1941." I agree that children's models were most important to the success of the industry but find the similar trends in bicycle and automobile consumption to be more convincing. That is, the same years that bicycle consumption was highest during the decade so too was automobile consumption. At the same time, the boost in popularity of cycling as sport and leisure among adults undoubtedly had a positive impact on the industry, even if it was a short-lived fad. Bicycle sales continued to increase after the Great Depression (ignoring the years of US involvement in World War II) so the resurgence in sales was not simply a result of Americans being unable to afford cars during an economic crisis.

6. "New Departure Coaster Brake," *American Bicyclist and Motorcyclist*, June 1930, 29.

7. William H. Young and Nancy K. Young, *The 1930s* (Westport, CT: Greenwood Press, 2002), xvii; Schwinn Bicycle Company, "U.S. Bicycle Market Statistics."

8. United States, *Historical Statistics of the United States* (US Department of Commerce, Bureau of the Census, 2001), no. HS 34, 64. Housing would not start to turn around until 1935.

9. Margaret Guroff, *The Mechanical Horse: How the Bicycle Reshaped American Life* (Austin: Univ. of Texas Press, 2016), 118–19; James Longhurst, *Bike Battles*, 125–28. Longhurst also argues that the "revival" was largely manufactured by the bicycle industry and built on over-reporting the increase in participation.

10. "Raquel Torres Rides at Malibu," *Toy World and Bicycle World*, August 1934, 53. Steven Rea reproduces this photo and many more in his book, *Hollywood Rides a Bike: Cycling with the Stars* (Santa Monica, CA: Angel City Press, 2012), 13.

11. Guroff, *The Mechanical Horse*, 119; "In the Balance," *Toy World and Bicycle World*, June 1935, cover. The image came from the set of *Break of Hearts* and dealers were encouraged to obtain photos from the film to use for window and counter displays.

12. "Tandem Is Revived," *Chicago Daily Tribune*, August 31, 1933, 15.

13. "Tandem Is Revived," 15.

14. Alan Brinkley, *Culture and Politics in the Great Depression* (Waco, TX: Markham Press Fund, 1999), 11–12. Brinkley offers Dale Carnegie's bestseller *How to Win Friends and Influence People*, "a paean to the positive value of conformity," as evidence.

15. City of New York Department of Parks, "Program of Proposed Facilities for Bicycling," New York Public Library (1938): 1–2.

16. Schwinn Bicycle Company, "U.S. Bicycle Market Statistics."

17. "Program of Proposed Facilities for Bicycling," 2.

18. Robert A. Caro, *The Power Broker: Robert Moses and the Fall of New York* (New York: Knopf, 1974), 927.

19. "Program of Proposed Facilities for Bicycling," 1.

20. Kenneth T. Jackson, *Crabgrass Frontier: Suburbanization of the United States* (New York: Oxford Univ. Press, 1985), 170.

21. "Program of Proposed Facilities for Bicycling," 1.

22. Marshall Sprague, "A Bicycle Army Takes to the Highroad," *New York Times*, May 15, 1938, 119.

23. Sprague, "A Bicycle Army Takes to the Highroad," 119.

24. Sprague, 119.

25. Sprague, 119.

26. "Program of Proposed Facilities for Bicycling," 2.

27. "Program of Proposed Facilities for Bicycling," 2.

28. Jackson, *Crabgrass Frontier*, 157–71. Jackson makes a convincing argument that public transportation lost out to the automobile because national transportation policy subsidized air and automobile traffic while taxing railroads.

29. Susan Currell, *The March of Spare Time: The Problem and Promise of Leisure in the Great Depression* (Philadelphia: Univ. of Pennsylvania Press, 2005), 2.

30. Currell, *The March of Spare Time*, 3.

31. Currell, 4.

32. Currell, 55.

33. Foster Rhea Dulles, *America Learns to Play: A History of Popular Recreation, 1607–1940* (New York: Appleton-Century Company, 1940), 373; Quoted in Currell, *The March of Spare Time*, 185. The WPA would help create over eight thousand parks in all. See Kennedy, *Freedom from Fear*, 253.

34. Currell, *The March of Spare Time*, 56.

35. "Program of Proposed Facilities for Bicycling," 3; Kennedy, *Freedom from Fear*, 253.

36. Sprague, "A Bicycle Army Takes to the Highroad"; "Franklin Quintet States Second-Half Drive to Defense and Work Progresses on Building Bicycle Track at Butler Fieldhouse," *Indianapolis Star*, February 12, 1937.

37. "Make Ready for Opening of Fair," *Shelbyville Democrat*, August 7, 1937.

38. Sprague, "A Bicycle Army Takes to the Highroad," 119.

39. Peter Nye, Jeff Groman, and Mark Tyson, *The Six-Day Bicycle Races*. (San Francisco: Van der Plas Publications, 2006), 68.

40. Nye, Groman, and Tyson, *The Six-Day Bicycle Races*, 149.

41. Cycle Trades of America, *Cycle-logical Ways to Happier Days* (New York: New Departure Press, 1930), 14.

42. Cycle Trades of America, *Cycle-logical Ways to Happier Days*, 3.

43. Cycle Trades of America, 3.

44. Cycle Trades of America, 3.

45. Cycle Trades of America, 8.

46. A century is when a cyclist rides a hundred miles in a single day.

47. Sprague, "A Bicycle Army Takes to the Highroad," 119.

48. Sprague, 119. Even though the number of sales in 1898 and 1938 were over one million, the price had come down significantly. Bicycles averaged around $60 in 1899 but were closer to $30 in average price in 1937.

49. Sprague, 119.

50. Sprague. 119. There was a similar parade in 1936 when Central Park privileges were returned to cyclists. See McCullough, *Old Wheelways*, 277, and "Bicyclists Have Their Day Again as Pedals Fly in Park Mall Parade," *New York Times*, April 12, 1936.

51. Morris Dickstein, *Dancing in the Dark: A Cultural History of the Great Depression* (New York: W. W. Norton, 2009), 358. Dickstein argues that scholars have "paid little attention to the seemingly frivolous, freewheeling side of the decade, [with an] entertainment culture often seen merely as escapist."

52. Currell, *The March of Spare Time*, 6.

53. Jay Pridmore and Jim Hurd, *Schwinn Bicycles* (St. Paul: MBI Publishing, 2001), 78; Matthew Gorski, "The Schwinn Paramount," Sheldonbrown.com/Chicago-schwinns.html.

54. Ohrt, "Optimism anent American Bicycles," 17.

55. Ohrt, 16.

56. Ohrt, 16.

57. Sears, Roebuck and Company, *A Year Ahead in Style and Value*, Catalog, Spring/Summer 1935, 395.

58. United States Rubber Company, "Ride 'Em Rough Fellows, They Thrive on It!" *Boys' Life*, June 1935, 27.

59. Herlihy, *Bicycle*, 327.

60. Judith Crown and Glenn Coleman, *No Hands: The Rise and Fall of the Schwinn Bicycle Company: An American Institution* (New York: Henry Holt, 1996), 35.

61. Crown and Coleman, *No Hands*, 16, 22, 26.

62. Crown and Coleman, 27–34. Crown and Coleman trace Schwinn's development as it made numerous innovations in design—most of those affecting children's models—and in its sales distribution methods, all of which contributed to the brand's phenomenal success from the 1940s through the 1980s.

63. Sears, Roebuck and Company, *A Year Ahead in Style and Value*, 395.

64. Ohrt, "Optimism anent American Bicycles," 17.

65. Sullivan, "Safety Vehicles as a Sales Plea," 20.

66. "Montgomery Ward & Co's Retail Department Store," *Chicago Daily Tribune*, July 22, 1928.

67. Sears, Roebuck and Company, *Wheels of Progress*, Catalog, Spring/Summer 1935, 569.

68. Huffman Manufacturing Company, "Fit As a Fiddle and Twice as Sweet," *Boys' Life*, May, 1940, 30.

69. Westfield Manufacturing Company, "Look at Lucky Ted on His Swell New Columbia," *Boys' Life*, May 1940, 32.

70. Shelby Bicycle Company, "100 Thrills and Hour!" *Boys' Life*, May 1940, 36.

71. Sears, Roebuck and Company, *Only Sears Elgins Have*, Catalog, Fall/Winter 1941, 1056.

72. "Juvenile Wheel Goods," *American Bicyclist and Motorcyclist*, January 1950, 70.

73. Cycle Trades of America, *Cycle-logical Ways to Happier Days*, 8.

74. Lisa Jacobson, *Raising Consumers: Children and the American Mass Market in the Early Twentieth Century* (New York: Columbia Univ. Press, 2004), 97–98, 116. There was a growing belief among ad agencies that the boy's opinion was critical even when peddling adults' consumer goods. Jacobson argues that "Thanks to the special affection middle class parents held for their sons, boys proved remarkably influential salesman." She reproduces advertisements proclaiming the boy was the "Dictator to the Universe" and another capturing an exchange between a son and father who had just come home with a new car battery. The boy asks, "Did'ja get the 'Super B' I told you about?"

75. Iver Johnson Manufacturing Company, "Gee! Dad Went the Limit and Got Me the Best There Is," *Boys' Life*, May 1929, 50.

76. Cromwell Publishing Company, "Boys Win this Bicycle," *Boys' Life*, May 1935, 41.

77. Huffman Manufacturing Company, "Fit As a Fiddle and Twice as Sweet," *Boys' Life*, May 1940, 30.

78. "Won't Need to Steal Another Bicycle Now," *Chicago Defender*, September 5, 1936, national edition. The assumption that the young boy was black is based on this

article's appearance in the *Chicago Defender*, a newspaper for African Americans, and because the article is specific about the race of the woman that contributed to the fund to buy the boy a bike. If it had been a white boy her race would have been assumed white as well. There was no bicycle advertising to speak of found in this and other issues of the *Chicago Defender*.

79. Sullivan, "Safety Vehicles as a Sales Plea," 20.

80. Sullivan, 20.

81. Schwinn Bicycle Company, "U.S. Bicycle Market Statistics."

82. Currell, *The March of Spare Time*, 51. Currell writes, "Recreation was of central importance to WPA administrator Harry Hopkins, who allocated at least 30 percent of the WPA budget (around $11 billion in all by 1943) toward recreation projects. While New Deal construction projects worked to repair or build more than two thousand swimming pools and create parks, playgrounds, stadiums, grandstands, bleachers, fairgrounds, athletic fields, tennis courts, golf courses, ice-skating rinks, ski runs, and bandstands, the recreation projects were concerned chiefly with organizing leadership programs so that facilities could receive proper use and supervision."

83. Pridmore and Hurd, *Schwinn Bicycles*, 49.

84. In the bicycle industry, much like the automotive industry, competitive success leads to increased purchases of nonracing models. NASCAR has often touted, "Win on Sunday, sale on Monday." See Robert Lipsyte, "Auto Racing; Success on the Track Leads to Sales in the Showroom," *New York Times*, June 10, 2001.

85. It is important to point out that total population in the United States had nearly doubled from 1900 to 1940, so the bicycle was not actually more popular than it had been during the golden age of cycling. By 1951, however, the percentage of bicycles sold per person would surpass that of the 1890s. This is not exact, but based on an estimated population of 76 million and approximately 1 million bicycles sold in 1898 versus an estimated population of 153 million and 2.1 million bicycles sold in 1951.

8. Bicycles in the Age of Affluence

1. "Cocomalt, Energy by the Glassful," *Boys' Life*, May 1938, 32.

2. Jacobson, *Raising Consumers*, 141–51.

3. See John Kenneth Galbraith, *The Affluent Society* (Boston: Houghton Mifflin, 1958); Harold G. Vatter, *The U.S. Economy in the 1950s* (New York: W. W. Norton, 1963); David Halberstam, *The Fifties* (New York: Villard Books, 1986); and James T. Patterson, *Grand Expectations: The United States, 1945–1974* (New York: Oxford Univ. Press, 1997).

4. Jacobson, *Raising Consumers*, 16–55. Jacobson traces the development back to the 1890s but some of her more convincing evidence comes from the 1910s–1920s.

5. Arnold, Schwinn & Company, *Fifty Years of Schwinn-Built Bicycles*, 57.

6. Suzanne Clark, *Cold Warriors: Manliness on Trial in the Rhetoric of the West* (Carbondale: Southern Illinois Univ. Press, 2000), 1–3. In her discussion of mass culture, Clark emphasizes the rise in popularity of the western, adventure, and crime fiction genres. She argues that this trend reveals a "hypermasculine crisis" that was difficult even to notice because "it called upon the nostalgia for the old discourses of the West (the national manliness asserted by Theodore Roosevelt) to claim that there was and always had been only one real American identity."

7. Seiler, *Republic of Drivers*, 85.

8. Seiler, 72.

9. Frederick Jackson Turner, "The Significance of the Frontier in American History," *Annual Report of the American Historical Association for the Year 1893*, 226–27; Seiler, *Republic of Drivers*, 47.

10. Patterson, *Grand Expectations*, 71; Russell Jacoby, *The Last Intellectuals: American Culture in the Age of Academe* (New York: Basic Books, 1987), 40–42.

11. Schwinn Bicycle Company, "U.S. Bicycle Market Statistics."

12. William Strand, "Adult Bicycles Sales Banned; Plan Rationing," *Chicago Tribune*, April 3, 1942.

13. "OPA Prepares to Put Bicycles on Ration List," *Chicago Tribune*, May 17, 1942.

14. Strand, "Adult Bicycles Sales Banned."

15. Strand.

16. "Bicycles Sales Soar in Advance of Steep Curb on Production," *Chicago Tribune*, March 15, 1942.

17. United States, *Victory: Official Weekly Bulletin of the Office of War Information*, January 13, 1942, 4. *Victory* details stories of how there were "runs" on items that were merely rumored to face curtailment such as car batteries and spark plugs.

18. United States, *Victory*, March 17, 1942, 5; Strand, "Adult Bicycles Sales Banned."

19. Arnold, Schwinn & Company, *Fifty Years of Schwinn-Built Bicycles*, 78.

20. Arnold, Schwinn & Company, 78.

21. Arnold, Schwinn & Company, 79.

22. Arnold, Schwinn & Company, 90.

23. Frank W. Schwinn to Mr. Johnson, November 1945, Interoffice notes to Mr. J. W. Fritz from Frank W. Schwinn, January 1945–December 1948. All correspondence from Schwinn came from the Bicycle Museum of America, New Bremen, Ohio.

24. Schwinn Bicycle Company, "U.S. Bicycle Market Statistics."

25. Schwinn Bicycle Company.

26. Vatter, *The U.S. Economy in the 1950s*, 64–67. He describes 1949 as a year of recession, part of a "pre-Korean slump."

27. Arnold, Schwinn & Company, "The Gift Nearest Their Hearts," *Life*, December 1, 1941, 88.

28. Arnold, Schwinn & Company, "The Gift Nearest Their Hearts," 88.

29. Frank W. Schwinn to Mr. Stoeffhuas, "1953 Loss of Percentage of Industry Volume," February 5, 1954. The company did so well during this era that its manufacturing facilities produced one quarter of all bicycles sold in the United States.

30. "The Bicycles' Aid to Rehabilitation of Our Wounded Veterans," *American Bicyclist and Motorcyclist*, April 1945, 20.

31. "The Bicycles' Aid to Rehabilitation of Our Wounded Veterans," 20.

32. For a discussion of the destruction of masculinity caused by World War I see Karen Petrone, *The Great War in Russian Memory* (Bloomington: Indiana Univ. Press, 2011), 75–126.

33. "The Bicycles' Aid to Rehabilitation of Our Wounded Veterans," 20.

34. Michael Roper, "Between Manliness and Masculinity: The 'War Generation' and the Psychology of Fear in Britain, 1914–1950," *Journal of British Studies* 44 (April 2005): 343–62.

35. Vatter, *The U.S. Economy in the 1950s*, 64–65.

36. Jon C. Teaford, *The American Suburb: The Basics* (New York: Routledge, 2008), 30–31; Patterson, *Grand Expectations*, 314–15.

37. Patterson, 317.

38. Halberstam, *The Fifties*, 487.

39. Patterson, *Grand Expectations*, 316.

40. Howard Chudacoff, *Children at Play: An American History* (New York: New York Univ. Press, 2007), 98.

41. The Sullivan Company, *Drive Your Bicycle*, 1954, http://www.youtube.com/watch?v=fDm6jiQz5BY.

42. Sally Joy Brown, "Hank Wants a Bicycle for Paper Route," *Chicago Daily Tribune*, December 18, 1953, B15.

43. Paul B. Ringel, *Commercializing Childhood: Children's Magazines, Urban Gentility, and the Ideal of the Child Consumer in the United States, 1823–1918* (Amherst: Univ. of Massachusetts Press, 2015), 151.

44. Gladys Huntington Bevans, "Give Teen-Age Child a Little Independence," *Chicago Daily Tribune*, March 23, 1945, 21.

45. Bevans, "Give Teen-Age Child a Little Independence," 21.

46. "Exhibits at the New York Toy Fair," *American Bicyclist and Motorcyclist*, March 1950, 60.

47. "Exhibits at the New York Toy Fair," 60.

48. "Juvenile Wheel Goods," *American Bicyclist and Motorcyclist*, January 1950, 70.

49. "Juvenile Wheel Goods," 70; Daniel Thomas Cook explains how segregating the stock by keeping girls' and boys' items separate was common. Retailers were told that clothing sections for boys and girls should be segregated by the age of two and that the boy should be treated like a little man in the interest of better sales. See Daniel

Thomas Cook, *The Commodification of Childhood: The Children's Clothing Industry and the Rise of the Child Consumer* (Durham, NC: Duke Univ. Press, 2004), 114.

50. *Dry Goods Economist*, May 29, 1920, 89; quoted in Cook, *The Commodification of Childhood*, 114.

51. "How Bicycle Design and Styling of Bicycles Affect Public Acceptance," *American Bicyclist and Motorcyclist*, January 1950, 55.

52. "How Bicycle Design and Styling of Bicycles Affect Public Acceptance," 55.

53. James Burkhart Gilbert, *A Cycle of Outrage: America's Reaction to the Juvenile Delinquent in the 1950s* (New York: Oxford Univ. Press, 1986), 3.

54. "Senators to Hold Teen Age Hearings: Subcommittee Plans Sessions Here and in 19 Other Cities—Local Assistance Sought," *New York Times*, September 19, 1953.

55. William H. Young and Nancy K. Young, *The 1950s* (Westport, CT: Greenwood Press, 2004), 281. See also Fredric Wertham, *Seduction of the Innocent* (New York: Rinehart, 1954).

56. Gilbert, *A Cycle of Outrage*, 5.

57. Gilbert, 10.

58. Steven Mintz, *Huck's Raft: A History of American Childhood* (Cambridge, MA: Belknap Press, 2004), 236. Steven Mintz argues that comic books, movie serials directed at juveniles, radio programs, and new toys designed specifically for children all were the direct result of "financially hard-pressed marketers and manufacturers [who] target[ed] children as independent consumers."

59. Frank W. Schwinn to Mr. Berry, Mr. Stoeffhuas, and Mr. Fritz, July 18, 1947, Interoffice notes to Advertising Department from Frank W. Schwinn, April 1943–December 1948.

60. Schwinn to Berry, Stoeffhuas, and Fritz, July 18, 1947.

61. Jacobson, *Raising Consumers*, 183–84.

62. Frank W. Schwinn to Mr. Fritz, August 24, 1948, Interoffice notes to Advertising Department from Frank W. Schwinn, April 1943–December 1948.

63. Bicycle Institute of America, *Bicycle Riding Clubs* (New York: Bicycle Institute of America, 1950), 4–5.

64. Bicycle Institute of America, *Bicycle Riding Clubs*, 4.

65. Bicycle Institute of America, 4.

66. Bicycle Institute of America, 57.

67. Bicycle Institute of America, 57.

68. Bicycle Institute of America, *How Your Community Can Participate in a Youth Fitness Bicycle Program* (New York: Bicycle Institute of America, n.d.). The date of this particular pamphlet is not known for sure. The New York Public Library has it catalogued as "195?" and there are no page numbers. It was probably at least 1957 or shortly thereafter since it specifically talks about President Eisenhower's Conference on Youth Fitness, which occurred in early 1957.

69. Bicycle Institute of America, *How Your Community Can Participate in a Youth Fitness Bicycle Program.*

70. Frank W. Schwinn to Mr. Barry, November 13, 1947, Interoffice notes to Advertising Department from Frank W. Schwinn, April 1943–December 1948.

71. Schwinn to Barry, November 13, 1947.

72. Roland C. Geist, *Bicycling as a Hobby* (New York: Harper & Brothers, 1940), 154.

73. John and Mavis Biesanz, "The School of the Youth Hostel," *Journal of Educational Sociology* (September 1941): 55; Thomas A. Campbell, "Youth Hosteling: An Educational and Recreational Experience," *Phi Delta Kappan*, December 1938, 120–21.

74. Edna V. Grodman, "American Youth Follows the Hostel Trail," *Clearing House*, January 1940, 261.

75. Geist, *Bicycling as a Hobby*, 154.

76. Campbell, "Youth Hosteling," 121.

77. *American Bicyclist and Motorcyclist*, January 1938, 35.

78. Sprague, "A Bicycle Army Takes to the Highroad," xx.

79. Bevans, "Give Teen-Age Child a Little Independence," 21.

80. Schwinn to Berry, Stoeffhuas, and Fritz, July 18, 1947.

81. Frank W. Scwhinn to Mr. Bond, November 12, 1948, Interoffice notes to Advertising Department from Frank W. Schwinn, April 1943–December 1948.

82. Arnold, Schwinn & Company, *Schwinn Bicycle Book* (1949). A copy of the 1949 edition is available at http://comicbookplus.com/?dlid=22101.

83. DC Comics, *Batman*, no. 108 (June 1957). Panels and information about this issue was accessed at http://thefifthbranch.com/gorilladaze/batman-jones/.

84. American Octanator Corporation, Letter to dealers with enclosed leaflet in binder titled "Bicycle Manufacturer Catalogs, A-D," Bicycle Museum of America.

85. Frank W. Schwinn to Mr. Bond, November 20, 1948, Interoffice notes to Advertising Department from Frank W. Schwinn, April 1943–December 1948.

86. J. Walter Thompson Representatives' Meeting, April 16, 1930, 3, RG 2, Box 2, J. Walter Thompson Archive. Quoted in McGovern, *Sold American*, 50–51.

87. Frank W. Schwinn to Mr. Bond, November 20, 1948.

88. Arnold, Schwinn & Company, "The Gift Nearest Their Hearts," 88.

89. Frank W. Schwinn to Mr. Barry, July 30, 1947, Interoffice notes to Advertising Department from Frank W. Schwinn, April 1943–December 1948.

90. Frank W. Schwinn to Mr. Anderson, August 6, 1946, Interoffice notes to Advertising Department from Frank W. Schwinn, April 1943–December 1948.

91. Schwinn to Anderson, August 6, 1946.

92. F. S. Anderson to Frank W. Schwinn, December 19, 1946, Interoffice notes to Advertising Department from Frank W. Schwinn, April 1943–December 1948.

93. Rea, *Hollywood Rides a Bike*, 7.

94. John Ford, dir. *The Quiet Man* (Hollywood, CA: Republic Pictures, 1952).

95. See Rea, *Hollywood Rides a Bike*.

96. Bicycle Institute of America, *How Your Community Can Participate in a Youth Fitness Bicycle Program* (New York: Bicycle Institute of America, 1950).

97. Frank W. Schwinn to Mr. Stoeffhaas, January 24, 1954, Memos General, Models, Prices, Dating, Statistics, Legal, Franchise, Individual Customer Instructions from FWS 1955.

98. Westfield Manufacturing Company, *By Columbia 'American' Lightweights 1955–56*, Bicycle Museum of America, "Bicycle Manufacturers' Catalogs."

99. Frank W. Schwinn to Mr. Stoeffhaas, "1953 Loss of Percentage of Industry Volume," February 5, 1951, Memos General, Models, Prices, Dating, Statistics, Legal, Franchise, Individual Customer Instructions from FWS 1955.

100. Frank W. Schwinn to Mr. Stoeffhaas. This is based on sales figures for 1953.

101. Ohrt, "Optimism anent American Bicycles," 16.

102. Ross D. Petty, "Peddling Schwinn Bicycles: Marketing Lessons from the Leading Post–WWII US Bicycle Brand," Conference on Historical Analysis and Research in Marketing, 2007, 165, http://faculty.quinnipiac.edu/charm. Petty's argument focuses on Schwinn's transformation from a "private label manufacturer to a brand marketer," how that transformation was successful, and the lesson it holds for contemporary marketing practices.

103. "President OK's 50 Pct. Boost in Bike Tariffs," *Toledo Blade*, August 19, 1955. See also "Tariff Hike on Bicycles is Ordered," *Times Daily*, August 19, 1955; "President Orders 50 P.C. Hike in Tariff on Bicycle Imports," *Christian Science Monitor*, August 19, 1955; "Costs Go Up Eisenhower Orders 50 Percent Boost in Tariff on Bicycles," *Kentucky New Era*, August 19, 1955.

104. "President OK's 50 Pct. Boost in Bike Tariffs."

105. Frank W. Schwinn to Mr. Stoeffhaas, "Increase in Imports," April 8, 1955, Memos General, Models, Prices, Dating, Statistics, Legal, Franchise, Individual Customer Instructions from FWS 1955.

106. "President OK's 50 Pct. Boost in Bike Tariffs."

107. "President OK's 50 Pct. Boost in Bike Tariffs."

108. "Ike Orders Duty Hike on Foreign Bicycles," *Rome News-Tribune*, August 19, 1955.

109. Schwinn to Stoeffhaas, "1953 Loss of Percentage of Industry Volume."

110. Frank W. Schwinn to Mr. Burch, January 22, 1955, Memos General, Models, Prices, Dating, Statistics, Legal, Franchise, Individual Customer Instructions from FWS 1955.

111. "Ike Orders Duty Hike on Foreign Bicycles." Specifically, Eisenhower scaled the tariff on lightweights to 11.25 percent because, in his opinion, American

manufactures "offered no direct competition in this category." See Petty, "Peddling Schwinn Bicycles," 165.

112. Bicycle Institute of America, *How Your Community Can Participate in a Youth Fitness Bicycle Program.*

113. Bess Furman, "Eisenhower Fears Softness in Youth: In Accord with Conference Experts, He Says 'Mode' Must be Overcome," *New York Times*, March 31, 1960.

114. Bicycle Institute of America, *How Your Community Can Participate in a Youth Fitness Bicycle Program.*

115. Jacoby, *The Last Intellectuals*, 42; Caro, *The Power Broker*, 952.

116. "Bike Rides Urged by Heart Doctor: White Also Says Alcohol and Diet May Have Effect on Coronary Attacks," *New York Times*, March 18, 1956.

117. "Bike Rides Urged by Heart Doctor."

118. Bicycle Institute of America, *How Your Community Can Participate in a Youth Fitness Bicycle Program.*

119. Bicycle Institute of America.

120. Bicycle Institute of America.

121. Bicycle Institute of America.

122. Alexander R. Hammer, "Wheels Roll as President's Push Helps Peddle Bicycles: President Spurs Sales of Bicycles," *New York Times*, January 13, 1957.

123. Hammer, "Wheels Roll as President's Push Helps Peddle Bicycles." This was based on sales over a two-week period compared with sales from the same period the previous year.

124. Hammer.

125. Schwinn Bicycle Company, "U.S. Bicycle Market Statics." There were a few years in which sales decreased but never more than a few hundred thousand.

126. Hammer, "Wheels Roll as President's Push Helps Peddle Bicycles."

127. Hammer.

128. Walter H. Waggoner, "Eisenhower's Enthusiasm for Bicycling Meets Warm Response in the Netherlands," *New York Times*, January 3, 1957. The figures the article gives is "one [bicycle] for every two people" and "one car for every forty people."

129. *Schwinn Reporter*, March 1, 1980; US Census Bureau, *Statistical Abstract of the United States: 2003*, 77.

130. Waggoner, "Eisenhower's Enthusiasm for Bicycling Meets Warm Response in the Netherlands."

131. Charles McGovern, "Consumption," in *A Companion to 20th-Century America*, ed. Stephen J. Whitfield (Malden, MA: Blackwell, 2004), 349. McGovern writes, "Indeed, the consumer economy recovered fully. In this era the phrase 'the American way of life' came into widespread use, and was practically synonymous with high levels of consumption and abundance."

132. In some instances, this was due, in part, to the fact that powerful members of the bicycle industry with the biggest advertising budgets were also tied to the automotive industry. Such was the case with the New Departure Coaster Brake Company, which had been a member of the United Motors Corporation (a subsidiary of General Motors) since 1916.

133. "After Lean War Years, Industry Hustles to Put Small Fry on Wheels," *Wall Street Journal*, September 20, 1945. The article claimed that 97 percent of children surveyed in 1945 wanted a bicycle.

9. High-Risers and Multi-Geared Redeemers

1. Bicycle Institute of America, *How Your Community Can Participate in a Youth Fitness Bicycle Program.*

2. "Will the Sixties Really Soar?" *American Bicyclist and Motorcyclist*, January 1960, 21–23.

3. See Bicycle Institute of America, *Bike Fun* (New York: Bicycle Institute of America, 1953); and Bicycle Institute of America, *Bike Regulation in the Community* (New York: Bicycle Institute of America, 1951).

4. James Godfrey Harmount, "55 Million Cyclists Can't Be Wrong," *Today's Health*, October 1964, 32.

5. Jay Pridmore and Jim Hurd, *Schwinn Bicycles* (St. Paul, MN: MBI Publishing, 2001), 90.

6. Jacobson, *Raising Consumers*, 122.

7. Herlihy, *Bicycle*, 352–25.

8. Frank J. Berto, "The Great American Bicycle Boom," in *Cycle History 10: Proceedings of the 10th International Cycling History Conference* (San Francisco: Van der Plas Publications, 2000), 135; "The 1960s: Two Profiles," *American Bicyclist and Motorcyclist*, September 1969, 130; Bicycle Manufacturers Association, "U.S. Bicycle Market: Major Trends in 1978," *American Bicyclist and Motorcyclist*, March 1979, 33–35. I use Berto's numbers for the 1960s and 1970s, which are derived from Schwinn's sales estimates for the entire industry. While differing slightly from numbers given in *American Bicyclist and Motorcyclist* they are very similar and provide the same trends aside from 1976. Schwinn's data list total sales as 7.8 million while *American Bicyclist* puts that figure at 8.1 million.

9. "Return of the Cycle," *Newsweek*, November 8, 1965, 102.

10. United States, *Victory*, March 17, 1942, 5; Strand, "Adult Bicycles Sales Banned."

11. "Return of the Cycle," 103.

12. Harmount, "55 Million Cyclists Can't Be Wrong," 32.

13. "Bicycle Popularity Sweeping Country," *Today's Health*, May 1965, 80.

14. Harmount, "55 Million Cyclists Can't Be Wrong"; David M. Earle, "Newsstand: 1925: Hygeia; A Virtual Newsstand from the Summer of 1925," http://uwf.edu/dearle/enewsstand/enewsstand_files/Page4115.htm.

15. Berto, "The Great American Bicycle Boom," 135.

16. Tom Sayler, "It's a Wonderful Year for Bicycles," *American Bicyclist and Motorcyclist*, February 1967, 57.

17. Sayler, "It's a Wonderful Year for Bicycles," 57.

18. Berto, "The Great American Bicycle Boom," 137.

19. Berto, 135, 137.

20. "Look Ma, No Engine," *Esquire*, December 1971, 169–73; "Bicycle Madness," *Life*, July 30, 1971, 28–33; "Bike Boom: A Way Out for Commuters?" *U.S. News*, December 6, 1971, 84–85; "Bike Comes Back," *Mechanics Illustrated*, April 1971, 73–74; "Bike is Back and Booming," *Reader's Digest*, December 1971, 185–88; "Riding a Bike for Health, Economy, and Ecology," *Consumer's Bulletin*, July 1971, 17; and "Bicycle Boom Still in High Gear," *U.S. News*, November 5, 1973, 88.

21. A. J. Hand, "Big Boom in the Hot New Bikes," *Popular Science*, July 1971, 72.

22. "Industry: They Like Bikes," *Time*, June 14, 1971, 81.

23. Mike Krawetz, "The Man Who Put New York City Back on Bikes," *American Bicyclist and Motorcyclist*, January 1967, 53–54.

24. "Industry: They Like Bikes," 81.

25. Henry S. Resnik, "Passion on a Bicycle," *Atlantic Monthly*, January 1968, 104.

26. Ken Cooper, *Aerobics* (Philadelphia: Lippincott, 1968), x. Quoted in Shelly McKenzie, *Getting Physical: The Rise of Fitness Culture in America* (Lawrence: Univ. Press of Kansas, 2013), 119.

27. McKenzie, *Getting Physical*, 13.

28. Quoted in McKenzie, 121.

29. Nelson Pena, "Beating Saddam," *Bicycling*, December 1990, 30.

30. Eileen Boris, "On Cowboys and Welfare Queens: Independence, Dependence, and Interdependence at Home and Abroad," *Journal of American Studies* (December 2007): 600.

31. Herlihy, *Bicycle*, 365; Berto, "The Great American Bicycle Boom," 133.

32. Natasha Zaretsky, *No Direction Home: The American Family and the Fear of National Decline, 1968–1980* (Chapel Hill: Univ. of North Carolina Press, 2007), 103.

33. Longhurst, *Bike Battles*, 188.

34. Herlihy, *Bicycle*, 368.

35. Samuel Wilkens, "Cycle-Industry Diagnosis: Image-Building: Mandatory . . . Growth Prospects: Impressive," *American Bicyclist and Motorcyclist*, January 1979, 89.

36. Wilkens, "Cycle-Industry Diagnosis," 89.

37. Wilkens, 90.

38. Wilkens, 90.

39. Frederick G. Vogel, "Bike Boom BMX–Style," *American Bicyclist and Motorcyclist*, March 1979, 73.

40. Ellyn E. Sprangins, "U.S. Bikemakers Gear Up to Beat Back Imports," *Business Week*, April 1, 1985, 97.

41. Sprangins, "U.S. Bikemakers Gear Up to Beat Back Imports," 97.

42. Sprangins, 97.

43. Hal Needham, dir., *Rad* (Los Angeles: Embassy Home Entertainment, 1986). The BMX boom also appeared to hit Australia, where the movie *BMX Bandits* was released in 1983. It soon made its way to American audiences.

44. Herlihy, *Bicycle*, 371.

45. Herlihy, 371; William Savage, dir., *Klunkerz: A Film About Mountain Bikes* (Los Angeles: Pumelo Pictures, 2007); "Tough Two-Wheelers," *Esquire*, May 1982, 40, 42; Trip Gabriel, "Mudslingers," *Rolling Stone*, November 7, 1985, 37, 42, 70. The name *Repack* came from the fact that by the time most riders made it to the bottom of the mountain they had to repack the rear hub with grease.

46. Sprangins, "U.S. Bikemakers Gear Up to Beat Back Imports," 97.

47. "The '88 Market in Review," *American Bicyclist and Motorcyclist*, April 1989, 55; "The 1992 Bicycle Market in Review," *American Bicyclist and Motorcyclist*, April 1993, 8.

48. Scott Martin, "Are Road Bikes Dead?" *Bicycling*, June 1990, 60.

49. Martin, "Are Road Bikes Dead?" 60.

50. Martin, 60.

51. Martin, 60.

52. Martin, 60.

53. "Bike Boom Inspires Bike Fashions," *American Bicyclist and Motorcyclist*, February 1972, 120.

54. For video footage of some of the races see *Klunkerz*.

55. Gabriel, "Mudslingers," 37.

56. Gabriel, 42.

57. Gabriel, 42.

58. Gillian Frank, "Discophobia: Antigay Prejudice and the 1979 Backlash against Disco," *Journal of the History of Sexuality* (May 2007): 278–79.

59. Peter Yates, dir., *Breaking Away* (Beverly Hills, CA: Twentieth Century Fox, 1979).

60. Gabriel, "Mudslingers," 70.

61. David Leverenz, "Manhood, Humiliation and Public Life: Some Stories," *Southwest Review* 71 (Autumn 1986): 451; quoted in Michael Kimmel, *Manhood in American: A Cultural History* (New York: Oxford Univ. Press, 2012), 6.

62. Gabriel, "Mudslingers," 42, 70.

63. "The '88 Market in Review," 55; "The 1992 Bicycle Market in Review," 8.

64. National Bicycle Dealers Association, "Industry Overview 2014," http://www.nbda.com.

65. Associated Press, "Bike Maker Rides High with Armstrong," *NBC News*, July 20, 2005, http://www.nbcnews.com/id/8645920/ns/business-small_business/t/bike-maker-rides-high-armstrong/. The argument that Lance Armstrong helped sell road bikes is perhaps more true for the Trek brand than the broader bicycle industry, however.

66. National Bicycle Dealers Association, "Industry Overview 2014." The National Sporting Goods Association only included those ages seven and up who had ridden a bicycle six times or more in a year. That represented 35.6 million Americans in 2014. Another organization, People for Bikes, used different methods and set their parameters at three years old and above. They found that over one hundred million people rode a bicycle at least once in 2014.

67. Guroff, *The Mechanical Horse*, 162; Gluskin Townley Group, "National Bicycle Dealers Association (NBDA) U.S. Bicycle Overview Report, 2013," section A, 6.

68. Michael Andersen, "Why is Kids' Bike Safety Soaring? It's not that Kids are Biking Less," People for Bikes, September 9, 2015, http://peopleforbikes.org/blog/why-is-kids-bike-safety-soaring-its-not-that-kids-are-biking-less.

69. National Bicycle Dealers Association, "Industry Overview 2015," http://www.nbda.com. The difficulty in estimating what percentage of the market children represent is compounded by the fact that many undoubtedly ride bicycles with wheels that are twenty inches or larger yet only the models with wheels smaller than that are considered "youth" models.

70. Brad Edmondson, "The U.S. Bicycle Market: A Trend Overview," Gluskin Townley Group, 2011, http://gluskintownleygroup.com.

71. National Bicycle Dealers Association, "Industry Overview 2015."

72. Gabriel, "Mudslingers" 42.

73. Guroff, *The Mechanical Horse*, 157.

74. "Bike Sharing in the United States: State of the Practice and Guide to Implementation," Toole Design Group and the Pedestrian and the Pedestrian and Bicycle Information Center, September, 2012, 10, http://www.pedbikeinfo.org/pdf/Programs_Promote_bikeshareintheus.pdf; Dan Malouff, "Bicycling," Greater Greater Washington, January 26, 2017, https://ggwash.org/view/62137/all-119-us-bikeshare-systems-ranked-by-size.

75. Brian McKenzie, "Modes Less Traveled—Bicycling and Walking to Work in the United States: 2008–2012," US Department of Commerce Economics and Statistics Administration, US Census Bureau, https://www.census.gov/prod/2014pubs/acs-25.pdf.

76. League of American Bicyclists, "Where We Ride: Analysis of Bicycling in American Cities," 2013, 6–7, http://bikeleague.org/sites/default/files/ACS_report_forweb.pdf; Longhurst, *Bike Battles*, 13.

77. Joe Lindsey, "The Secret to Safer Cities," *Bicycling*, July 2015, 34; Guroff, *The Mechanical Horse*, 158, 235.

78. Guroff, *The Mechanical Horse*, 158.

79. "Modes Less Traveled." Out of the categories included in the survey—car/truck/van, walking, work at home, public transportation, other means, or bicycle—the bicycle was used least as a means of commuting to work. It is important to note that the number of commutes made on a bicycle is higher in some cities. For instance, in 2013 Portland, Oregon, saw 6 percent of all commutes made on a bicycle. The number is higher than the 1 percent cited earlier in numerous cities including Washington, DC; Minneapolis, Minnesota; Davis, California; and Cambridge, Massachusetts. See League of American Bicyclists, "Where We Ride: Analysis of Bicycling in American Cities," 2013, 3, http://bikeleauge.org/sites/default/files/ACS_report_forweb.pdf; and Evan Friss, *The Cycling City: Bicycles and Urban America in the 1890s* (Chicago: Univ. of Chicago Press, 2015), 205–6.

80. John Pucher and Ralph Buehler, "Cycling For Everyone: Lessons from Europe," *Transportation Research Record* no. 2074 (2008): 3.

Conclusion

1. Andre Siegfried, "The Gulf Between," *Atlantic Monthly*, March 1928, 289–95. This argument is widely accepted at this point and has been reiterated by countless scholars over the years but Siegfried seems to be one of the first to point this out.

2. Evan Friss comes to a similar conclusion independently. See Friss, *The Cycling City*, 9.

Bibliography

Archives

Benson Ford Research Center
Bicycle Museum of America
Chicago Public Library
Cincinnati Public Library
Indiana Historical Society
New York Public Library
University of Kentucky Special Collections
University of Louisville Ekstrom Library

Periodicals

American Bicyclist and Motorcyclist
American Boy
American Quarterly
Arena
Atlantic Monthly
Bicycle News
Bicycling News
Bicycling World and L.A.W. Bulletin
Bicycling World & Motorcycle Review
Blackwood's Edinburgh Magazine
Boys' Life
Business Week
Century Illustrated
Century Magazine
Chicago Tribune
Chicago Defender
Christian Science Monitor
Consumer's Bulletin
Cycling Life
Ebony
Esquire
Harper's Weekly
Harper's Monthly
Indianapolis Star
Kentucky New Era
L.A.W. Bulletin and Good Roads
Leavenworth Times
Life
Louisville Courier Journal
Mechanics Illustrated
Monticello Herald-Journal
Motorcycling
MotorCycling and Bicycling
Motorcycling (Including the Bicycling World)
Motorcyclist and Bicyclist Illustrated
Newsweek
New York Evening Post
New York Sun
New York Times
Outing: An Illustrated Monthly Magazine of Recreation

Pittsburgh Courier
Popular Mechanics
Popular Science
Printers' Ink
Puck
Reader's Digest
Referee
Rolling Stone
Rome News-Tribune
Saturday Evening Post
Schwinn Reporter
Scientific American
Shelbyville Democrat
Sports Historian
St. Nicholas
Terre Haute Star
Time
Times Daily
Today's Health
Toledo Blade
U.S. News
Victory: Official Weekly Bulletin of the Office of War Information
Wall Street Journal
Wheelmen's Gazette

Audiovisual Materials

Apatow, Judd, dir. *The 40 Year Old Virgin*. Universal City, CA: Universal Pictures, 2005.

Cohen, Ethan, and Joel Cohen, dir. *Burn After Reading*. Universal City, CA: Universal Studios Home Entertainment, 2008.

Fleming, Victor, dir. *The Wizard of Oz*. Hollywood, CA: Warner Bros. Pictures, 1939.

Ford, John, dir. *The Quiet Man*. Hollywood, CA: Republic Pictures, 1952.

McElhenney Rob, dir. *It's Always Sunny in Philadelphia*, season 3, episode 9, "Sweet Dee's Dating a Retarded Person." Aired October 11, 2007, on FX.

Savage, William. *Klunkerz: A Film about Mountain Bikes*. Los Angeles: Pumelo Pictures, 2007.

Needham, Hal, dir. *Rad*. Los Angeles: Embassy Home Entertainment, 1986.

Sullivan Company. *Drive Your Bicycle*, 1954. http://www.youtube.com/watch?v=fDm6jiQz5BY.

Yates, Peter, dir. *Breaking Away*. Beverly Hills, CA: Twentieth Century Fox, 1979.

Books, Journals, and Other Printed Material

Acme Cycle Company. *Acme Bicycles*. Elkhart, IN: Acme Cycle Company, 1898.

Adelman, Melvin A. *A Sporting Time: New York City and the Rise of Modern Athletics, 1820–70*. Urbana: Univ. of Illinois Press, 1986.

Anderson, Benedict. *Imagined Communities: Reflections on the Origin and Spread of Nationalism*. London: Verso, 1991.

Anderson, Benjamin. *Economics and the Public Welfare: Financial and Economic History of the United States, 1914–1946*. Princeton, NJ: D. Van Nostrand Company, 1963.

Aronson, Sidney H. "The Sociology of the Bicycle." *Social Forces* 30, no. 3 (March 1952): 305–12.

Arnold, Schwinn & Company. *Fifty Years of Schwinn-Built Bicycles: The Story of the Bicycle and Its Contributions to Our Way of Life, 1895–1945*. Chicago: Arnold, Schwinn & Company, 1945.

———. *Schwinn Bicycles*. Chicago: Arnold, Schwinn & Company, 1955.

Axelrod, Alan. *Selling the Great War: The Making of American Propaganda*. New York: Palgrave Macmillan, 2009.

Balf, Todd. *Major: A Black Athlete, A White Era, and the Fight to be the World's Fastest Human Being*. New York: Crown Publishers, 2008.

Bardou, Jean Pierre. *The Automobile Revolution: The Impact of an Industry*. Chapel Hill: Univ. of North Carolina Press, 1982.

Bederman, Gail. *Manliness and Civilization: A Cultural History of Gender and Race in the United States, 1880–1917*. Chicago: Univ. of Chicago Press, 1995.

Beeley, Serena. *A History of Bicycles*. Secaucus, NJ: Wellfleet Books, 1992.

Beezley, William H. *Judas at the Jockey Club and Other Episodes of Porfirian Mexico*. Lincoln: Univ. of Nebraska Press, 1987.

Bell, Ida Trafford. *Bicycling for Women*. Hartford, CT: Pope Manufacturing Company, 1890.

Berto, Frank, Ron Shepherd, and Raymond Henry. *The Dancing Chain: History and Development of the Derailleur Bicycle*. San Francisco: Van der Plas Publications, 2005.

Berto, Frank. "The Great American Bicycle Boom." In *Cycle History 10: Proceedings of the 10th International Cycling History Conference*. San Francisco: Van der Plas Publications, 2000.

Bicycle Institute of America. *Bike Fun*. New York: Bicycle Institute of America, 1953.

———. *Bike Regulation in the Community*. New York: Bicycle Institute of America, 1951.

———. *Bicycle Riding Clubs*. New York: BIA, 1950.

———. *How Your Community Can Participate in a Youth Fitness Bicycle Program*. New York: Bicycle Institute of America, n.d.

Biesanz, John, and Mavis Biesanz. "The School of the Youth Hostel." *Journal of Educational Sociology* 26 (September 1941): 55–60.

Bloom, John, and Michael Nevin Willard, eds. *Sports Matters: Race, Recreation, and Culture*. New York: New York Univ. Press, 2002.

Boris, Eileen. "On Cowboys and Welfare Queens: Independence, Dependence, and Interdependence at Home and Abroad." *Journal of American Studies* 41, no. 3 (December 2007): 599–621.

Breen, T. H. *The Marketplace of Revolution: How Consumer Politics Shaped American Independence*. New York: Oxford Univ. Press, 2004.

Brinkley, Alan. *Culture and Politics in the Great Depression*. Waco, TX: Markham Press Fund, 1999.

Brinkley, Douglas. *Wheels for the World: Henry Ford, His Company, and a Century of Progress, 1903–2003*. New York: Viking, 2003.

Brock, Julia Marie. "The Bicycle as Vehicle to Women's Emancipation as Reflected in Popular Culture, 1888–1900." Master's thesis, University of Houston–Clear Lake, 2004.

Bromley, Michael L. *William Howard Taft and the First Motoring Presidency*. Jefferson, NC: McFarland, 2003.

Brown, Bill. *The Material Unconscious: American Amusement, Stephen Crane, and the Economics of Play*. Cambridge, MA: Harvard Univ. Press, 1996.

Brownlee, W. Elliot. *Dynamics of Ascent: A History of the American Economy*. Chicago: Dorsey Press, 1988.

Burr, Thomas Cameron. "Markets as Producers and Consumers: The French and U.S. National Bicycle Markets, 1875–1910." PhD diss., University of California, Davis, 2005.

Butler University. *Official Program: Indianapolis First International Six Days Bicycle Races*. Indianapolis: s.n., 1937.

———. *Official Program: Indianapolis Second Six Day Bike Race*. Indianapolis: s.n., 1938.

Cahn, Susan K. *Coming on Strong: Gender and Sexuality in Twentieth-Century Women's Sport*. New York: Free Press, 1994.

Carnes, Mark C., and Clyde Griffen, eds., *Meanings for Manhood: Constructions of Masculinity in Victorian America*. Chicago: Univ. of Chicago Press, 1990.

Caro, Robert A. *The Power Broker: Robert Moses and the Fall of New York*. New York: Knopf, 1974.

Carter, Susan B. *Historical Statistics of the United States: Earliest Times to the Present*. New York: Cambridge Univ. Press, 2006.

Chudacoff, Howard. *Children at Play: An American History*. New York: New York Univ. Press, 2007.

City of New York Department of Parks. *Programs of Proposed Facilities for Bicycling*. 1938.

Clark, Suzanne. *Cold Warriors: Manliness on Trial in the Rhetoric of the West*. Carbondale: Southern Illinois Univ. Press, 2000.

Cohen, Lizabeth. *A Consumers' Republic: The Politics of Mass Consumption in Postwar America*. New York: Knopf, 2003.

———. "From Town Square to Shopping Center: The Reconfiguration of Community Marketplaces in Postwar America." *American Historical Review* 101 no. 4 (October 1996): 1050–81.

———. *Making a New Deal: Industrial Workers in Chicago, 1919–1939*. Cambridge: Cambridge Univ. Press, 1990.

Cook, Bruce. *The Beat Generation*. New York: Scribner, 1971.

Cook, Daniel Thomas. *The Commodification of Childhood: The Children's Clothing Industry and the Rise of the Child Consumer*. Durham, NC: Duke Univ. Press, 2004.

Cooper, Ken. *Aerobics* (Philadelphia: Lippincott, 1968).

Cresswell, Tim. *On the Move: Mobility in the Modern Western World*. New York: Routledge, 2006.

Cross, Gary. *Kids' Stuff: Toys and the Changing World of American Childhood*. Cambridge, MA: Harvard Univ. Press, 1997.

Cross, Gary S. *A Social History of Leisure since 1600*. State College, PA: Venture Publishing, 1990.

Crown, Judith, and Glenn Coleman. *No Hands: The Rise and Fall of the Schwinn Bicycle Company: An American Institution*. New York: Henry Holt, 1996.

Currell, Susan. *The March of Spare Time: The Problems and Promise of Leisure in the Great Depression*. Philadelphia: Univ. of Pennsylvania Press, 2005.

Cycle Trades of America. *Cycle-Logical Ways to Happier Days*. New York: New Departure Press, 1930.

———. *Sixth Annual Year Book 1924–1925*. New York: Peter J. Carey and Sons, 1925.

De Grazia, Victoria, and Ellen Furlough. *The Sex of Things: Gender and Consumption in Historical Perspective*. Berkeley: Univ. of California Press, 1996.

de Wilde, A. "Sport History's Atlantis: How Resurrecting the History of American Cycling Influences Our View of the Field." *North American Society for Sport History Proceedings & Newsletter* (2007): 38–39.

Dickstein, Morris. *Dancing in the Dark: A Cultural History of the Great Depression*. New York: W. W. Norton, 2009.

Dowell, Glen, and Anand Swaminathan. "Racing and Back-Pedaling into the Future: New Product Introduction and Organizational Mortality in the US Bicycle Industry, 1880–1918." *Organization Studies* 21, no. 2 (March 2000): 405–31.

Downey, Gregory J. *Telegraph Messenger Boys: Labor, Technology, and Geography, 1850–1950*. New York: Routledge, 2002.

Dulles, Foster Rhea. *America Learns to Play: A History of Popular Recreation, 1607–1940*. New York: Appleton-Century Company, 1940.

———. *The United States since 1865*. Ann Arbor: Univ. of Michigan Press, 1969.

Dunham, Norman Leslie. "The Bicycle Era in American History." PhD diss., Harvard University, 1956.

Dzierzak, Lou. *The Evolution of American Bicycle Racing*. Guilford, CT: Globe Pequot Press, 2007.

Elias, Norbert, and Eric Dunning. *Quest for Excitement: Sport and Leisure in the Civilizing Process*. Oxford: Basil Blackwell, 1986.

Enloe, Cynthia H. "Was It 'The Good War' for Women?" *American Quarterly* 37 no. 4, (Autumn 1985): 627–31.

Epperson, Bruce. "How Many Bikes: An Investigation into the Quantification of Bicycling, 1878–1914." In *Cycle History 11: Proceedings of the 11th International Cycling History Conference*, edited by Andrew Ritchie and Rob Van der Plas (San Francisco: Van der Plas Publications, 2001), 49.

———. *Peddling Bicycles to America: The Rise of an Industry*. Jefferson, NC: McFarland, 2010.

Faulkner, Harold Underwood. *American Economic History*. New York: Harper & Row, 1960.

Filene, Peter G. *Him/Her/Self: Sex Roles in Modern America*. Baltimore, MD: Johns Hopkins Univ. Press, 1986.

Fox, Richard Wightman, and T. J. Jackson Lears, eds. *The Culture of Consumption: Critical Essays in American History, 1880–1980*. New York: Pantheon Books, 1983.

Frank, Gillian. "Discophobia: Antigay Prejudice and the 1979 Backlash against Disco." *Journal of the History of Sexuality* 16, no. 2 (May 2008): 276–306.

Friss, Evan. *The Cycling City: Bicycles and Urban America in the 1890s*. Chicago: Univ. of Chicago Press, 2015.

Furness, Zach. *One Less Car: Bicycles and the Politics of Automobility*. Philadelphia: Temple Univ. Press, 2010.

Galbraith, John Kenneth. *The Affluent Society*. Boston: Houghton Mifflin, 1958

Garvey, Ellen Gruber. "Reframing the Bicycle: Advertising-Supported Magazines and Scorching Women." *American Quarterly* 47, no. 1 (March 1995): 66–101.

———. *The Admen in the Parlor: Magazines and the Gendering of Consumer Culture, 1880s to 1910s*. New York: Oxford Univ. Press, 1996.

Geist, Roland C. *Bicycling As a Hobby*. New York: Harper & Brothers, 1940.

Gerstle, Gary. *Working-Class Americanism: The Politics of Labor in an Industrial City, 1914–1960*. New York: Cambridge Univ. Press, 1989.

Gilbert, James Burkhart. *A Cycle of Outrage: America's Reaction to the Juvenile Delinquent in the 1950s*. New York: Oxford Univ. Press, 1986.

Goddard, Stephen B. *Colonel Albert Pope and His American Dream Machines: The Life and Times of a Bicycle Tycoon Turned Automotive Pioneer*. Jefferson, NC: McFarland, 2000.

Goodman, Phil. "'Patriotic Femininity': Women's Morals and Men's Morale During the Second World War." *Gender and History* 10, no. 2 (August 1998): 278–93.

Guroff, Margaret. *The Mechanical Horse: How the Bicycle Reshaped American Life*. Austin: Univ. of Texas Press, 2016.

Guttman, Allen. "Sport, Politics and the Engaged Historian." *Journal of Contemporary History* 38, no. 3 (2003): 363–75.

Halberstam, David. *The Fifties*. New York: Villard Books, 1986.

Hallenbeck, Sarah. *Claiming the Bicycle: Women, Rhetoric, and Technology in Nineteenth-Century America*. Carbondale: Southern Illinois Univ. Press, 2016.

Harmond, Richard. "Progress and Flight: An Interpretation of the American Cycle Craze of the 1890s." *Journal of Social History* 5, no. 2 (Winter 1971–72): 235–57.

Harrison, A. E. "The Competitiveness of the British Cycle Industry, 1890–1940." *Economic History Review* 22, no. 2 (August 1969): 287–303.

Hart, David M. *Forged Consensus: Science, Technology, and Economic Policy in the United States, 1921–1953*. Princeton, NJ: Princeton Univ. Press, 1998.

Hay and Willits Manufacturing Company. *Outing Bicycles*. Indianapolis: WMB Burford, 1896.

Hayes, Kevin J. *The Two-Wheeled World of George B. Thayer*. Lincoln: Univ. of Nebraska Press, 2015.

Herlihy, David V. *Bicycle: The History*. New Haven, CT: Yale Univ. Press, 2004.

———. *The Lost Cyclist: The Epic Tale of an American Adventurer and His Mysterious Disappearance*. Boston: Houghton Mifflin Harcourt, 2010.

Higham, John, ed. *Writing American History*. Bloomington: Indiana Univ. Press, 1970.

Hobsbawm, E. J. *Nations and Nationalism since 1780: Programme, Myth, Reality*. Cambridge: Cambridge Univ. Press, 1990.

Hoganson, Kristin. *Fighting For American Manhood: How Gender Politics Provoked the Spanish-American and Philippine-American Wars*. New Haven, CT: Yale Univ. Press, 1998.

Holt, Richard. *Sport and Society in Modern France*. Hamden, CT: Archon Books, 1981.

Horton, Dave, Paul Rosen, and Peter Cox, eds. *Cycling and Society*. Abingdon, United Kingdom: Ashgate, 2007.

Indiana Bicycle Company. *Evolution of the Bicycle*. Indianapolis: Indiana Bicycle Company, 1897.

Jacobson, Lisa. *Raising Consumers: Children and the American Mass Market in the Early Twentieth Century*. New York: Columbia Univ. Press, 2004.

Jacoby, Russell. *The Last Intellectuals: American Culture in the Age of Academe*. New York: Basic Books, 1987.

Jackson, Kenneth T. *Crabgrass Frontier: Suburbanization of the United States*. New York: Oxford Univ. Press, 1985.

Jefferson Post 15 American Legion. *Official Program: 6-Day Bike Race, Louisville's 1st International Six-Day Bike Race*. Louisville, Kentucky, Jefferson Post 15, American Legion Incorporated, 1935.

Jones, Stephen G. *Sport, Politics, and the Working Class: Organised Labour and Sport in Inter-War Britain*. Manchester: Manchester Univ. Press, 1988.

Kennedy, David M. *Freedom from Fear: The American People in Depression and War, 1929–1945*. New York: Oxford Univ. Press, 2005.

———. *Over Here: The First World War and American Society*. New York: Oxford Univ. Press, 1980.

Kimmel, Michael S. *Manhood in America: A Cultural History*. New York: Free Press, 1996.

Laird, Pamela. *Advertising Progress: American Business and the Rise of Consumer Marketing*. Baltimore, MD: Johns Hopkins Univ. Press, 1998.

League of American Wheelmen. *Proceedings of 3rd Annual Good Roads Convention of Boards of Supervisors of State of New York, Held in Albany, New York, January 28 and 29, 1902*. Washington, DC: US GPO, 1902.

Lears, T. J. Jackson. *No Place of Grace: Antimodernism and the Transformation of American Culture, 1880–1920*. Chicago: Univ. of Chicago Press, 1945.

Leuchtenburg, William E. *The Perils of Prosperity, 1914–32*. Chicago: Univ. of Chicago Press, 1958.

Lloyd-Jones, Roger, M. J. Lewis, and Mark Eason. *Raleigh and the British Bicycle Industry: An Economic and Business History, 1870–1960*. Abingdon, United Kingdom: Ashgate, 2000.

Longhurst, James. *Bike Battles: A History of Sharing the American Road*. Seattle: Univ. of Washington Press, 2015.

Longstreth, Richard. "The Neighborhood Shopping Center in Washington, D.C., 1930–1941." *Journal of the Society of Architectural Historians* 51, no. 1 (March 1992): 5–34.

Mangan, J. A., ed. *Making European Masculinities: Sport, Europe, Gender*. London: Frank Cass, 2000.

Marchand, Roland. *Advertising the American Dream: Making Way for Modernity, 1920–1940*. Berkeley: Univ. of California Press, 1985.

Marks, Patricia. *Bicycles, Bangs, and Bloomers: The New Woman in the Popular Press*. Lexington: Univ. Press of Kentucky, 1990.

Mason, Phillip P. "The League of American Wheelmen and the Good-Roads Movement, 1880–1905." Master's thesis, University of Michigan, 1958.

McCullough, Robert L. *Old Wheelways: Traces of Bicycle History on the Land*. Cambridge, MA: MIT Press, 2015.

McGerr, Michael. *A Fierce Discontent: The Rise and Fall of the Progressive Movement in America, 1870–1920*. New York: Free Press, 2003.

McGovern, Charles F. *Sold American: Consumption and Citizenship, 1890–1945*. Chapel Hill: Univ. of North Carolina Press, 2006.

McKenzie, Shelly. *Getting Physical: The Rise of Fitness Culture in America*. Lawrence: Univ. Press of Kansas, 2013.

McNally, Evaline Grumbine. *Reaching Juvenile Markets: How to Advertise, Sell, and Merchandise through Boys and Girls*. New York: McGraw-Hill, 1938.

McShane, Clay. *Down the Asphalt Path: The Automobile and the American City*. New York: Columbia Univ. Press, 1994.

Mintz, Steven. *Huck's Raft: A History of American Childhood*. Cambridge, MA: Belknap Press, 2004.

Morison, Samuel Eliot. *The Oxford History of the American People*. New York: Oxford Univ. Press, 1965.

National Recovery Administration. "Code of Fair Competition for the Bicycle Manufacturing Industry." 437, registry no. 1407-1-02, 1934.

Norcliffe, Glen, ed. *Critical Geographies of Cycling: History, Political Economy and Culture*. Abingdon, United Kingdom: Ashgate, 2015.

———. *The Ride to Modernity: The Bicycle in Canada, 1869–1900*. Toronto: Univ. of Toronto Press, 2001.

Norton, Peter D. *Fighting Traffic: The Dawn of the Motor Age in the American City*. Cambridge, MA: MIT Press, 2008.

Nye, Peter. *Hearts of Lions: The History of American Bicycle Racing*. New York: W. W. Norton, 1988.

Nye, Peter, Jeff Groman, and Mark Tyson. *The Six-Day Bicycle Races*. San Francisco: Van der Plas Publications, 2006.

Painter, Nell Irvin. *Standing at Armageddon: The United States, 1877–1919*. New York: W. W. Norton, 1987.

Palmer, Arthur Judson. *Riding High: The Story of the Bicycle*. New York: Dutton, 1956.

Patterson, James T. *Grand Expectations: The United States, 1945–1974*. New York: Oxford Univ. Press, 1997.

Pendergast, Tom. *Creating the Modern Man: American Magazines and Consumer Culture 1900–1950*. Jackson: Univ. Press of Mississippi, 2000.

Perry, David B. *Bike Cult: The Ultimate Guide to Human-Powered Vehicles*. New York: Four Walls Eight Windows, 1995.

Petrone, Karen. *The Great War in Russian Memory*. Bloomington: Indiana Univ. Press, 2011.

Petty, Ross. "Peddling Schwinn Bicycles: Marketing Lessons from the Leading Post–WWII U.S. Bicycle Brand." Quinnipiac University CHARM Symposium Papers, 2007.

Pope, Albert Augustus. *The Relation of Good Streets to the Prosperity of a City: An Address*. Boston: s.n., 1892.

Potter, Isaac B., Edward P. North, and Lewis M. Haupt. *Roads Improvement: The Common Roads of Europe and America*. N.p., s.n.: 1891.

Poulson, Barry W. *Economic History of the United States*. New York: Macmillan, 1981.

Pratt, Charles. *The American Bicycler: A Manual for the Observer, the Learner, and the Expert*. Boston: Osgood and Company, 1879.

Pridmore, Jay, and Jim Hurd. *Schwinn Bicycles*. St. Paul, MN: MBI Publishing, 2001.

Pucher, John, and Ralph Buehler. "Cycling for Everyone: Lessons from Europe." *Transportation Research Record* no. 2074 (2008).

Putney, Clifford. *Muscular Christianity: Manhood and Sports in Protestant America, 1880–1920*. Cambridge, MA: Harvard Univ. Press, 2001.

Rae, John Bell. *American Automotive Manufacturers: The First Forty Years*. Philadelphia: Chilton Publishing Company, 1959.

Rea, Steven. *Hollywood Rides a Bike: Cycling with the Stars*. Santa Monica, CA: Angel City Press, 2012.

Register, Woody. *The Kid of Coney Island: Fred Thompson and the Rise of American Amusements*. New York: Oxford Univ. Press, 2001.

Riess, Steven A. *City Games: The Evolution of American Urban Society and the Rise of Sports*. Urbana: Univ. of Illinois Press, 1989.

Ringel, Paul D. *Commercializing Childhood: Children's Magazines, Urban Gentility, and the Ideal of the Child Consumer in the United States, 1823–1918*. Amherst: Univ. of Massachusetts Press, 2015.

Ritchie, Andrew. *King of the Road: An Illustrated History of Cycling*. London: Wildwood House, 1975.

———. "The League of American Wheelmen, Major Taylor and the 'Color Question' in the United States in the 1890s." *Sport in Society* 6 no. 2/3 (June/October 2003): 13–43.

Ritchie, Andrew. *Major Taylor: The Extraordinary Career of a Champion Bicycle Racer*. San Francisco: Bicycle Books, 1988.

Roper, Michael. "Between Manliness and Masculinity: The 'War Generation' and the Psychology of Fear in Britain, 1914–1950." *Journal of British Studies* 44 (April 2005): 343–62.

Scanlon, Jennifer, ed. *The Gender of Consumer Culture Reader*. New York: New York Univ. Press, 2000.

Schrum, Kelly. *Some Wore Bobby Sox: The Emergence of Teenage Girls' Culture, 1920–1945*. New York: Palgrave Macmillan, 2004.

Schudson, Michael. *Advertising, the Uneasy Persuasion: Its Dubious Impact on American Society*. New York: Basic Books, 1984.

———. "Citizens, Consumers, and the Good Society." *Annals of the American Academy of Political and Social Science* 611, no. 1 (2007): 274–75.

Schwarb, John. *The Little 500: The Story of the World's Greatest College Weekend.* Bloomington: Indiana Univ. Press, 1999.

Schwinn, Frank W. *Letters, Memos, Reports, and Experimental.* N.p., s.n., 1945.

Sears & Roebuck Company. *Sears & Roebuck Company.* Chicago: Sears & Roebuck Company, 1910–1950.

Seiler, Cotten. *Republic of Drivers: A Cultural History of Automobility in America.* Chicago: Univ. of Chicago Press, 2008.

Shah, Dhavan V., Lewis A. Friedland, Douglas Malcolm McLeod, and Michelle R. Nelson, eds. *The Politics of Consumption/The Consumption of Politics.* Thousand Oaks, CA: SAGE Publications, 2007.

Smethurst, Paul. *The Bicycle: Towards a Global History.* New York: Palgrave, 2015.

Smith, Robert. *A Social History of the Bicycle.* New York: American Heritage Press, 1972.

Smith, Susan Harris, and Melanie Dawson. *The American 1890s: A Cultural Reader.* Durham, NC: Duke Univ. Press, 2000.

Stewart, Mary Lynn. *For Health and Beauty: Physical Culture for Frenchwomen, 1880s–1930s.* Baltimore, MD: Johns Hopkins Univ. Press, 2001.

Strange, Lisa S., and Robert S. Brown. "The Bicycle, Women's Rights, and Elizabeth Cady Stanton." *Women's Studies* 31, no. 5 (2002): 609–26.

Sucher, Harry V. *Inside American Motorcycling and the American Motorcycle Association, 1900–1990.* Laguna Niguel, CA: Infosport, 1995.

Swann, Dick, and James C. McCullagh. *American Bicycle Racing.* Emmaus, PA: Rodale, 1976.

Taylor, Major. *The Fastest Bicycle Rider in the World: The Autobiography of Major Taylor.* Brattleboro, VT: S. Greene Press, 1972.

Teaford, Jon C. *The American Suburb: The Basics.* New York: Routledge, 2008.

Thompson, Christopher S. *The Tour De France: A Cultural History.* Berkeley: Univ. of California Press, 2006.

Tuchman, Barbara W. *The Proud Tower: A Portrait of the World Before the War, 1890–1914.* New York: Macmillan, 1966.

Turner, Frederick Jackson. "The Significance of the Frontier in American History." *Annual Report of the American Historical Association for the Year 1893.* N.p.: s.n., 1894.

Tygiel, Jules. *Baseball's Great Experiment: Jackie Robinson and His Legacy*. New York: Oxford Univ. Press, 1983.

Urry, John. "The System of Automobility." *Theory, Culture & Society* 21, no. 4/5 (2016): 25–39.

Van der Plas, Rob, ed. *Cycle History: Proceedings of the 7th International Cycle History Conference, Buffalo, New York, September 4–6, 1996*. San Francisco: Van der Plas Publications, 1997.

Vanguard Cycle Company. *Vanguard Cycle Company Catalog*. Indianapolis: Vanguard Cycle Company, 1900.

Vatter, Harold G. *The U.S. Economy in the 1950s: An Economic History*. New York: W. W. Norton, 1963.

Veblen, Thorstein, and John Kenneth Galbraith. *The Theory of the Leisure Class*. Norwalk, CT: Easton Press, 1994.

Vivanco, Luis A. *Reconsidering the Bicycle: An Anthropological Perspective on a New (Old) Thing*. New York: Routledge, 2013.

Vogel, Andrew Richard. "Narrating the Geography of Automobility: American Road Story 1893–1921." PhD diss., Ohio State University, 2007.

Wells, Christopher W. *Car Country: An Environmental History*. Seattle: Univ. of Washington Press, 2012.

Wertham, Ferdric. *Seduction of the Innocent*. New York: Rinehart, 1954.

Whitfield, Stephen J. *A Companion to 20th-Century America*. Malden, MA: Blackwell, 2004.

Willard, Frances E. *A Wheel within a Wheel: How I Learned to Ride the Bicycle with Some Reflections by the Way*. Bedford, MA: Applewood Books, 1997 (1895).

Williamson, Joel. *A Rage for Order: Black-White Relations in the American South since Emancipation*. New York: Oxford Univ. Press, 1986.

Withers, Jeremy, and Daniel P. Shea, eds. *Culture on Two Wheels: The Bicycle in Literature and Film*. Lincoln: Univ. of Nebraska Press, 2016.

Young, William H., and Nancy K. Young. *The 1930s*. Westport, CT: Greenwood Press, 2002.

Zaretsky, Natasha. *No Direction Home: The American Family and the Fear of National Decline, 1968–1980*. Chapel Hill: Univ. of North Carolina Press, 2007.

Zheutlin, Peter. *Around the World on Two Wheels: Annie Londonderry's Extraordinary Ride*. New York: Kensington Books, 2013.

Index

advertising: in comics, 1, 138, 171–73, 175, 178–80, 194–95, 253n58; and movie stars, 139, 182–83, 191; targeting fathers, 71, 79, 81, 110, 145, 153–54, 194–95; tie-ins, 59, 158–59; use of envy, 110–11, 153–54
aerobics, 200
African American. *See under* cyclists
age of affluence, 159
amateurism, 26–27
American Bicycler, The. *See* Pratt, Charles E.
American Bicyclist and Motorcyclist, 206, 257n8
American Boy, 75, 80, 108–10, 138
American culture, compared to European, 5, 119–22, 143, 167, 184–90
American Girl, 182
American Medical Association, 197
American Octanator Corporation, 179
American Rolling Mill Company, 97
American Youth Hostel, 176–78
Ankeney, S. H., 80
anti-bicycle attitudes, 48–49
Armstrong, Lance, 209–10, 260n65
Arnhem, Edward, 100
Arnold, Schwinn & Company. *See* Schwinn
Aronson, Sidney A., 242n3
Aspen, Colorado, 208
Atherton Coaster Brakes. *See* Buffalo Metal Goods
Atlantic Monthly, 200
automobile age, 72, 119, 125
automobiles: attitudes against, 57, 125–29; as fad, 121, 132–34, 214; fatalities involving, 118, 129, 132; influence on bicycle marketing, 52, 57, 59, 72–73, 78, 99, 117–21, 123, 131–34, 148–54, 157, 161–62, 168, 191–92, 215; influence on ideals of mobility, 38–41, 52, 72, 78, 124–25, 214–15; prices, 39, 51, 99; production, 37–38; relationship with bicycles, 3, 5–6, 37, 40–42, 45, 242n3
automobility, 39–40, 93, 141, 161, 236n17
automotive culture, 117–18, 161
Autry, Gene, 170

baby boom, 194, 216
Bacall, Lauren, 183
banana seat, 197–98
Barbie, 204
Barthelmess, Dick, 145
Bartsch, A. H., 103
Batman, 179; Batman Jones, 179
Beard, Dan, 114
Beck, Irving, 103

Bederman, Gail, 18, 225n44
Bendix Corporation, 116
Berto, Frank, 197, 201, 257n8
Bicycle Day, 65, 111, 200
Bicycle Institute of America (BIA), 174–76, 181, 183, 188, 190, 193, 196, 206
bicycle manufacturers: Asian, 203. *See also specific manufacturing companies*
Bicycle Manufacturers' Association of America (BMA), 50, 118–19, 205
bicycle motocross. *See* BMX
Bicycle Week, 65, 111–12
bicycling. *See* cycling
bike parade, 14, 112, 146, 154, 248n50
bike-share programs, 211
Black Beauty bicycles, 88
black cyclists. *See* cyclists: African American
BMX (bicycle moto-cross), 203–4, 259n43
BMX Bandits, 2, 259n43
boneshaker bicycle, 8, 11, 142. *See also* velocipede
boom of 1890s, 2–4, 16–17, 20, 31–34, 52, 62, 72, 213, 217, 222n14, 233n37; institutional memory of, 63, 104, 155, 214
boosters, 35, 57, 132, 156, 183, 215; assumptions of, 56, 65–66, 82, 95, 133, 179; suggestions of, 48, 52, 55, 85, 93, 100–101
Bowden, Frank, 121
boys: bicycles as birthright, 111, 145, 159, 192; influence on family spending, 82, 116, 249n74; restrictions on activities, 87, 161; share of market, 108–10, 147
Boy Scout movement, 84, 88, 90, 92–93, 105, 114, 240n53
Boys' Life, 80, 85–86, 89, 91, 112, 114, 131
Boys' World, 108
Breaking Away, 207–8
Brinkley, Alan, 140, 247n14
British bicycle industry, 185
British Cycle and Motorcycle Manufacturers' Union, 185
Brown, Bill, 92
Brown, Robert S., 30
Brownlee, W. Elliot, 101, 103
Bryan, William Jennings, 101
Buffalo Metal Goods, 67–68, 83–84, 233n44
Burch, Ray, 186
Burleson, Albert S., 48–49
Burr, Thomas, 33, 120–21, 222n14, 233n37, 234n46, 243n13
Butler Fieldhouse, 144

Callender, W. D., 104–5
Campbell, David, 206
Campbell-Ewald, 181
Cannondale, 206
Capone, Al, 145
Captain Marvel, 179
cardiac crisis, 200
Central Park, 144, 146, 248n50
Chain Bike Corporation. *See* Ross Bicycle Organization
Chicago, Illinois, 55, 69, 87, 128, 142, 144, 188
Chicago Defender, 250n78
Chicago Tribune, 31, 129, 140, 178
children: bicycles as investment, 9, 79; bicycles as lesser form of movement, 78, 150–51, 157; as conspicuous consumers, 153–54; and consumerism, 2, 10, 75, 153, 157, 173; as controllable, 99–100, 239;

and envy as sales tactic, 110–11, 153–54; share of bicycle market, 76–77, 108–9, 147; training for cars, 157, 168, 213
Childs, Kennedy, 20, 29
Christmas, 111, 113, 132, 200; sales campaign, 79–81, 93, 112–13, 115, 164–65, 170, 242n84
Chudacoff, Howard, 168
citizenship, 39; consumption as, 44–46, 76, 88–90, 93–94, 114–15, 175, 215; health and manhood as requisites for, 77, 105–6
Clark, Suzanne, 160, 251n6
class associations, 1–9, 53–58, 72–73, 120–21, 124–25; children, 6, 119, 158–59; lower classes, 14, 26–27, 97, 104, 116, 120, 222n14; manliness, 21, 23–25, 32–33, 36, 213–14; middle class, 19–20, 99; upper class, 12, 72, 183
Cleveland, Grover, 41
Cleveland, Ohio, 57
Cleveland bicycle, 60
Cleveland Welding Company, 170
club movement, 145–46
coaster brakes: as safety feature, 57, 130–31
Cocomalt, 158
Cohen, Lizabeth, 136
Cold War, 160, 191
Collier, Price, 18
comeback, 55, 137; predictions of, 131
comics, 1, 138, 160, 171–73, 175, 178–80, 182, 194–95, 253n58
community builder: bicycles as, 175–76
commuting, 122, 126, 132, 134, 155–57, 210–11, 261n79; bike lanes, 211–12
conspicuous consumption, 10, 34, 39, 125, 153–54
consumer culture, 162
consumers, adult, 95, 118, 121, 124, 159, 162, 193, 195–97, 200, 202, 210, 215–16, 246n5; bicycle industry's lack of confidence in, 115, 120, 133–34, 137, 147, 155–56
consumer testimonials, 114–15
Cooper, Gary, 183
Crawford, Joan, 139
Cresswell, Tim, 78, 229n12
Crested Butte, Colorado, 208
cult of fitness, 17, 25, 166, 200, 213
culture of sacrifice, 44–46, 72, 116, 230n44
Currell, Susan, 143, 146, 250n82
Cycle Jobbers Association of America, 60
Cycle Tradesmen of Dayton, 120
Cycle Trades of America (CTA), 96–97, 99, 130, 132, 140, 145; advertising, 106–8, 181; campaigns, 111–12, 125; membership, 125, 127, 132, 140, 237n40, 240n53, 245n63
cycling: as adventure, 178; advocacy groups, 142; clothing and fashion, 183, 206–7; clubs, 14, 19, 26–27, 30, 53, 55–56, 82–83, 87, 106–7, 142, 144–46, 173–76, 178, 237n35; decline in youth participation, 210; and developing bodies, 178; as escapism, 146, 155; as fad, 17, 36, 45, 120, 140, 214, 246n5; governmental support of, 143, 155–56, 161, 186; health benefits of, 19–20, 25, 35, 125, 145, 174, 183, 188–89, 196; as idea of progress, 22, 151; and masculinity, 6, 9, 15, 18–19, 22–23, 26–27, 30, 32, 145, 225n44, 240n55; as patriotic, 44–45, 175, 178; as rejuvenating, 21, 143;

cycling (*cont.*)
resurgence of, 155; as sacrifice, 116; safety of, 187; and self-reliance, 178; as sociable, 144; as social statement, 9; as work, 69; for women, 15, 27–32, 36, 56, 87
cyclists: African American, 27, 53–54, 82–83, 154, 231n1, 249n7; as hazard to motorists, 141–42. *See also* consumers

Daley, Richard J., 161, 188
Davis Sewing Machine Company, 80, 236n22. *See also* Huffy
dealers, 1, 79, 112–13, 150, 197; bad examples, 233n39; dead, 83; good examples, 56, 66, 81–83, 97, 131; industry support of, 55–71, 80, 83–84, 128–29, 182; instructions to, 43–45, 55, 64, 77, 92, 97, 104–5, 110, 242n84; live, 56, 232n7; opinions of, 53–54, 108, 123–24, 127, 132–33; and repair work, 154, 185; window displays, 92, 247n11. *See also* retailers
Delaney, Martin A., 87
Dempsey, Jack, 145
derailleur, 195
design: adornments, 126, 148, 150–52; differences between boys' and girls' models, 152, 170–71; heavy and inefficient, 122, 126, 147–48, 150–51, 169; inspired by automobiles, 6, 134, 148; lightweight models, 156; streamlined, 167–68; trends after World War II, 160, 169
Dickinson, Robert, 28
Directorate. *See* United Cycle Trade Directorate
doctors, and bicycle usage, 50
doctors' advice. *See* health advocates
Donald Duck, 160
Downey, Fairfax, 130
Downey, Gregory, 52
D. P. Harris Hardware and Manufacturing Company, 169
draisine, 7
Drive Your Bicycle, 168
Dulles, Foster Rhea, 144
Dutch attitudes, toward cycling, 189–90, 212

Eagan, Frank, 48
education reformers, 77, 177
Eisenhower, Dwight D., 161, 184–90, 253n68, 255n111
electronic bicycles (e-bikes), 217
Elgin Blackhawk, 148
Emerson, W. F., 83–84, 233n44
energy crisis of 1973, 201
English style models, 184
environmentalism, 2, 200, 211
Epperson, Bruce, 223n15, 228n4, 233n25
Erie Medical Company, 26
E.T., 2, 204
exercise boom, 25
exports, 42, 51–52, 101–4, 116, 243n23

facilities for bicycles, 140–44, 189
factories, 9, 44, 46, 60, 68–69, 72, 147, 164, 167
Farrell, W. P., 77–78
Farwell, W. T., Jr., 69–70, 124–25, 234n59
fashion trends, 15, 56, 71, 140, 183, 206–7; fashionability of cycling, 5, 36, 56, 121, 133, 139–40, 214
Federal Aid Road Act of 1916, 40

female cyclists, 14, 26, 28–33, 36, 54–55, 87, 122, 169, 208; and growth of bicycle sales, 17; and ordinary, 14–15; and safety bicycle, 17, 30
Fetter, Sam, 101–2
fiction, 114
Fifty Years of Schwinn-Built Bicycles, 74, 164
film stars, 59, 139–40, 182–83
Fisher, Gary, 204
flaming youth, 172
Ford, 148, 232n10; cost of Model T, 38, 51, 228n8, 231n68, 232n10
Ford, Henry, 105
40-Year-Old Virgin, The, 2
Fox, Richard, 74
Frank, Gillian, 207
French bicycle industry, 147, 195
Friss, Evan, 5, 24, 225n32, 226n58, 261n2

Garvey, Ellen Gruber, 28, 31
Gates, Charles, 66
gearing, 8, 16, 73, 150, 183–84, 195, 199, 204–5, 234n56; importance of, 68–70
gender: feminine, 28–30, 154; ideals of, 2, 7, 32, 39, 54, 78, 124–25, 190, 214; initiation to manhood, 88, 93, 160, 165, 190–92, 215; masculine, 9, 26, 99, 251n6; middle class, 19–20, 22–23, 57, 158–61, 213
General Motors, 60, 132–33, 257n132
German cycling, 5, 12, 42, 119, 122, 212, 222n13
Gilbert, James, 172
Girl Scouts, 106
Goodyear Company, 58–59, 61, 79
Goonies, The, 2, 204
Gorski, Mark, 203
Great American Bike Boom, 196–202, 206, 210, 216–17
Green Lantern, 194
gymnacyclidium, 11

Hallenbeck, Sarah, 30
Hamilton, C. B. T., 110–11
Harbison and Garthright Bicycle Company, 24
Harley-Davidson, 70, 84–85, 110
Harmond, Richard, 22, 242n3
Harmount, James G., 196–97
Hawthorne Cycle Company, 170
Hayes, James, 196
Hayes, Kevin, 18
health advocates, 19, 21, 28–30, 87–88, 125, 187–89, 194
health and fitness, benefits of cycling, 19–21, 25, 35, 125, 143, 145, 174, 183, 188–89, 196
health-care experts. *See* health advocates
Health on Wheels, 21
Henderson, T. W., 48–49
Hendrickson, Robert C., 171
Hepburn, Katherine, 139
Herlihy, David, 12, 17, 99, 117, 119, 137, 148, 201–2, 226n54, 228n10
Higham, John, 17
high-rise bicycle, 197–98, 204, 216–17
high-wheel bicycle, 8, 13–16, 118, 214
hobbyhorse, 7
Hoover, Herbert, 44–45, 230n44
Hopalong Cassidy, 169–70, 180
horses, 7–8, 37, 49, 55, 130, 170
hostels, 142, 176–78, 190; movement for, 161, 177; youth, 176–77
Hoving, Thomas P. F., 200
Howdy Doody, 182

Huffman bicycles. *See* Huffy
Huffy, 151, 203
Hutchinson, Carl, 170

image, of bicycle: as backward, 2; as child's toy, 10, 113, 199; damage to, 71, 118; managing, 5–7, 10, 32, 34, 148, 157, 216; as serious or masculine, 15, 88, 210–11; in transition, 30, 202; as youthful, 93, 115, 159, 190, 193–94
imports, 42–43, 167, 184–86, 189, 196–97, 203–4, 243n23
Indian bicycles, 80, 133
industrialization, 2, 10, 18, 26, 32, 225n38
industry: diversifying consumers, 36, 51, 54, 66; divisions within, 138, 155; report, 61–62, 115, 118
installment plans, 97, 112
Interstate Highway System, 161, 187
isolationism, 101

Jacobson, Lisa, 74–74, 159, 173, 241n67, 249n74, 250n4
Jefferis, Howard, 132–33
jobbers, 60–61, 64, 105
jogging, 200–201
juveniles: and delinquency, 171–76, 190; masculinity, 4–5, 87, 90, 93, 165, 167, 170, 178
J. Walter Thompson, 181

Karate Kid, The, 204
Keds shoes, 158
Kelly, Charlie, 208
Kennedy, David, 235–36n13
Kerr, Robert W. (America Machine Foundry), 189
Kopchovsky, Annie Cohen. *See* Annie Londonderry

La Guardia, Fiorello H., 141
Laird, Pamela, 32
Lash LaRue Western, 180
League of American Bicyclists (LAB), 211
League of American Wheelmen (LAW), 19, 130, 177–78, 227n67
Lears, T. J. Jackson, 24, 74
legal classification, 40–41, 130
LeMond, Greg, 209
Lenz, Frank, 23
Letourneur, Alfred (Alf), 179–80, 234n56
Leverenz, David, 208
liberty, notions of, 88–89, 169, 229n12
Life, 165
Lifebuoy soap, 158
lightweight bicycles, 68, 147, 156, 162–63, 183–84, 196–97, 199, 205, 209, 216, 255n111; consumer preference for, 147, 184–85
Lindbergh, Charles, 145
Little Orphan Annie, 173
Lobdell-Emery Manufacturing Company, 130
Londonderry, Annie, 28, 31, 224n19
Longhurst, James, 139, 202, 230n46, 240n53, 246n9

MacCarthy, Shane, 187
Madison Square Garden, 126, 144–45
mail carriers, 46, 48–49, 51, 90
manhood. *See* gender
manliness. *See* gender
Marchand, Roland, 23
Marin County, California, 204

masculinity, Peter Pan, 106, 211. *See also* gender
Mason, Shirley, 145
mass consumption, 159
mass culture, 160–61, 172, 178, 251n6
mass media, 158, 169, 171
Masters Incorporated, 189
Masters of the Universe, 204
Maxim, Hiram P., 242n3
McClure, Samuel Sidney, 22
McGavin, A. E., 103–4
McGerr, Michael, 25, 225n45
McGovern, Charles, 76, 88–90, 256n131
McKenzie, Shelly, 200
McNally, E. Evalyn Grumbine, 239n20
merchandising advice, 66–68
merchants. *See* dealers; retailers
messenger boys. *See* telegraph messengers
Miami Cycle and Manufacturing Company, 70, 111
middleweight bicycles, 189, 196–97, 199
militarism, training, 84
Million Bicycles Committee (MBC), 57–62, 64–65, 72, 79, 96
Mintz, Steven, 74, 253n58
mobility, 157, 162, 191; ideals of, 2, 12, 39, 52, 72, 78, 138, 161, 192, 214, 229n12; masculinity of, 93, 161, 213, 229n14; politicization of, 40; social, 175
model bicycle shops, 66–67
modernity, 22, 125, 222n14, 226n46
Monark Bicycles, 170
Montgomery Ward & Company, 151
Moore, Elizabeth Skelding, 56
Moses, Robert, 141–43, 187
Motorcycle & Bicycle Illustrated, 96
motorcycle industry, 48, 102
Motorcycle Manufacturers' Association, 48
motorcycles, as competition for bicycles, 47, 59, 70–72
MotorCycling and Bicycling, 43–44, 50, 63, 67, 70, 79–80, 97, 100, 104, 111
motorists, as threat to cyclists, 119, 122, 127–28
mountain bike, 203–11, 216–17; competition with road bike, 205–6
Mount Tamalpais, 204
movement. *See* mobility
Murdoch, Neal, 207–8
Murray Ohio Manufacturing, 203–4
Mutt & Jeff, 194

National Bicycle Dealers' Association (NBDA), 197, 210
National Board of Trade of Cycle Manufacturers, 20
National Boys' Week, 111–12
National Cash Register Company, 98
nationalism: American, 84, 188, 199; material, 76, 88
National Sporting Goods Association, 210
nature and bicycles, 9, 19, 22, 24–25, 32, 35–36, 56, 92–93, 110, 174, 196
Netherlands, 119–20, 189–90
New Deal, 143–44, 146, 250n82
New Departure Manufacturing Company, 46, 50, 57–61, 68, 79, 88–90, 131, 138, 151, 181, 245n63, 257n132
New York Central Wheelmen, 30
New York City, 58, 143–44; cycling in, 141–42, 144, 196, 200

New York Department of Parks, 144
New York Times, 46, 120, 126, 131, 142, 146, 188
Nixon, Richard, 188, 201
Norton, Peter, 40, 128, 242n6
nostalgia, 153, 251n6; for happy days of 1890s, 146

Office of Price Administration (OPA), 163
Office of War Information, 166
O'Hara, Maureen, 182
Ohrt, Hans, 121–22, 139, 147, 150
oil shortage. *See* energy crisis of 1973
Olin, Charles F., 46, 57–58
One Hundred Percent Bicycle Merchant, The, 62
ordinary bicycle, 8, 13–15, 23, 118
Otto Todry and Son, 194
Outing, 19, 22, 31, 234n59
overcivilized lifestyle, 18, 21–22

Paddock, Charlie, 145
Page, DeWitt, 57, 132, 245n63
Palin, H. M., 185
Palm Beach, Florida, 44–45
parts manufacturers, 59–61, 67–68, 137, 190, 232nn24–25
paternalism, 126, 169; of manufacturers, 110
paths, 187; advocacy for, 126–27, 129–30, 141–42, 144, 155–56, 178, 188, 243n22. *See also* commuting
payment plans, 97, 112
Payne-Aldrich Act, 41, 229n28
pecuniary emulation, 214
peer society, 110, 158, 169
Petticord, Charles, 23
Petty, Ross, 255n102
physicians' advice. *See* health advocates
Pierce-Arrow Motor Car Company, 97–98
Pierce Bicycles, 203n52
playground access, 129, 132
police and bicycle usage, 40, 46–48
political policy, and impact on bicycle, 48–49, 141–45, 161–62
Pope, Albert A., 8, 13, 15, 17, 30, 231n64
Pope Manufacturing, 8, 13, 23–24, 32, 50, 70, 222n15, 233n37
popular entertainment, use of bicycles in, 1–2, 179–83, 187–88, 204
Popular Mechanics, 80, 165
Pratt, Charles E., 19
President's Council on Youth Fitness, 187–88, 253n68
Prince of Wales, 145
Printer's Ink, 89, 98, 116, 239n16
prizes, bicycles as consumer incentive, 81–82
Progressivism, 22, 35
Project Independence, 201
Puck, 25, 32–33
Pugh, L. Stanton, 44–45

Quiet Man, The, 182
Quine, Harry S., 58–59

racing, 55, 147, 179, 204, 206–9, 233n37, 237n49; amateur, 112–13, 142, 144–45, 156; exclusion from, 27, 53, 82; impact on sales, 38, 64, 70, 139, 250n84; six-day, 38, 126, 144; spectators, 17, 38, 228n10
racism. *See* cyclists: African American
Rad, 204
radio advertising, 1, 171, 172, 182, 217; value of, 180–81
Rainbow Bright, 204

Raleigh Cycle Company, 121, 182
recession of 1921, 100–105, 131, 136
Reed, Thomas, 1
reform, bicycle as agent of, 25, 30
Register, Woody, 106
regulations, bicycle, 41
Repack (mountain bike race), 204, 259n45
republican motherhood, 45
retailers, 43, 45, 62–63, 72, 76, 81–83, 112, 131, 164, 174, 199–200, 206, 252n49; ideas about increasing sales, 123–24; stigmatization of profession, 65. *See also* dealers
retail market, diversification of, 6, 36, 44, 51–52, 54, 66–67
Ride a Bicycle marketing campaign, 62–63
rider psychology, 170–71
Riess, Steven, 117
rights to the road, 130
Rinck, Walter, 50
Ringel, Paul, 75, 77, 169
Ritchey, Tom, 204
road bikes, 205–6, 209, 217; and elitism, 207–9. *See also* ten-speeds
roller skates, 4, 71, 78, 128, 132
Rollfast, 182
Roosevelt, Franklin D., 118–19
Roosevelt, Theodore, 40–41, 251n6
Ross Bicycle Organization, 202
Rover-style bicycle. *See* safety bicycle
Rugg, Harold, 143
Runners' World, 201
Rural Free Delivery (RFD), 48–49, 51
Ruth, Babe, 145

safety bicycle, 8–9, 15, 17, 214; and masculinity, 9, 30; and sales boom, 15–16; women's use of, 15, 17, 30
safety films, 168
sales, bicycle, 193–94; compared to automobile sales, 5, 37–38; slump of 1907, 100–101; slump of 1914, 54, 100–101; slump of 1921, 100–105, 111, 115; and unemployment, 103, 116, 138–39
Santa Claus, 81, 87–88, 113
Saturday Evening Post (Post), 106, 138
Schirrmann, Richard, 177
Scholastic, 177
school programs, 177–78
Schwinn, 1, 74, 100, 147–49, 156, 159–60, 163–65, 167, 182–84, 194, 255n102; *Bicycle Comic Book*, 178–80; cyclorama catalog, 182; Paramount, 147, 156, 179; Sting-Ray, 198; Varsity, 195
Schwinn, Frank, 147, 156, 164, 172–74, 176, 178, 181–83, 185–86, 232n25
Schwinn, Ignaz, 148, 211
scorcher position, 20, 28
Sears & Roebuck, 152, 233n37
Seduction of the Innocent. *See* Wertham, Fredric
Seiler, Cotton, 39–41, 161
sexual health, of women, 28–29
Shea, Daniel, 4
Shelby Cycle Company, 182
shops and sales tactics. *See* retailers
sidewalks, 12, 134, 141, 187, 205; bikes, 52, 76, 150
six-day racing. *See* racing
Smethurst, Paul, 12
Smith, Robert, 17, 20, 244n35
Smith College, 56–57
social emulation, 214
social mobility, 175
society women, 55, 140, 183, 214
Sprague, Marshall, 142, 146

Sprague Publishing Company, 108–11
Stables, W. Gordon, 21
Stanton, Elizabeth Cady, 30–31
Stephenson, W. B., 140
St. Nicholas, 114
Stock Market Crash of 1929, 243n23
Strange, Lisa, 30
Stranger Things, 2
strenuous life, 10, 31, 213, 251n6
suburbanization, 2, 5, 117–18, 132, 134, 156, 167
suburbs: as safe for kids' bikes, 126, 131, 189; stores move to, 132–33, 156
Sullivan, T. J., 127–29, 131, 141–42, 150, 154, 235n66, 244n50
symbolism, 6, 32, 118, 158–59, 215, 222n14; youth and vigor, 191

Taft, William H., 40–41, 229n28
tariffs, 41–42, 184–86, 189, 229n28, 255n11
telegraph messengers, 50, 52, 92–93, 133
television, 167, 169–72, 183, 209, 217; children's programs, 1, 160, 173, 175, 180; commercials, 181–82
ten-speeds, 205–7, 209–10, 216. *See also* lightweight bicycles; road bikes
Thayer, George B., 18
Time, 199–200
tires: balloon, 137–38, 147–49, 151, 169, 183–84, 204; pneumatic, 8, 16, 214
Today's Health, 194, 196–97
Torres, Raquel, 139
Tour de France, 147, 209
Toy Fair, of 1950, 169
toys: attempts to make bicycles less like, 10, 193–95, 199, 202, 210–12, 216; of elites, 24
trade journals, 7, 47, 52–53, 66, 70–72, 82, 138, 182. *See also specific titles*
transportation, bicycles as, 115–22, 155, 190, 212, 242n3, 261n79; alternative to public transportation, 23–24, 64, 95, 97–99, 116, 137–38; for children, 129, 170; as ideal form, 71, 174, 207; social conceptions of, 2; for work, 47–48. *See also* commuting
Trek Bicycle Corporation, 210, 260n65
tricycles, 12, 15–17, 29, 236n15
Tulsa, Oklahoma, 211
Turner, Frederick Jackson, 161

Uncle Sam, 43, 88–90
Underwood Tariff Act, 41–42, 229n28
Underwood Typewriter Company, 97–98
United Cycle Trade Directorate, 50, 61–65, 69, 72, 80–81, 96, 174, 234n59, 237n40
United States Rubber Company, 90–92, 148, 181
United States Tires, 80
United States Trade Commission, 184–85
utilitarian, bicycles as, 24, 51, 66, 73, 97, 116, 119, 134, 156, 205, 211, 217. *See also* transportation

Vatter, Harold, 167
velocipede, 7–8, 11–16, 77–78, 223n4, 236n15
velodromes, 5, 55, 144, 155–56
Victorian ideals, 54
Victory model, 163
Volstead Act, 123–24

Wall Street Journal, 172
War Production Board (WPB), 162–63, 167
Washington, DC, 196, 211
Wayne, John, 182
Weed, Hugh, 102
weight. *See* design
Wells, Christopher, 40
Wertham, Fredric, 171–72
Wessel, W. C., 114
Wheel within a Wheel. *See* Willard, Frances
White, Paul Dudley, 188–89, 194
wholesalers, 60–61, 64, 105
Wide World of Sports, 209
Wilkens, Samuel, 202–3
Wilkinson, Bill, 206
Willard, Frances, 27–28, 30–31
Williams Rims, 194
Willis, Helen, 146
Wilson, Woodrow, 39, 41–42, 44, 101, 229n28, 236n13
window displays, 55, 59, 61, 68, 92, 154, 170, 233n30
Withers, Jeremy, 4
Witty, Calvin, 13
Wizard of Oz, The, 2
women, of college age, 56–57, 145
women's bicycles. *See* female cyclists
women's television programming, 182–83
Wonder Woman, 194
working class, 9, 18, 57, 71–72, 99, 104
Works Progress Administration (WPA), 142–44, 155, 250n82
World War I: contract for 10,000 bicycles, 50–51; impact on bicycle industry, 51–52, 54, 62, 93–94, 113–16
World War II: bicycle as rehabilitation from, 165–67, 191–92; bicycle rationing, 163, 167, 246n5; impact on culture, 160–62, 169; impact on policy, 159; postwar production, 159, 167; retooling, 163–65

X Games, ESPN, 204

YMCA, 57, 176
Yosemite National Park, 164
Youth's Companion, 80

Zaretsky, Natasha, 201
Zheutlin, Peter, 29

Robert J. Turpin is an assistant professor of history at Lees-McRae College. Originally from Crab Orchard, Kentucky, he now lives in North Wilkesboro, North Carolina, with his beautiful wife, two lovely daughters, and four neglected bicycles.